Ancient States and Empires
For Colleges And Schools
Book II

by

John Lord

Ancient States and Empires
For Colleges And Schools
Book II
by John Lord

Copyright © 2024

All Rights reserved.

ISBN: 978-93-62204-29-5

Published by

DOUBLE 9 BOOKS
2/13-B, Ansari Road
Daryaganj, New Delhi – 110002
info@double9books.com
www.double9books.com
Tel. 011-40042856

ABOUT THE AUTHOR

John Lord (September 10, 1810 – December 15, 1894) was a professor and historian from the United States. He graduated from Dartmouth College in 1833 and then entered the Andover Theological Seminary, where in his second year he produced a series of lectures on the Dark Ages, which he presented the following fall during a trip through northern New York. He joined the American Peace Society after graduating from Andover. He was summoned to a Congregational Church in New Marlborough, Massachusetts, and subsequently to one in Stockbridge, Massachusetts, despite not being ordained. In 1840, he resigned from his pastoral duties to become a public lecturer and devote more attention to literary pursuits. In 1843-46, he lectured about the Middle Ages in England, and upon his return to the United States, he lectured for many years in the major towns and cities, giving almost 6,000 lectures in total. He obtained his LL.D. from the City University of New York in 1864. He taught history at Dartmouth College from 1866 to 1876.

CONTENTS

BOOK II
THE GRECIAN STATES

CHAPTER XIII
THE GEOGRAPHY OF ANCIENT GREECE AND ITS EARLY INHABITANTS

Degeneracy of the oriental states.

We have seen that the Oriental-world, so favored by nature, so rich in fields, in flocks, and fruits, failed to realize the higher destiny of man. In spite of all the advantages of nature, he was degraded by debasing superstitions, and by the degeneracy which wealth and ease produced. He was enslaved by vices and by despots. The Assyrian and Babylonian kingdom, that "head of gold," as seen in Nebuchadnezzar's dream, became inferior to the "breast and arms of silver," as represented by the Persian Empire, and this, in turn, became subject to the Grecian States, "the belly and the thighs of brass." It is the nobler Hellenic race, with its original genius, its enterprise, its stern and rugged nature, strengthened by toil, and enterprise, and war, that we are now to contemplate. It is Greece—the land of song, of art, of philosophy—the land of heroes and freemen, to which we now turn our eyes—the most interesting, and the most famous of the countries of antiquity.

Boundaries of Greece.

Let us first survey that country in all its stern ruggedness and picturesque beauty. It was small compared with Assyria or Persia. Its original name was Hellas, designated by a little district of Thessaly, which lay on the southeast verge of Europe, and extended in length from the thirty-sixth to the fortieth degree of latitude. It contained, with its islands, only twenty-one thousand two hundred and ninety square miles—less than Portugal or Ireland, but its coasts exceeded the whole Pyrenean peninsula. Hellas is itself a peninsula, bounded on the north by the Cambunian and Ceraunian mountains, which separated it from Macedonia; on the east by the Ægean Sea, (Archipelago), which separated it from Asia Minor; on the south by the Cretan Sea, and on the west by the Ionian Sea.

The mountains of Greece. Between Ossa and Olympus is the famous vale of Tempe.

The northern part of this country of the Hellenes is traversed by a range of mountains, commencing at Acra Ceraunia, on the Adriatic, and tending southeast above Dodona, in Epirus, till they join the Cambunian mountains, near Mount Olympus, which run along the coast of the Ægean till they terminate in the southeastern part of Thessaly, under the names of Ossa, Pelion, and Tisæus. The great range of Pindus enters Greece at the sources of the Peneus, where it crosses the Cambunian mountains, and extends at first south, and then east to the sea, nearly inclosing Thessaly, and dividing it from the rest of Greece. After throwing out the various spurs of Othrys, Œta, and Corax, it loses itself in those famous haunts of the Muses—the heights of Parnassus and Helicon, in Phocis and Bœotia, In the southern part of Greece are the mountains which intersect the Peloponnesus in almost every part, the principal of which are Scollis, Aroanii, and Taygetus. We can not enumerate the names of all these mountains; it is enough to say that no part of Europe, except Switzerland, is so covered with mountains as Greece, some of which attain the altitude of perpetual snow. Only a small part of the country is level.

The rivers.

The rivers, again, are numerous, but more famous for associations than for navigable importance. The Peneus which empties itself into the Ægean, a little below Tempe; the Achelous, which flows into the Ionian Sea; the Alpheus, flowing into the Ionian Sea; and the Eurotas, which enters the Laconican Gulf, are among the most considerable. The lakes are numerous, but not large. The coasts are lined by bays and promontories, favorable to navigation in its infancy, and for fishing. The adjacent seas are full of islands, memorable in Grecian history, some of which are of considerable size.

Natural advantages for political independence.

Thus intersected in all parts with mountains, and deeply indented by the sea, Greece was both mountainous and maritime. The mountains, the rivers, the valleys, the sea, the islands contributed to make the people enterprising and poetical, and as each State was divided from every other State by mountains, or valleys, or gulfs, political liberty was engendered. The difficulties of cultivating a barren soil on the highlands inured the inhabitants to industry and economy, as in Scotland and New England, while the configuration of the country strengthened the powers of defense, and shut the people up from those invasions which have so often subjugated a plain and level country. These natural divisions also kept the States from political union, and fostered a principle of repulsion, and led to an indefinite multiplication of self-governing towns, and to great individuality of character.

Natural productions.

Situated in the same parallels of latitude as Asia Minor, and the south of Italy and Spain, Greece produced wheat, barley, flax, wine, oil, in the earliest times. The cultivation of the vine and the olive was peculiarly careful. Barley cakes were more eaten than wheaten. All vegetables and fish were abundant and cheap. But little fresh meat was eaten. Corn also was imported in considerable quantities by the maritime States in exchange for figs, olives, and oil. The climate, clear and beautiful to modern Europeans, was less genial than that of Asia Minor, but more bracing and variable. It also varied in various sections.

These various sections, or provinces, or states, into which Greece was divided, claim a short notice.

Epirus.

The largest and most northerly State was Epirus, containing four thousand two hundred and sixty square miles, bounded on the north by Macedonia, on the east by Thessaly, on the south by Acarnania, and on the west by the Ionian Sea. Though mountainous, it was fertile, and produced excellent cattle and horses. Of the interesting places of Epirus, memorable in history, ranks first Dodona, celebrated for its oracle, the most ancient in Greece, and only inferior to that of Delphi. It was founded by the Pelasgi before the Trojan war and was dedicated to Jupiter. The temple was surrounded by a grove of oak, but the oracles were latterly delivered by the murmuring of fountains. On the west of Epirus is the island of Corcyra (Corfu), famous for the shipwreck of Ulysses, and for the gardens of Aleinous, and for having given rise to the Peloponnesian war. Epirus is also distinguished as the country over which Pyrrhus ruled. The Acheron, supposed to communicate with the infernal regions, was one of its rivers.

Thessaly.

West of Epirus was Thessaly, and next to it in size, containing four thousand two hundred and sixty square miles. It was a plain inclosed by mountains; next to Bœotia, the most fertile of all the States of Greece, abounding in oil, wine, and corn, and yet one of the weakest and most insignificant politically. The people were rich, but perfidious. The river Peneus flowed through the entire extent of the country, and near its mouth was the vale of Tempe, the most beautiful valley in Greece, guarded by four strong fortresses.

The famous places.

At some distance from the mouth of the Peneus was Larissa, the city of Achilles, and the general capital of the Pelasgi. At the southern extremity of the lake Cælas, the largest in Thessaly, was Pheræ, one of the most ancient cities in Greece, and near it was the fountain of Hyperia. In the southern part of Thessaly was Pharsalia, the battle-ground between Cæsar and Pompey, and near it was Pyrrha, formerly called Hellas, where was the tomb of Hellen, son of Deucalion, whose descendants, Æolus, Dorus and Ion, are said to have given name to the three nations, Æolians, Dorians, and Ionians, Still further south, between the inaccessible cliffs of Mount Œta and the marshes which skirt the Maliaeus Bay, were the defiles of Thermopylæ, where Leonidas and three hundred heroes died defending the pass, against the army of Xerxes, and which in one place was only twenty-five feet wide, so that, in so narrow a defile, the Spartans were able to withstand for three days the whole power of Persia. In this famous pass the Amphictyonic council met annually to deliberate on the common affairs of all the States.

Acarnania.

South of Epirus, on the Ionian Sea, and west of Ætolia, was Acarnania, occupied by a barbarous people before the Pelasgi settled in it. It had no historic fame, except as furnishing on its waters a place for the decisive battle which Augustus gained over Antony, at Actium, and for the islands on the coast, one of which, Ithaca, a rugged and mountainous island, was the residence of Ulysses.

Ætolia.

Ætolia, to the east of Acarnania, and south of Thessaly, and separated from Achaia by the Corinthian Gulf, contained nine hundred and thirty square miles. Its principal city was Thermon, considered impregnable, at which were held splendid games and festivals. The Ætolians were little known in the palmy days of Athens and Sparta, except as a hardy race, but covetous and faithless.

Doris.

Doris was a small tract to the east of Ætolia, inhabited by one of the most ancient of the Greek tribes—the Dorians, called so from Dorus, son of Deucalion, and originally inhabited that part of Thessaly in which were the mountains of Olympus and Ossa. From this section they were driven by the Cadmeans. Doris was the abode of the Heraclidæ when exiled from the Peloponnesus, and which was given to Hyllas, the son of Hercules, in gratitude by Ægiminius, the king, who was reinstated by the hero in his dispossessed dominion.

Locri Ozolæ.

Locri Ozolæ was another small State, south of Doris, from which it is separated by the range of the Parnassus situated on the Corinthian Gulf, the most important city of which was Salona, surrounded on all sides by hills. Naupactus was also a considerable place, known in the Middle Ages as Lepanto, where was fought one of the decisive naval battles of the world, in which the Turks were defeated by the Venetians. It contained three hundred and fifty square miles.

Phocis.

Phocis was directly to the east, bounded on the north by Doris and the Locri Epicnemidii, and south by the Corinthian Gulf. This State embraced six hundred and ten square miles. The Phocians are known in history from the sacred or Phocian war, which broke out in 357 B.C., in consequence of refusing to pay a fine imposed by the Amphictyonic council. The Thebans and Locrians carried on this war successfully, joined by Philip of Macedon, who thus paved the way for the sovereignty of Greece. One among the most noted places was Crissa, famed for the Pythian games, and Delphi, renowned for its oracle sacred to Apollo. The priestess, Pythia, sat on a sacred tripod over the mouth of a cave, and pronounced her oracles in verse or prose. Those who consulted her made rich presents, from which Delphi became vastly enriched. Above Delphi towers Parnassus, the highest mountain in central Greece, near whose summit was the supposed residence of Deucalion.

Bœotia.

Bœotia was the richest State in Greece, so far as fertility of soil can make a State rich. It was bounded on the north by the territory of the Locri, on the west by Phocis, on the south by Attica, and on the east by the Eubœan Sea. It contained about one thousand square miles. Its inhabitants were famed for their stolidity, and yet it furnished Hesiod, Pindar, Corinna, and Plutarch to the immortal catalogue of names. Its men, if stupid, were brave, and its women were handsome. It was originally inhabited by barbarous tribes, all connected with the Leleges. In its southwestern part was the famous Helicon, famed as the seat of Apollo and the Muses, and on the southern border was Mount Cithæron, to the north of which was Platea, where the Persians were defeated by the confederate Greeks under Pausanias. Bœotia contained the largest lake in Greece—Copaias, famed for eels. On the borders of this lake was Coronea, where the Thebans were defeated by the Spartans. To the north of Coronea was Chæronea, where was fought the great battle with

Philip, which subverted the liberties of Greece. To the north of the river Æsopus, a sluggish stream, was Thebes, the capital of Bœotia, founded by Cadmus, whose great generals, Epaminondas and Pelopidas, made it, for a time, one of the great powers of Greece.

Attica.

The most famous province of Greece was Attica, bounded on the north by the mountains Cithæron and Parnes, on the west by the bay of Saronicus, on the east by the Myrtoum Sea. It contained but seven hundred square miles. It derived its name from Atthis, a daughter of Cranaus; but its earliest name was Cecropia, from its king, Cecrops. It was divided, in the time of Cecrops, into four tribes. On its western extremity, on the shores of the Saronic Gulf, stood Eleusis, the scene of the Eleusinian mysteries, the most famous of all the religious ceremonials of Greece, sacred to Ceres, and celebrated every four years, and lasting for nine days. Opposite to Eleusis was Salamis, the birthplace of Ajax, Teucer, and Solon. There the Persian fleet of Xerxes was defeated by the Athenians. The capital, Athens, founded by Cecrops, 1556 B.C., received its name from the goddess Neith, an Egyptian deity, known by the Greeks as Athena, or Minerva. Its population, in the time of Pericles, was one hundred and twenty thousand. The southernmost point of Attica was Sunium, sacred to Minerva; Marathon, the scene of the most brilliant victory which the Athenians ever fought, was in the eastern part of Attica. To the southeast of Athens was Mount Hymettus, celebrated for its flowers and honey. Between Hymettus and Marathon was Mount Pentelicus, famed for its marbles.

Megaris.

Megaris, another small State, was at the west of Attica, between the Corinthian and the Saronican gulfs. Its chief city, Megara, was a considerable place, defended by two citadels on the hills above it. It was celebrated as the seat of the Megaric school of philosophy, founded by Euclid.

The Peloponnesus and its states.

The largest of the Grecian States was the famous peninsula known as the Peloponnesus, entirely surrounded by water, except the isthmus of Corinth, four geographical miles wide. On the west was the Ionian Sea; on the east the Saronic Gulf and the Myrtoum Sea; on the north the Corinthian Gulf. It contained six thousand seven hundred and forty-five square miles. It was divided into several States. It was said to be left by Hercules on his death to the Heraclidæ, which they, with the assistance of the Dorians, ultimately succeeded in regaining, about eighty years after the Trojan war.

Of the six States into which the Peloponnesus was divided, Achaia was the northernmost, and was celebrated for the Achæan league, composed of its principal cities, as well us Corinth, Sicyon, Phlius, Arcadia, Argolis, Laconia, Megaris, and other cities and States.

Elis.

Southwest of Achaia was Elis, on the Ionian Sea, in which stood Olympia, where the Olympic games were celebrated every four years, instituted by Hercules.

Arcadia.

Arcadia occupied the centre of the Peloponnesus, surrounded on all sides by lofty mountains—a rich and pastoral country, producing fine horses and asses. It was the favorite residence of Pan, the god of shepherds, and its people were famed for their love of liberty and music.

Argolis.

Argolis was the eastern portion of the Peloponnesus, watered by the Saronic Gulf, whose original inhabitants were Pelasgi. It boasted of the cities of Argos and Mycenæ, the former of which was the oldest city of Greece. Agamemnon reigned at Mycenæ, the most powerful of the kings of Greece during the Trojan war.

Laconia.

Laconia, at the southeastern extremity of the peninsula, was the largest and most important of the States of the Peloponnesus. It was rugged and mountainous, but its people were brave and noble. Its largest city, Sparta, for several generations controlled the fortune of Greece, the most warlike of the Grecian cities.

Messenia.

Messenia was the southwestern part of the peninsula—mountainous, but well watered, and abounding in pasture. It was early coveted by the Lacedæmonians, inhabitants of Laconia, and was subjugated in a series of famous wars, called the Messenian.

Such were the principal States of Greece. But in connection with these were the islands in the seas which surrounded it, and these are nearly as famous as the States on the main land.

Crete.

The most important of these was Crete, at the southern extremity of the Ægean Sea. It was the fabled birthplace of Jupiter. To the south of Thrace were Thasos, remarkable for fertility, and for mines of gold and silver; Samothrace, celebrated for the mysteries of Cybele; Imbros, sacred to Ceres and Mercury. Lemnos, in latitude forty, equidistant from Mount Athos and the Hellespont, rendered infamous by the massacre of all the male inhabitants of the island by the women. The island of Eubœa stretched along the coast of Attica, Locris, and Bœotia, and was exceedingly fertile, and from this island the Athenians drew large supplies of corn—the largest island in the Archipelago, next to Crete. Its principal city was Chalcis, one of the strongest in Greece.

The Cyclades.

To the southeast of Eubœa are the Cyclades—a group of islands of which Delos, Andros, Tenos, Myeonos, Naxos, Paros, Olearos, Siphnos, Melos, and Syros, were the most important. All these islands are famous for temples and the birthplace of celebrated men.

The Sporades.

The islands called the Sporades lie to the south and east of the Cyclades, among which are Amorgo, Ios, Sicinos, Thera, and Anaphe—some of which are barren, and others favorable to the vine.

Lesbos, and other islands.

Besides these islands, which belong to the continent of Europe, are those which belong to Asia—Tenedos, small but fertile; Lesbos, celebrated for wine, the fourth in size of all the islands of the Ægean; Chios, also famed for wine; Samos, famous for the worship of Juno, and the birthplace of Pythagoras; Patmos, used as a place of banishment; Cos, the birthplace of Apelles and Hippocrates, exceedingly fertile; and south of all, Rhodes, the largest island of the Ægean, after Crete and Eubœa. It was famous for the brazen and colossal statue of the sun, seventy cubits high. Its people were great navigators, and their maritime laws were ultimately adopted by all the Greeks and Romans. It was also famous for its schools of art.

Such were the States and islands of Greece, mountainous, in many parts sterile, but filled with a hardy, bold, and adventurous race, whose exploits and arts were the glory of the ancient world.

Origin of the Grecian nations. The Pelasgians.

The various tribes and nations all belonged to that branch of the Indo-European race to which ethnographers have given the name of Pelasgian. They were a people of savage manners, but sufficiently civilised to till the earth, and build walled cities. Their religion was polytheistic—a personification of the elemental powers and the heavenly bodies. The Pelasgians occupied insulated points, but were generally diffused throughout Greece; and they were probably a wandering people before they settled in Greece. The Greek traditions about their migration rests on no certain ground. Besides this race, concerning which we have no authentic history, were the Leleges and Carians. But all of them were barbarous, and have left no written records. Argos and Sicyon are said to be Pelasgian cities, founded as far back as one thousand eight hundred and fifty-six years before Christ. It is also thought that Oriental elements entered into the early population of Greece. Cecrops imported into Attica Egyptian arts. Cadmus, the Phœnician, colonized Bœotia, and introduced weights and measures. Danaus, driven out of Egypt, gave his name to the warlike Danai, and instructed the Pelasgian women of Argos in the mystic rites of Demetus. Pelope is supposed to have passed from Asia into Greece, with great treasures, and his descendants occupied the throne of Argos.

The Hellenes. The Æolians. The Achæans.

At a period before written history commences, the early inhabitants of Greece, whatever may have been their origin, which is involved in obscurity, were driven from their settlements by a warlike race, akin, however, to the Pelasgians. These conquerors were the Hellenes, who were believed to have issued from the district of Thessaly, north of Mount Othrys. They gave their name ultimately to the whole country. Divided into small settlements, they yet were bound together by language and customs, and cherished the idea of national unity. There were four chief divisions of this nation, the Dorians, Æolians, Achæans, and Ionians, traditionally supposed to be descended from the three sons of Hellen, the son of Deucalion, Dorus, Æolus, and Xuthus, the last the father of Achæus, and Jon. So the Greek poets represented the origin of the Hellenes—a people fond of adventure, and endowed by nature with vast capacities, subsequently developed by education.

The Dorians and Ionians.

Of these four divisions of the Hellenic race, the Æolians spread over northern Greece, and also occupied the western coast of the Peloponnesus and the Ionian islands. It continued, to the latest times, to occupy the greater part of Greece. The Achæans were the most celebrated in epic poetry, their name being used by Homer to denote all the Hellenic tribes which fought at Troy. They were the dominant people of the Peloponnesus, occupying the south and east, and the Arcadians the centre. The Dorians and Ionians were of later celebrity; the former occupying a small patch of territory on the slopes of Mount Œta, north of Delphi; the latter living on a narrow slip of the country along the northern coast of the Peloponnesus, and extending eastward into Attica.

Settlements of the Æolians.

The principal settlements of the Æolians lay around the Pagasæan Gulf, and were blended with the Minyans, a race of Pelasgian adventurers known in the Argonautic expedition, under Æolian leaders. In the north of Bœotia arose the city of Orchomenus, whose treasures were compared by Homer to those of the Egyptian Thebes. Another seat of the Æolians was Ephyra, afterward known as Corinth, where the "wily Sisyphus" ruled. He was the father of Phocus, who gave his name to Phocis. The descendants of Æolus led also a colony to Elis, and another to Pylus. In general, the Æolians sought maritime settlements in northern Greece, and the western side of the Peloponnesus.

Of the Achæans.

The Achæans were the dominant race, in very early times, of the south of Thessaly, and the eastern side of the Peloponnesus, whose chief seats were Phthia, where Achilles reigned, and Argolis. Thirlwall seems to think they were a Pelasgian, rather than an Hellenic people. The ancient traditions represent the sons of Achæus as migrating to Argos, where they married the daughters of Danaus the king, but did not mount the throne.

Of the Dorians.

The early fortunes of the Dorians are involved in great obscurity, nor is there much that is satisfactory in the early history of any of the Hellenic tribes. Our information is chiefly traditional, derived from the poets. Dorus, the son of Deucalion, occupied the country over against Peloponnesus, on the opposite side of the Corinthian Gulf, comprising Ætolia, Phocis, and the Ozolian Locrians. Nor can the conquests of the Dorians on the Peloponnesus be reconciled upon any other ground than that they occupied a considerable tract of country.

Of the Ionians.

The early history of the Ionians is still more obscure. Ion, the son of Xuthus, is supposed to have led his followers from Thessaly to Attica, and to have conquered the Pelasgians, or effected peaceable settlements with them. Then follows a series of legends which have more poetical than historical interest, but which will be briefly noticed in the next chapter.

CHAPTER XIV
THE LEGENDS OF ANCIENT GREECE

The heroic ages of Greece.

The Greeks possessed no authentic written history of that period which included the first appearance of the Hellenes in Thessaly to the first Olympiad, B.C. 776. This is called the heroic age, and is known to us only by legends and traditions, called myths. They pertain both to gods and men, and are connected with what we call mythology, which possesses no historical importance, although it is full of interest for its poetic life. And as mythology is interwoven with the literature and the art of the ancients, furnishing inexhaustible subjects for poets, painters, and sculptors, it can not be omitted wholly in the history of that classic people, whose songs and arts have been the admiration of the world.

The legends.

We have space, however, only for those legends which are of universal interest, and will first allude to those which pertain to gods, such as appear most prominent in the poems of Hesiod and Homer.

Zeus.

Zeus, or Jupiter, is the most important personage in the mythology of Greece. Although, chronologically, he comes after Kronos and Uranos, he was called the "father of gods and men," whose power it was impossible to resist, and which power was universal. He was supposed to be the superintending providence, whose seat was on Mount Olympus, enthroned in majesty and might, to whom the lesser deities were obedient. With his two brothers, Poseidon, or Neptune, and Hades, or Pluto, he reigned over the heavens, the earth, the sea, and hell. Mythology represents him as born in Crete; and when he had gained sufficient mental and bodily force, he summoned the gods to Mount Olympus, and resolved to wrest the supreme power from his father, Kronos, and the Titans. Ten years were spent in the mighty combat, in which all nature was convulsed, before victory was obtained, and the Titans hurled into Tartarus. With Zeus now began a different order of beings. He is represented as having many wives and a numerous offspring. From his own head came Athene, fully armed, the goddess of wisdom, the patron deity of Athens. By Themis he begat the Horæ; by Eurynome, the three Graces; by Mnemosyne, the Muses; by Leto (Latona), Apollo, and Artemis (Diana); by Demeter (Ceres), Persephone; by Here (Juno), Hebe, Ares (Mars), and Eileithyia; by Maia, Hermes (Mercury).

The other deities.

Under the presidency of Zeus were the twelve great gods and goddesses of Olympus—Poseidon (Neptune), who presided over the sea; Apollo, who was the patron of art; Ares, the god of war; Hephaestos (Vulcan), who forged the thunderbolts; Hermes, who was the messenger of omnipotence and the protector of merchants; Here, the queen of heaven, and general protector of the female sex; Athene (Minerva), the goddess of wisdom and letters; Artemis (Diana), the protectress of hunters and shepherds; Aphrodite (Venus), the goddess of beauty and love; Hertia (Vesta), the goddess of the hearth and altar, whose fire never went out; Demeter (Ceres), mother earth, the goddess of agriculture.

Scarcely inferior to these Olympian deities were Hades (Pluto), who presided over the infernal regions; Helios, the sun; Hecate, the goddess of expiation; Dionysus (Bacchus), the god of the vine; Leto (Latona), the goddess of the concealed powers; Eos (Aurora), goddess of the morn; Nemesis, god of vengeance; Æolus, the god of winds; Harmonia; the Graces, the Muses, the Nymphs, the Nereids, marine nymphs—these were all invested with great power and dignity.

Besides these were deities who performed special services to the greater gods, like the Horæ; and monsters, offspring of gods, like the gorgons, chimera, the dragon of the Hesperides, the Lernæan hydra, the Nemean lion, Scylla and Charybdis, the centaurs, the sphinx, and others.

Who represent the powers of Nature.

It will be seen that these gods and goddesses represent the powers of nature, and the great attributes of wisdom, purity, courage, fidelity, truth, which belong to man's higher nature, and which are associated with the divine. It was these powers and attributes which were worshiped— superhuman and adorable. Homer and Hesiod are the great authorities of the theogonies of the pagan world, and we can not tell how much of this was of their invention, and how much was implanted in the common mind of the Greeks, at an age earlier than 700 B.C. The Orphic theogony belongs to a later date, but acquired even greater popular veneration than the Hesiodic.

The worship of these deities.

The worship of these divinities was attended by rites more or less elevated, but sometimes by impurities and follies, like those of Bacchus and

Venus. Sometimes this worship was veiled in mysteries, like those of Eleusis. To all these deities temples were erected, and offerings made, sometimes of fruits and flowers, and then of animals. Of all these deities there were legends—sometimes absurd, and these were interwoven with literature and religious solemnities. The details of these fill many a large dictionary, and are to be read in dictionaries, or in poems. Those which pertain to Ceres, to Apollo, to Juno, to Venus, to Minerva, to Mercury, are full of poetic beauty and fascination. They arose in an age of fertile imagination and ardent feeling, and became the faith of the people.

Legends which pertain to heroes.

Besides the legends pertaining to gods and goddesses, are those which relate the heroic actions of men. Grote describes the different races of men as they appear in the Hesiodic theogony—the offspring of gods. First, the golden race: first created, good and happy, like the gods themselves, and honored after death by being made the unseen guardians of men— "terrestrial demons." Second, the silver race, inferior in body and mind, was next created, and being disobedient, are buried in the earth. Third, the brazen race, hard, pugnacious, terrible, strong, which was continually at war, and ultimately destroyed itself, and descended into Hades, unhonored and without privilege. Fourth, the race of heroes, or demigods, such as fought at Thebes and Troy, virtuous but warlike, which also perished in battle, but were removed to a happier state. And finally, the iron race, doomed to perpetual guilt, care, toil, suffering—unjust, dishonest, ungrateful, thoughtless—such is the present race of men, with a small admixture of good, which will also end in due time. Such are the races which Hesiod describes in his poem of the "Works and Days," —penetrated with a profound sense of the wickedness and degeneracy of human life, yet of the ultimate rewards of virtue and truth. His demons are not gods, nor men, but intermediate agents, essentially good—angels, whose province was to guard and to benefit the world. But the notions of demons gradually changed, until they were regarded as both good and bad, as viewed by Plato, and finally they were regarded as the causes of evil, as in the time of the Christian writers. Hesiod, who lived, it is supposed, four hundred years before Herodotus, is a great ethical poet, and embodied the views of his age respecting the great mysteries of nature and life.

The legends which Hesiod, Homer, and other poets made so attractive by their genius, have a perpetual interest, since they are invested with all the fascinations of song and romance. We will not enter upon those which relate to gods, but confine ourselves to those which relate to men—the early heroes of the classic land and age; nor can we allude to all—only a few— those which are most memorable and impressive.

The Danaides.

Among the most ancient was the legend relating to the Danaides, which invest the early history of Argos with peculiar interest. Inachus, who reigned 1986 B.C., according to ancient chronology, is also the name of the river flowing beneath the walls of the ancient city, situated in the eastern part of the Peloponnesus. In the reign of Krotopos, one of his descendants, Danaus came with his fifty daughters from Egypt to Argos in a vessel of fifty oars, in order to escape the solicitations of the fifty sons of Ægyptos, his brother, who wished to make them their wives. Ægyptos and the sons followed in pursuit, and Danaus was compelled to assent to their desires, but furnished each of his daughters with a dagger, on the wedding night, who thus slew their husbands, except one, whose husband, Lynceus, ultimately became king of Argos. From Danaus was derived the name of Danai, applied to the people of the Argeian territory, and to the Homeric Greeks generally. We hence infer that Argos—one of the oldest cities of Greece, was settled in part by Egyptians, probably in the era of the shepherd kings, who introduced not only the arts, but the religious rites of that ancient country. Among the regal descendants of Lynceus was Danae, whose son Perseus performed marvelous deeds, by the special favor of Athene, among which he brought from Libya the terrific head of the Gorgon Medusa, which had the marvelous property of turning every one to stone who looked at her. Stung with remorse for the accidental murder of his grandfather, the king, he retired from Argos, and founded the city of Mycenæ, the ruins of whose massive walls are still to be seen—Cyclopean works, which seem to show that the old Pelasgians derived their architectural ideas from the Egyptian Danauns. The Perseids of Mycenæ thus boasted of an illustrious descent, which continued down to the last sovereign of Sparta.

Hercules.

The grand-daughter of Perseus was Alcmena, whom mythology represents as the mother of Hercules by Jupiter. The labors of Hercules are among the most interesting legends of pagan antiquity, since they are types of the endless toils of a noble soul, doomed to labor for others, and obey the commands of worthless persecutors. But the hero is finally rewarded by admission to the family of the gods, and his descendants are ultimately restored to the inheritance from which they were deprived by the wrath and jealousy of Juno. A younger branch of the Perseid family reigned in Lacedæmon—Eurystheus, to whom Hercules was subject; but he, with all his sons, lost their lives in battle, so that the Perseid family was represented only by the sons of Hercules—the Heracleids, or Heraclidæ. They endeavored to regain their possessions, and invaded the Peloponnesus, from which they had been expelled. Hyllos, the oldest son, proposed to the army of Ionians, Achæans, and Arcadians, which met them in defense, that the combat should be decided between himself and any champion of the invading army, and that, if he were victorious, the Heracleids should be restored to their sovereignty, but if defeated, should forego their claim for three generations. Hyllos was vanquished, and the Heracleids retired and resided with the Dorians. When the stipulated period had ended, they, assisted by the Dorians, gained possession of the Peloponnesus. Hence the great Dorian settlement of Argos, Sparta, and Messenia, effected by the return of the Heracleids.

Deucalion.

Another important legend is that which relates to Deucalion and the deluge, as it is supposed to shed light on the different races that colonized Greece. The wickedness of the world induced Zeus to punish it by a deluge; a terrible rain laid the whole of Greece under water, except a few mountain tops. Deucalion was saved in an ark, or chest, which he had been forewarned to construct. After floating nine days, he landed on the summit of Mount Parnassus. Issuing from his ark, he found no inhabitants, they having been destroyed by the deluge. Instructed, however, by Zeus, he and his wife, Pyrrha, threw stones over their heads, and those which he threw became men, and those thrown by his wife became women. Thus does mythology account for the new settlement of the country—a tradition doubtless derived from the remote ages through the children of Japhet, from whom the Greeks descended, and who, after many wanderings and migrations, settled in Greece.

Hellen and Pyrrha.

Deucalion and Pyrrha had two sons, Hellen and Amphictyon. The eldest, Hellen, by a nymph was the father of Dorus, Æolus, and Xuthus, and he gave his name to the nation—Hellenas. In dividing the country among his sons, Æolus received Thessaly; Xuthus, Peloponnesus; and Dorus, the country lying opposite, on the northern side of the Corinthian Gulf, as has been already mentioned in the preceding chapter. Substitute Deucalion for Noah, Greece for Armenia, and Dorus, Æolus, and Xuthus for Shem, Ham, and Japhet, and we see a reproduction of the Mosaic account of the second settlement of mankind.

As it is natural for men to trace their origin to illustrious progenitors, so the Greeks, in their various settlements, cherished the legends which represented themselves as sprung from gods and heroes—those great benefactors, whose exploits occupy the heroic ages. As Hercules was the Argine hero of the Peloponnesus, so Æolus was the father of heroes sacred in the history of the Æolians, who inhabited the largest part of Greece. Æolus reigned in Thessaly, the original seat of the Hellenes.

Pelias and Neleus.

Among his sons was Salmoneus, whose daughter, Tyro, became enamored of the river Eneipus, and frequenting its banks, the god Poseidon fell in love with her. The fruits of this alliance were the twin brothers, Pelias and Neleus, who quarreled respecting the possession of Iolchos, situated at the foot of Mount Pelion, celebrated afterward as the residence of Jason. Pelias prevailed, and Neleus returned into Peloponnesus and founded the kingdom of Pylos. His beautiful daughter, Pero, was sought in marriage by princes from all the neighboring countries, but he refused to entertain the pretensions of any of them, declaring that she should only wed the man who brought him the famous oxen of Iphiklos, in Thessaly. Melampus, the nephew of Neleus, obtained the oxen for his brother Bias, who thus obtained the hand of Pero. Of the twelve sons of Neleus, Nestor was the most celebrated. It was he who assembled the various chieftains for the siege of Troy, and was pre-eminent over all for wisdom.

Admetus.

Another descendant of Æolus was the subject of a beautiful legend. Admetus, who married a daughter of Pelias, and whose horses were tended by Apollo, for a time incarnated as a slave in punishment for the murder of the Cyclopes. Apollo, in gratitude, obtained from the Fates the privilege that the life of Admetus should be prolonged if any one could be found to die voluntarily for him. His wife, Alkestes, made the sacrifice, but was released from the grasp of death (Thanatos) by Hercules, the ancient friend of Admetus.

Jason and the Argonauts.

But a still more beautiful legend is associated with Jason, a great grandson of Æolus. Pelias, still reigning at Iolchos, was informed by the oracle to beware of the man who should appear before him with only one sandal. He was celebrating a festival in honor of Poseidon when Jason appeared, having lost one of his sandals in crossing a river. As a means of averting the danger, he imposed upon Jason the task, deemed desperate, of bringing back to Iolchos the "Golden Fleece." The result was the memorable Argonautic expedition of the ship Argo, to the distant land of Colchis, on the eastern coast of the Black Sea. Jason invited the noblest youth of Greece to join him in this voyage of danger and glory. Fifty illustrious persons joined him, including Hercules and Theseus, Castor and Pollux, Mopsus, and Orpheus. They proceeded along the coast of Thrace, up the Hellespont, past the southern coast of the Propontis, through the Bosphorus, onward past Bithynia and Pontus, and arrived at the river Phasis, south of the Caucasian mountains, where dwelt Æetes, whom they sought. But he refused to surrender the golden fleece except on conditions which were almost impossible. Medea, however, his daughter, fell in love with Jason, and by her means, assisted by Hecate, he succeeded in yoking the ferocious bulls and plowing the field, and sowing it with dragons' teeth. Still Æetes refused the reward, and meditated the murder of the Argonauts; but Medea lulled to sleep the dragon which guarded the fleece, and fled with her lover and his companions on board the Argo. The adventurers returned to Iolchos in safety, after innumerable perils, and by courses irreconcilable with all geographical truths. But Jason could avenge himself on Pelias only through the stratagem of his wife, and by her magical arts she induced the daughters of Pelias to cut up their father, and to cast his limbs into a cauldron, believing that by this method he would be restored to the vigor of youth, and Jason was thus revenged, and obtained possession of the kingdom, which he surrendered to a son of Pelias, and retired with his wife to Corinth. Here he lived ten years in prosperity, but repudiated Medea in order to marry Glance, the daughter of the king of Corinth; Medea avenged the insult by the poisoned robe she sent to Glance as a marriage present, while Jason perished, while asleep, from a fragment of his ship Argo, which fell upon him. Such is the legend of the Argonauts, which is typical of the naval adventures of the maritime Greeks, and their restless enterprises.

Sisyphus.

The legend of Sisyphus is connected with the early history of Corinth. Sisyphus was the son of Æolus, and founded this wealthy city. He was distinguished for cunning and deceit. He detected Antolycus, the son of Hermes, by marking his sheep under the foot, so that the arch-thief was obliged to acknowledge the superior craft of the Æolid, and restore the plunder. He discovered the amour of Zeus with the nymph Ægina, and told her mother where she was carried, which so incensed the "father of gods and men," that he doomed Sisyphus, in Hades, to the perpetual punishment of rolling up a hill a heavy stone, which, as soon as it reached the summit, rolled back again in spite of all his efforts. This legend illustrates the never ending toils and disappointments of men.

Bellerophon.

Sisyphus was the grandfather of Bellerophon, whose beauty made him the object of a violent passion on the part of Antea, the wife of a king of Argos. He rejected her advances, and became as violently hated. She made false accusations, and persuaded her husband to kill him. Not wishing to commit the murder directly, he sent him to his son-in-law, the king of

Sykia, in Asia Minor, with a folded tablet full of destructive symbols, which required him to perform perilous undertakings, which he successfully performed. He was then recognized as the son of a god, and married the daughter of the king. This legend reminds us of Joseph in Egypt.

Æolus.

We are compelled to omit other interesting legends of the Æolids, the sons and daughters of Æolus, among which are those which record the feats of Atalanta, and turn to those which relate to the Pelopids, who gave to the Peloponnesus its early poetic interest. Of this remarkable race were Tantalus, Pelops, Atreus, Thyestes, Agamemnon, Menelaus, Helen, and Hermione, all of whom figured in the ancient legendary genealogies.

Tantalus.

Tantalus resided, at a remote antiquity, near Mount Sipylus, in Lydia, and was a man of immense wealth, and pre-eminently favored both by gods and men. Intoxicated by prosperity, he stole nectar and ambrosia from the table of the gods, and revealed their secrets, for which he was punished in the under world by perpetual hunger and thirst, yet placed with fruit and water near him, which eluded his grasp when he attempted to touch them. He had two children, Pelops and Niobe. The latter was blessed with seven sons and seven daughters, which so inflamed her with pride that she claimed equality with the goddesses Latona and Diana, who favored her by their friendship. This presumption so incensed the goddesses, that they killed all her children, and Niobe wept herself to death, and was turned into a stone, a striking image of excessive grief.

Pelops.

Pelops was a Lydian king, but was expelled from Asia by Ilus, king of Troy, for his impieties. He came to Greece, and beat Hippodamenia, whose father was king of Pisa, near Olympia, in Elis, in a chariot race, when death was the penalty of failure. He succeeded by the favor of Poseidon, and married the princess, and became king of Pisa. He gave his name to the whole peninsula, which he was enabled to do from the great wealth he brought from Lydia, thus connecting the early settlements of the Peloponnesus with Asia Minor. He had numerous children, who became the sovereigns of different cities and states in Argos, Elis, Laconia, and Arcadia. One of them, Atreus, was king of Mycenæ, who inherited the sceptre of Zeus, and whose wealth was proverbial. The sceptre was made by Hephæstus (Vulcan) and given to Zeus; he gave it to Hermes; Hermes presented it to Pelops; and Pelops gave it to Atreus, the ruler of men. Atreus and his brother, Thyestes, bequeathed it to Agamemnon, who ruled at Mycenæ, while his brother, Menelaus, reigned at Sparta. It was the wife of Menelaus, Helen, who was carried away by Paris, which occasioned the Trojan war. Agamemnon was killed on his return from Troy, through the treachery of his wife Clytemnestra, who was seduced by Ægisthus, the son of Thyestes. His only son, Orestes, afterward avenged the murder, and recovered Mycenæ. Hermione, the only daughter of Menelaus and Helen, was given in marriage to the son of Achilles, Neoptolemas, who reigned in Thessaly. Mycenæ maintained its independence to the Persian invasion, and is rendered immortal by the Iliad and Odyssey. On the subsequent ascendency of Sparta, the bones of Orestes were brought from Tegea, where they had reposed for generations, in a coffin seven cubits long.

The other States of the Peloponnesus, have also their genealogical legends, which trace their ancestors to gods and goddesses, which I omit, and turn to those which belong to Attica.

The Deucalian deluge.

The great Deucalian deluge, according to legend, happened during the reign of Ogyges, 1796 years B.C., and 1020 before the first Olympiad. After a long interval, Cecrops, half man and half serpent, became king of the country. By some he is represented as a Pelasgian, by others, as an Egyptian. He introduced the first elements of civilized life—marriage, the twelve political divisions of Attica, and a new form of worship, abolishing the bloody sacrifices to Zeus. He gave to the country the name of Cecropia. During his reign there ensued a dispute between Athenæ and Poseidon, respecting the possession of the Acropolis. Poseidon struck the rocks with his trident, and produced a well of salt water; Athenæ planted an olive tree. The twelve Olympian gods decided the dispute, and awarded to Athenæ the coveted possession, and she ever afterward remained the protecting deity of Athens.

Theseus.

Among his descendants was Theseus, the great legendary hero of Attica, who was one of the Argonauts, and also one of those who hunted the Calidomian boar. He freed Attica from robbers and wild beasts, conquered the celebrated Minotaur of Crete, and escaped from the labyrinth by the aid of Ariadne, whom he carried off and abandoned. In the Iliad he is represented as fighting against the centaurs, and in the Hesiodic poems he is an amorous knight-errant, misguided by the beautiful Ægle. Among his other feats, inferior only to those of Hercules, he vanquished the Amazons—a nation of courageous and hardy women, who came from the country about Caucasus, and whose principal seats were near the modern Trezibond. They invaded Thrace, Asia Minor, Greece, Syria, Egypt, and the islands of the Ægean. The foundation of several towns in Asia Minor is ascribed to them. In the time of Theseus, this semi-mythical and semi-historical race of female warriors invaded Attica, and even penetrated to Athens, but were conquered by the hero king. Allusion is made to their defeat throughout the literature of Athens. Although Theseus was a purely legendary personage, the Athenians were accustomed to regard him as a great political reformer and legislator, who consolidated the Athenian commonwealth, distributing the people into three classes.

Theban legends. Cadmus. Œdipus.

The legends pertaining to Thebes occupy a prominent place in Grecian mythology. Cadmus, the son of Agenor, king of Phœnicia, leaves his country in search of his sister Europa, with whom Zeus, in the form of a bull, had fallen in love, and carried on his back to Crete. He first goes to Thrace, and thence to Delphi, to learn tidings of Europa, but the god directs him not to prosecute his search; he is to follow the guidance of a cow, and to found a city where the animal should lie down. The cow stops at the site of Thebes. He marries Harmonia, the daughter of Ares and Aphrodite, after having killed the dragons which guarded the fountain Allia, and sowed their teeth. From these armed men sprang up, who killed each other, except five. From these arose the five great families of Thebes, called Sparti. One of the Sparti marries a daughter of Cadmus, whose issue was Pentheus, who became king. It was in his reign that Dionysus appears as a god in Bœotia, the giver of the vine, and obtains divine honors in Thebes. Among the descendants of Cadmus was Laius. He is forewarned by an oracle that any son he should beget would destroy him, and hence he caused the infant Œdipus to be exposed on Mount Cithanon. Here the herdsmen of Polybus, king of Corinth, find him, and convey him to their lord who brings him up as his own child. Distressed by the taunts of companions as to his unknown parentage, he goes to Delphi, to inquire the name of his real father. He is told not to return to his own country, for it was his destiny to kill his father and become the husband of his mother. Knowing no country but Corinth, he pursues his way to Bœotia, and meets Laius in a chariot drawn by mules. A quarrel ensues from the insolence of attendants, and Œdipus kills Laius. The brother of Laius, Creon, succeeds to the throne of Thebes. The country around is vexed with a terrible monster, with the face of a woman, the wings of a bird, and the tail of a lion, called the Sphinx, who has learned from the Muses a riddle, which she proposed to the Thebans, and on every failure to resolve it one of them was devoured. But no person can solve the riddle. The king offers his crown and his sister Jocasta, wife of Laius, in marriage to any one who would explain the riddle. Œdipus solves it, and is made king of Thebes, and marries Jocasta. A fatal curse rests upon him. Jocasta, informed by the gods of her relationship, hangs herself in agony. Œdipus endures great miseries, as well as his children, whom he curses, and who quarrel about their inheritance, which quarrel leads to the siege of Thebes by Adrastus, king of Argos, who seeks to restore Polynices—one of the sons of Œdipus, to the throne of which he was dispossessed. The Argetan chieftains readily enter into the enterprise, assisted by numerous auxiliaries from Arcadia and Messenia. The Cadmeans, assisted by the Phocians, march out to resist the invaders, who are repulsed, in consequence of the magnanimity of a generous youth, who offers himself a victim to Ares. Eteocles then proposed to his brother, Polynices, the rival claimants, to decide the quarrel by single combat. It resulted in the death of both, and then in the renewal of the general contest, and the destruction of the Argeian chiefs, and Adrastus's return to Argos in shame and woe.

Creon.

But Creon, the father of the self-sacrificing Menæceus, succeeds on the death of the rival brothers, to the administration of Thebes. A second siege takes place, conducted by Adrastus, and the sons of those who had been slain. Thebes now falls, and Thereander, the son of Polynices, is made king. The legends of Thebes have furnished the great tragedians Sophocles and Euripides, with their finest subjects. In the fable of the Sphinx we trace a connection between Thebes and ancient Egypt.

But all the legends of ancient Greece yield in interest to that of Troy, which Homer chose as the subject of his immortal epic.

Dardanus.

Dardanus, a son of Zeus, is the primitive ancestor of the Trojan kings, whose seat of power was Mount Ida. His son, Erichthonius, became the richest of mankind, and had in his pastures three thousand mares. His son, Tros, was the father of Ilus, Assarcus, and Ganymede. The latter was stolen by Zeus to be his cup-bearer.

Ilus.

Ilus was the father of Laomedon, under whom Apollo and Poseidon, in mortal form, went through a temporary servitude—the former tending his flocks, the latter building the walls of Ilium. Laomedon was killed by Hercules, in punishment for his perfidy in giving him mortal horses for his destruction of a sea monster, instead of the immortal horses, as he had promised, the gift of Zeus to Tros.

Priam. Helen.

Among the sons of Laomedon was Priam, who was placed upon the throne. He was the father of illustrious sons, among whom were Hector and

Paris. The latter was exposed on Mount Ida, to avoid the fulfillment of an evil prophecy, but grew up beautiful and active among the flocks and herds. It was to him that the three goddesses, Here, Athenæ, and Aphrodite (Juno, Minerva, and Venus), presented their respective claims to beauty, which he awarded to Aphrodite, and by whom he was promised, in recompense, Helen, wife of the Spartan king, Menelaus, and daughter of Zeus. Aphrodite caused ships to be built for him, and he safely arrived in Sparta, and was hospitably entertained by the unsuspecting monarch. In the absence of Menelaus in Crete, Paris carries away to Troy both Helen, and a large sum of money belonging to the king. Menelaus hastens home, informed of the perfidy, and consults his brother, Agamemnon, and the venerable Nestor. They interest the Argeian chieftains, who resolve to recover Helen. Ten years are spent in preparations, consisting of one thousand one hundred and eighty-six ships, and one hundred thousand men, comprised of heroes from all parts of Greece, among whom are Ajax, Diomedes, Achilles, and Odysseus. The heroes set sail from Aulis, and after various mistakes, reach Asia.

The Trojan war.

Meanwhile the Trojans assemble, with a large body of allies, to resist the invaders, who demand the redress of a great wrong. The Trojans are routed in battle, and return within their walls. After various fortunes, the city is taken, at the end of ten years, by stratagem, and the Grecian chieftains who were not killed seek to return to their own country, with Helen among the spoils. They meet with many misfortunes, from the anger of the gods, for not having spared the altars of Troy. Their chieftains quarrel among themselves, and even Agamemnon and Menelaus lose their fraternal friendship. After long wanderings, and bitter disappointments, and protracted hopes, the heroes return to their homes—such as war had spared—to recount their adventures and sufferings, and reconstruct their shattered States, and mend their broken fortunes—a type of war in all the ages, calamitous even to conquerors. The wanderings of Ulysses have a peculiar fascination, since they form the subject of the Odyssey, one of the noblest poems of antiquity. Nor are the adventures of Æneas scarcely less interesting, as presented by Virgil, who traces the first Settlement of Latium to the Trojan exiles. We should like to dwell on the siege of Troy, and its great results, but the subject is too extensive and complicated. The student of the great event, whether historical or mystical, must read the detailed accounts in the immortal epics of Homer. We have only space for the grand outlines, which can be scarcely more than allusions.

The legend of the Heraclidæ.

Scarcely inferior to the legend of Troy, is that which recounts the return of the descendants of Hercules to the ancient inheritance on the Peloponnesus, which, it is supposed, took place three or four hundred years before authentic history begins, or eighty years after the Trojan war.

We have briefly described the geographical position of the most important part of ancient Greece—the Peloponnesus—almost an island, separated from the continent only by a narrow gulf, resembling in shape a palm-tree, indented on all sides by bays, and intersected with mountains, and inhabited by a simple and warlike race.

We have seen that the descendants of Perseus, who was a descendant of Danaus, reigned at Mycenæ in Argolis—among whom was Amphitryon, who fled to Thebes, on the murder of his uncle, with Alemena his wife. Then Hercules, to whom the throne of Mycenæ legitimately belonged, was born, but deprived of his inheritance by Eurystheus—a younger branch of the Perseids—in consequence of the anger and jealousy of Juno, and to whom, by the fates, Hercules was made subject. We have seen how the sons of Hercules, under Hyllos, attempted to regain their kingdom, but were defeated, and retreated among the Dorians.

Their settlement in Sparta.

After three generations, the Heraclidæ set out to regain their inheritance, assisted by the Dorians. They at length, after five expeditions, gained possession of the country, and divided it, among the various chieftains, who established their dominion in Argos, Mycenæ, and Sparta, which, at the time of the Trojan war, was ruled by Agamemnon and Menelaus, descendants of Pelops. In the next generation, Corinth was conquered by the Dorians, under an Heraclide prince.

The wanderings of the dispossessed Achæans.

The Achæans, thus expelled by the Dorians from the south and east of the Peloponnesus, fell back upon the northwest coast, and drove away the Ionians, and formed a confederacy of twelve cities, which in later times became of considerable importance. The dispossessed Ionians joined their brethren of the same race in Attica, but the rugged peninsula was unequal to support the increased population, and a great migration took place to the Cyclades and the coasts of Lydia. The colonists there built twelve cities, about one hundred and forty years after the Trojan war. Another body of Achæans, driven out of the Peloponnesus by the Dorians, first settled in Bœotia, and afterward, with Æolians, sailed to the isle of Lesbos, where they founded six cities, and then to the opposite mainland. At the foot of Mount Ida they founded the twelve Æolian cities, of which Smyrna was the principal.

Crete.

Crete was founded by a body of Dorians and conquered Achæans. Rhodes received a similar colony. So did the island of Cos. The cities of Lindus, Ialysus, Camirus, Cos, with Cnidus and Halicarnassus, on the mainland, formed the Dorian Hexapolis of Caria, inferior, however, to the Ionian and Æolian colonies.

The Dorians and Ionians become the leading tribes.

At the beginning of the mythical age the dominant Hellenic races were the Achæans and Æolians; at the close, the Ionians and Dorians were predominant. The Ionians extended their maritime possessions from Attica to the Asiatic colonies across the Ægean, and gradually took the lead of the Asiatic Æolians, and formed a great maritime empire under the supremacy of Athens. The Hellenic world ultimately was divided and convulsed by the great contest for supremacy between the Dorians and Ionians, until the common danger from the Persian invasion united them together for a time.

First Olympiad, the era of the historic period.

Thus far we have only legend to guide us in the early history of Greece. The historical period begins with the First Olympiad, B.C. 776. Before this all is uncertain, yet as probable as the events of English history in the mythical period between the departure of the Romans and the establishment of the Anglo-Saxon kingdom. The history is not all myth; neither is it clearly authenticated.

Grecian leagues.

The various Hellenic tribes, though separated by political ambition, were yet kindred in language and institutions. They formed great leagues, or associations, of neighboring cities, for the performance of religious rites. The Amphictyonic Council, which became subsequently so famous, was made up of Thessalians, Bœotians, Dorians, Ionians, Achæans, Locrians, and Phocians—all Hellenic in race. Their great centre was the temple of Apollo at Delphi. The different tribes or nations also came together regularly to take part in the four great religious festivals or games—the Olympic, Pythian, Isthmian, and Nemæan—the two former of which were celebrated every four years.

Early dominant states.

In the Homeric age the dominant State was Achæa, whose capital was Mycenæ. The next in power was Lacedæmon. After the Dorian conquest, Argos was the first, Sparta the second, and Messenia the third State in importance. Argos, at the head of a large confederacy of cities on the northeast of the Peloponnesus, was governed by Phidon—an irresponsible ruler, a descendant of Hercules, to whom is inscribed the coinage of silver and copper money, and the introduction of weights and measures. He flourished B.C. 747.

Interest to be attached to the legends of Greece.

All these various legends, though unsupported by history, have a great ethical importance, as well as poetic interest. The passions, habits, and adventures of a primitive and warlike race are presented by the poets with transcendent effect, and we read lessons of human nature as in the dramas of Shakespeare. Hence, one of the most learned and dignified of the English historians deems it worthy of his pen to devote to these myths a volume of his noble work. Nor is it misplaced labor. These legends furnished subjects to the tragic and epic poets of antiquity, as well as to painters and sculptors, in all the ages of art. They are identified with the development of Grecian genius, and are as imperishable as history itself. They were to the Greeks realities, and represent all that is vital in their associations and worship. They stimulated the poetic faculty, and taught lessons of moral wisdom which all nations respect and venerate. They contributed to enrich both literature and art. They make Æschylus, Euripides, Pindar, Homer, and Hesiod great monumental pillars of the progress of the human race. Therefore, we will not willingly let those legends die in our memories or hearts.

Their historical importance.

They are particularly important as shedding light on the manners, customs, and institutions of the ancient Greeks, although they give no reliable historical facts. They are memorials of the first state of Grecian society, essentially different from the Oriental world. We see in them the germs of political constitutions—the rise of liberty—the pre-eminence of families which forms the foundation for oligarchy, or the ascendency of nobles. We see also the first beginnings of democratic influence—the voice of the people asserting a claim to be heard in the market-place. We see again the existence of slavery—captives taken in war doomed to attendance in princely palaces, and ultimately to menial labor on the land. In those primitive times a State was often nothing but a city, with the lands surrounding it, and therefore it was possible for all the inhabitants to assemble in the agora with the king and nobles. We find, in the early condition of Greece, kings, nobles, citizens, and slaves.

The early government of the Hellenes. The king.

The king was seldom distinguished by any impassable barrier between himself and subjects. He was rather the chief among his nobles, and his supremacy was based on descent from illustrious ancestors. It passed generally to the eldest son. In war he was a leader; in peace, a protector. He offered up prayers and sacrifices for his people to the gods in whom they all alike believed. He possessed an ample domain, and the produce of his lands was devoted to a generous but rude hospitality. He had a large share of the plunder taken from an enemy, and the most alluring of the female captives. It was, however, difficult for him to retain ascendency without great personal gifts and virtues, and especially bravery on the field of battle, and wisdom in council. To the noblest of these kings the legends ascribe great bodily strength and activity.

The councils.

The kings were assisted by a great council of chieftains or nobles, whose functions were deliberation and consultation; and after having talked over their intentions with the chiefs, they announced them to the people, who assembled in the market-place, and who were generally submissive to the royal authority, although they were regarded as the source of power. Then the king, and sometimes his nobles, administered justice and heard complaints. Public speaking was favorable to eloquence, and stimulated intellectual development, and gave dignity to tho people to whom the speeches were addressed.

Religious and social life.

In those primitive times there was a strong religious feeling, great reverence for the gods, whose anger was deprecated, and whose favor was sought. The ties of families were strong. Paternal authority was recognized and revered. Marriage was a sacred institution. The wife occupied a position of great dignity and influence. Women were not secluded in a harem, as were the Asiatics, but employed in useful labors. Children were obedient, and brothers, sisters, and cousins were united together by strong attachments. Hospitality was a cherished virtue, and the stranger was ever cordially welcome, nor questioned even until refreshed by the bath and the banquet. Feasts were free from extravagance and luxury, and those who shared in them enlivened the company by a recital of the adventures of gods and men. But passions were unrestrained, and homicide was common. The murderer was not punished by the State, but was left to the vengeance of kindred and friends, appeased sometimes by costly gifts, as among the ancient Jews.

Early forms of civilization.

There was a rude civilization among the ancient Greeks, reminding us of the Teutonic tribes, but it was higher than theirs. We observe the division of the people into various trades and occupations—carpenters, smiths, leather-dressers, leeches, prophets, bards, and fishermen, although the main business was agriculture. Cattle were the great staple of wealth, and the largest part of the land was devoted to pasture. The land was tilled chiefly by slaves, and women of the servile class were doomed to severe labor and privations. They brought the water, and they turned the mills. Spinning and weaving were, however, the occupations of all, and garments for men and women were alike made at home. There was only a limited commerce, which was then monopolized by the Phœnicians, who exaggerated the dangers of the sea. There were walled cities, palaces, and temples. Armor was curiously wrought, and arms were well made. Rich garments were worn by princes, and their palaces glittered with the precious metals. Copper was hardened so as to be employed in weapons of war. The warriors had chariots and horses, and were armed with sword, dagger, and spear, and were protected by helmets, breastplates, and greaves. Fortified cities were built on rocky elevations, although the people generally lived in unfortified villages. The means of defense were superior to those of offense, which enabled men to preserve their acquisitions, for the ancient chieftains resembled the feudal barons of the Middle Ages in the passion for robbery and adventure. We do not read of coined money nor the art of writing, nor sculpture, nor ornamental architecture among the Homeric Greeks; but they were fond of music and poetry. Before history commences, they had their epics, which, sung by the bards and minstrels, furnished Homer and Hesiod with materials for their noble productions. It is supposed by Grote that the Homeric poems were composed eight hundred and fifty years before Christ, and preserved two hundred years without the aid of writing—of all poems the most popular and natural, and addressed to unlettered minds.

Such were the heroic ages with their myths, their heroes, their simple manners, their credulity, their religious faith, their rude civilization. We have now to trace their progress through the historical epoch.

CHAPTER XV
THE GRECIAN STATES AND COLONIES
TO THE PERSIAN WARS

We come now to consider those States which grew into importance about the middle of the eighth century before Christ, at the close of the legendary period.

Lycurgus.

The most important of these was Sparta, which was the leading State. We have seen how it was conquered by Dorians, under Heraclic princes. Its first great historic name was Lycurgus, whom some historians, however, regard as a mythical personage.

His legislation.

Sparta was in a state of anarchy in consequence of the Dorian conquest, a contest between the kings, aiming at absolute power, and the people, desirous of democratic liberty. At this juncture the king, Polydectes, died, leaving Lycurgus, his brother, guardian of the realm, and of the infant heir to the throne. The future lawgiver then set out on his travels, visiting the other States of Greece, Asia Minor, Egypt, and other countries, and returned to Sparta about the period of the first Olympiad, B.C. 776, with a rich store of wisdom and knowledge. The State was full of disorders, but he instituted great reforms, aided by the authority of the Delphic oracle, and a strong party of influential men. His great object was to convert the citizens of Sparta into warriors united by the strongest bonds, and trained to the severest discipline, governed by an oligarchy under the form of the ancient monarchy. In other words, his object was to secure the ascendency of the small body of Dorian invaders that had conquered Laconia.

Spartan citizens.

The descendants of these invaders, the Spartans, alone possessed the citizenship, and were equal in political rights. They were the proprietors of the soil, which was tilled by Helots. The Spartans disdained any occupation but war and government. They lived within their city, which was a fortified camp, and ate in common at public tables, and on the simplest fare. Every virtue and energy were concentrated on self-discipline and sacrifice, in order to fan the fires of heroism and self-devotion. They were a sort of stoics—hard, severe, proud, despotic, and overbearing. They cared nothing for literature, or art, or philosophy. Even eloquence was disdained, and the only poetry or music they cultivated were religions hymns and heroic war songs. Commerce was forbidden by the constitution, and all the luxuries to which it leads. Only iron was allowed for money, and the precious metals were prohibited. Every exercise, every motive, every law, contributed to make the Spartans soldiers, and nothing but soldiers. Their discipline was the severest known to the ancients. Their habits of life were austere and rigid. They were trained to suffer any hardship without complaint.

The old Achæan population.

Besides these Spartan citizens were the *Periœci*—remnants of the old Achæan population, but mixed with an inferior class of Dorians. They had no political power, but possessed personal freedom. They were landed proprietors, and engaged in commerce and manufactures.

The Helots.

Below this class were the Helots—pure Greeks, but reduced to dependence by conquest. They were bound to the soil, like serfs, but dwelt with their families on the farms they tilled. They were not bought and sold as slaves. They were the body servants of the Spartan citizens, and were regarded as the property of the State. They were treated with great haughtiness and injustice by their masters, which bred at last an intense hatred.

The Ecclesia.

All political power was in the hands of the citizen warriors, only about nine thousand in number in the time of Lycurgus. From them emanated all delegated authority, except that of kings. This assembly, or *ecclesia*, of Spartans over thirty years of age, met at stated intervals to decide on all important matters submitted to them, but they had no right of amendment— only a simple approval or rejection.

The Senate.

The body to which the people, it would seem, delegated considerable power, was the Senate, composed of thirty members, not under sixty years of age, and elected for life. They were a deliberative body, and judges in all capital charges against Spartans. They were not chosen for noble birth or property qualifications, but for merit and wisdom.

The kings.

At the head of the State, at least nominally, were two kings, who were numbered with the thirty senators. They had scarcely more power than the Roman consuls; they commanded the armies, and offered the public sacrifices, and were revered as the descendants of Hercules.

The Ephors.

The persons of most importance were the ephors, chosen annually by the people, who exercised the chief executive power, and without responsibility. They could even arrest kings, and bring them to trial before the Senate. Two of the five ephors accompanied the king in war, and were a check on his authority.

Aristocratic form of government. The citizen lost in the State.

It would thus seem that the government of Sparta was a republic of an aristocratic type. There were no others nobler than citizens, but these citizens composed but a small part of the population. They were Spartans—a handful of conquerors, in the midst of hostile people—a body of lords among slaves and subjects. They sympathized with law and order, and detested the democratical turbulence of Athens. They were trained, by their military education, to subordination, obedience, and self-sacrifice. They, as citizens or as soldiers, existed only for the *State*, and to the State every thing was subordinate. In our times, the State is made for the people; in Sparta, the people for the State. This generated an intense patriotism and self-denial. It also permitted a greater interference of the State in personal matters than would now be tolerated in any despotism in Europe. It made the citizens submissive to a division of property, which if not a perfect community of goods, was fatal to all private fortunes. But the property which the citizens thus shared was virtually created by the Helots, who alone tilled the ground. The wealth of nations is in the earth, and it is its cultivation which is the ordinary source of property. The State, not individual masters, owned the Helots; and they toiled for the citizens. In the modern sense of liberty, there was very little in Sparta, except that which was possessed by the aristocratic citizens—the conquerors of the country—men, whose very occupation was war and government, and whose very amusement were those which fostered warlike habits. The Roman citizens did not disdain husbandry, nor the Puritan settlers of New England, but the Spartan citizens despised both this and all trade and manufacture. Never was a haughtier class of men than these Spartan soldiers. They exceeded in pride the feudal chieftain.

Number of citizens.

Such an exclusive body of citizens, however, jealous of their political privileges, constantly declined in numbers, so that, in the time of Aristotle, there were only one thousand Spartan citizens; and this decline continued in spite of all the laws by which the citizens were compelled to marry, and those customs, so abhorrent to our Christian notions, which permitted the invasion of marital rights for the sake of healthy children.

Spartan armies.

As it was to war that the best energies of the Spartans were directed, so their armies were the admiration of the ancient world for discipline and effectiveness. They were the first who reduced war to a science. The general type of their military organization was the phalanx, a body of troops in close array, armed with a long spear and short sword. The strength of an army was in the heavy armed infantry; and this body was composed almost entirely of citizens, with a small mixture of Periœci. From the age of twenty to sixty, every Spartan was liable to military service; and all the citizens formed an army, whether congregated at Sparta, or absent on foreign service.

Such, in general, were the social, civil, and military institutions of Sparta, and not peculiar to her alone, but to all the Dorians, even in Crete; from which we infer that it was not Lycurgus who shaped them, but that they existed independent of his authority. He may have re-established the old regulations, and gave his aid to preserve the State from corruption and decay. And when we remember that the constitution which he re-established resisted both the usurpations of tyrants and the advances of democracy, by which other States were revolutionized, we can not sufficiently admire the wisdom which so early animated the Dorian legislators.

The Spartans obtain the ascendency on the Peninsula.

The Spartans became masters of the country after a long struggle, and it was henceforth called Laconia. The more obstinate Achæans became Helots. After the conquest, the first memorable event in Spartan history was the reduction of Messenia, for which it took two great wars.

Messenia. The war with Sparta.

Messenia has already been mentioned as the southwestern part of the Peloponnesus, and resembling Laconia in its general aspects. The river Parnisus flows through its entire length, as Eurotas does in Laconia, forming fertile valleys and plains, and producing various kinds of cereals and fruits, even as it now produces oil, silk, figs, wheat, maize, cotton, wine, and honey. The area of Messenia is one thousand one hundred and ninety-two square miles, not so large as one of our counties. The early inhabitants had been conquered by the Dorians, and it was against the descendants of these conquerors that the Spartans made war. The murder of a Spartan king, Teleclus, at a temple on the confines of Laconia and Messenia, where sacrifices were offered in common, gave occasion for the first war, which lasted nineteen years, B.C. 743. Other States were involved in the quarrel—Corinth on the side of Sparta, and Sicyon and Arcadia on the part of the Messenians. The Spartans having the superiority in the field, the Messenians retreated to their stronghold of Ithome, where they defended themselves fifteen years. But at last they were compelled to abandon it, and the fortress was razed to the ground. The conquered were reduced to the condition of Helots—compelled to cultivate the land and pay half of its produce to their new masters. The Spartan citizens became the absolute owners of the whole soil of Messenia.

Aristomenes. Conquest of Messenia.

After thirty-nine years of servitude, a hero arose among the conquered Messenians, Aristomenes, like Judas Maccabeus, or William Wallace, who incited his countrymen to revolt. The whole of the Peloponnesus became involved in the new war, and only Corinth became the ally of Sparta; the remaining States of Argos, Sicyon, Arcadia, and Pisa, sided with the Messenians. The Athenian poet, Tyrtæus, stimulated the Spartans by his war-songs. In the first great battle, the Spartans were worsted; in the second, they gained a signal victory, so that the Messenians were obliged to leave the open country and retire to the fortress on Mount Ira. Here they maintained themselves eleven years, the Spartans being unused to sieges, and trained only to conflict in the open field. The fortress was finally taken by treachery, and the hero who sought to revive the martial glories of his State fled to Rhodes. Messenia became now, B.C. 668, a part of Laconia, and it was three hundred years before it appeared again in history.

Aggrandizement of Sparta.

The Spartans, after the conquest of Messenia, turned their eyes upon Arcadia—that land of shepherds, free and simple and brave like themselves. The city of Tegea long withstood the arms of the Spartans, but finally yielded to superior strength, and became a subject ally, B.C. 560. Sparta was further increased by a part of Argos, and a great battle, B.C. 547, between the Argives and Spartans, resulted in the complete ascendency of Sparta in the southern part of the Peloponnesus, about the time that Cyrus overthrew the Lydian empire. The Ionian Greeks of Asia Minor invoked their aid against the Persian power, and Sparta proudly rallied in their defense.

Political changes. The age of Tyrants.

Meanwhile, a great political revolution was going on in the other States of Greece, in no condition to resist the pre-eminence of Sparta, The patriarchal monarchies of the heroic ages had gradually been subverted by the rising importance of the nobility, enriched by conquered lands. Every conquest, every step to national advancement, brought the nobles nearer to the crown, and the government passed into the hands of those nobles who had formerly composed the council of the king. With the growing power of nobles was a corresponding growth of the political power of the people or citizens, in consequence of increased wealth and intelligence. The political changes were rapid. As the nobles had usurped the power of the kings, so the citizens usurped the power of the nobles. The everlasting war of classes, where the people are intelligent and free, was signally illustrated in the Grecian States, and democracy succeeded to the oligarchy which had prostrated kings. Then, when the people had gained the ascendency, ambitious and factious demagogues in turn, got the control, and these adventurers, now called Tyrants, assumed arbitrary powers. Their power was only maintained by cruelty, injustice, and unscrupulous means, which caused them finally to be so detested that they were removed by assassination. These natural changes, from a monarchy, primitive and just and limited, to an oligarchy of nobles, and the gradual subversion of their power by wealthy and enlightened citizens, and then the rise of demagogues, who became tyrants, have been illustrated in all ages of the world. But the rapidity of these changes in the Grecian States, with the progress of wealth and corruption, make their history impressive on all generations. It is these rapid and natural revolutions which give to the political history of Greece its permanent interest and value. The age of the Tyrants is generally fixed from B.C. 650 to B.C. 500—about one hundred and fifty years.

Corinthia.

No State passed through these changes of government more signally than Corinthia, which, with Megaris, formed the isthmus which connected the Peloponnesus with Greece Proper. It was a small territory, covered with the ridges and the spurs of the Geranean and and Oneian mountains, and useless for purposes of agriculture. Its principal city was Corinth; was favorably situated for commerce, and rapidly grew in population and wealth. It also commanded the great roads which led from Greece Proper through the defiles of the mountains into the Peloponnesus. It rapidly monopolized the commerce of the Ægean Sea, and the East through the Saronic Gulf; and through the Corinthian Gulf it commanded the trade of the Ionian and Sicilian seas.

Changes in Corinth.

Corinth, by some, is supposed have been a Phœnician colony. Before authentic history begins, it was inhabited by a mixed population of Æolians and Ionians, the former of whom were dominant. Over them reigned Sisyphus, according to tradition, the grandfather of Bellerophon who laid the foundation of mercantile prosperity. The first historical king was Aletes,

B.C. 1074, the leader of Dorian invaders, who subdued the Æolians, and incorporated them with their own citizens. The descendants of Aletes reigned twelve generations, when the nobles converted the government into an oligarchy, under Bacchis, who greatly increased the commercial importance of the city. In 754, B.C., Corinth began to colonize, and fitted out a war fleet for the protection of commerce. The oligarchy was supplanted by Cypselus, B.C. 655, a man of the people, whose mother was of noble birth, but rejected by her family, of the ruling house of the Bacchiadæ, on account of lameness. His son Periander reigned forty years with cruel despotism, but made Corinth the leading commercial city of Greece, and he subjected to her sway the colonies planted on the islands of the Ionian Sea, one of which was Corcyra (Corfu), which gained a great mercantile fame. It was under his reign that the poet Arion, or Lesbos, flourished, to whom he gave his patronage. In three years after the death of Periander, 585 B.C., the oligarchal power was restored, and Corinth allied herself with Sparta in her schemes of aggrandizement.

Changes in Megara.

The same change of government was seen in Megara, a neighboring State, situated on the isthmus, between Corinth and Attica, and which attained great commercial distinction. As a result of commercial opulence, the people succeeded in overthrowing the government, an oligarchy of Dorian conquerors, and elevating a demagogue, Theagenes, to the supreme power, B.C. 630. He ruled tyrannically, in the name of the people, for thirty years, but was expelled by the oligarchy, which regained power. During his reign all kinds of popular excesses were perpetrated, especially the confiscation of the property of the rich.

Changes in other States.

Other States are also illustrations of this change of government from kings to oligarchies, and oligarchies to demagogues and tyrants, as on the isle of Lesbos, where Pittacus reigned dictator, but with wisdom and virtue—one of the seven wise men of Greece—and in Samos, where Polycrates rivaled the fame of Periander, and adorned his capital with beautiful buildings, and patronized literature and art. One of his friends was Anacreon, the poet. He was murdered by the Persians, B.C. 522.

But the State which most signally illustrates the revolutions in government was Athens.

"Where on the Ægean shore a city stands,—

Built nobly; pure the air, and light the soil:

Athena, the eye of Greece, mother of arts

And eloquence, native to famous wits."

Early history of Athens. Theseus. Codrus.

Every thing interesting or impressive in the history of classical antiquity clusters round this famous city, so that without Athens there could be no Greece. Attica, the little State of which it was the capital, formed a triangular peninsula, of about seven hundred square miles. The country is hilly and rocky, and unfavorable to agriculture; but such was the salubrity of the climate, and the industry of the people, all kinds of plants and animals flourished. The history of the country, like that of the other States, is mythical, to the period of the first Olympiad. Ogyges has the reputation of being the first king of a people who claimed to be indigenous, about one hundred and fifty years before the arrival of Cecrops, who came, it is supposed, from Egypt, and founded Athens, and taught the simple but savage natives a new religion, and the elements of civilized life, 1556 B.C. It received its name from the goddess Neith, introduced by him from Egypt, under the name of Athena, or Minerva. It was also called Cecropia, from its founder. Until the time of Theseus it was a small town, confined to the Acropolis and Mars Hill. This hero is the great name of ancient Athenian legend, as Hercules is to Greece generally. He cleared the roads of robbers, and formed an aristocratical constitution, with a king, who was only the first of his nobles. But he himself, after having given political unity, was driven away by a conspiracy of nobles, leaving the throne to Menesthius, a descendant of the ancient kings. This monarch reigned twenty-four years, and lost his life at the siege of Troy. The whole period of the monarchy lies within the mythical age. Tradition makes Codrus the last king, who was slain during an invasion of the Dorians, B.C. 1045. Resolving to have no future king, the Athenians substituted the office of archon, or ruler, and made his son, Medus, the superior magistrate. This office remained hereditary in the family of Codrus for thirteen generations. In B.C. 752, the duration of the office was fixed for ten years. It remained in the family of Codrus thirty-eight years longer, when it was left open for all the nobles. In 683 B.C. nine archons were annually elected from the nobles, the first having superior dignity.

Draco.

The first of these archons, of whom any thing of importance is recorded, was Draco, who governed Athens in the year 624 B.C., who promulgated written laws, exceedingly severe, inflicting capital punishment for slight offenses. The people grew weary of him and his laws, and he was banished to Ægina, where he died, from a conspiracy headed by Cylon, one of the nobles, who seized the Acropolis, B.C. 612. His insurrection, however, failed, and he was treacherously put to death by one of the archons, which led to the expulsion of the whole body, and a change in the constitution.

Solon.

This was effected by Solon, the Athenian sage and law-giver—himself of the race of Codrus, whom the Athenians chose as archon, with full power to make new laws. Intrusted with absolute power, he abstained from abusing it—a patriot in the most exalted sense, as well as a poet and philosopher. Urged by his friends to make himself tyrant, he replied that tyranny might be a fair country, only there was no way out of it.

His institutions.

When he commenced his reforms, the nobles, or Eupatridæ, were in possession of most of the fertile land of Attica, while the poorer citizens possessed only the sterile highlands. This created an unhappy jealousy between the rich and poor. Besides, there was another class that had grown rich by commerce, animated by the spirit of freedom. But their influence tended to widen the gulf between the rich and poor. The poor got into debt, and fell in the power of creditors, and sunk to the condition of serfs, and many were even sold in slavery, for the laws were severe against debtors, as in ancient Rome. Solon, like Moses in his institution of the Year of Jubilee, set free all the estates and persons that had fallen in the power of creditors, and ransomed such as were sold in slavery.

Loss of aristocratic power. Different classes.

Having removed the chief source of enmity between the rich and poor, he repealed the bloody laws of Draco, and commenced to remodel the political constitution. The fundamental principles which he adopted was a distribution of power to all citizens according to their wealth. But the nobles were not deprived of their ascendency, only the way was opened to all citizens to reach political distinction, especially those who were enriched by commerce. He made an assessment of the landed property of all the citizens, taking as the medium a standard of value which was equivalent to a drachma of annual produce. The first class, who had no aristocratic titles, were called Pentacosio medimni, from possessing five hundred medimni or upward. They alone were eligible to the archonship and other high offices, and bore the largest share of the public burdens. The second class was called Knights, because they were bound to serve as cavalry. They filled the inferior offices, farmed the revenue, and had the commerce of the country in their hands.

Other political changes.

The third class was called Zeugitæ (yokesmen), from their ability to keep a yoke of oxen. They were small farmers, and served in the heavy-armed infantry, and were subject to a property-tax. All those whose incomes fell short of two hundred medimni formed the fourth class, and served in the light-armed troops, and were exempt from property-tax, but disqualified for public office, and yet they had a vote in popular elections, and in the judgment passed upon archons at the expiration of office. "The direct responsibility of all the magistrates to the popular assembly, was the most democratic of all the institutions of Solon; and though the government was still in the hands of the oligarchy, Solon clearly foresaw, if he did not purposely prepare for, the preponderance of the popular element." "To guard against hasty measures, he also instituted the Senate of four hundred, chosen year by year, from the four Ionic tribes, whose office was to prepare all business for the popular assembly, and regulate its meetings. The Areopagus retained its ancient functions, to which Solon added a general oversight over all the public institutions, and over the private life of the citizens. He also enacted many other laws for the administration of justice, the regulation of social life, the encouragement of commerce, and the general prosperity of the State." His whole legislation is marked by wisdom and patriotism, and adaptation to the circumstances of the people who intrusted to him so much power and dignity. The laws were, however, better than the people, and his legislative wisdom and justice place him among the great benefactors of mankind, for who can tell the ultimate influence of his legislation on Rome and on other nations. The most beautiful feature was the responsibility of the chief magistrates to the people who elected them, and from the fact that they could subsequently be punished for bad conduct was the greatest security against tyranny and peculation.

Departure of Solon from Athens. Pisistratus. His reign. Hippias.

After having given this constitution to his countrymen, the lawgiver took his departure from Athens, for ten years, binding the people by a solemn oath to make no alteration in his laws. He visited Egypt, Cyprus, and Asia Minor, and returned to Athens to find his work nearly subverted by one of his own kinsmen. Pisistratus, of noble origin, but a demagogue, contrived, by his arts and prodigality, to secure a guard, which he increased, and succeeded in seizing the Acropolis, B.C. 560, and in usurping the supreme authority—so soon are good laws perverted, so easily are constitutions overthrown, when demagogues and usurpers are sustained by the people. A combination of the rich and poor drove him into exile; but their divisions and hatreds favored his return. Again he was exiled by popular dissension, and a third time he regained his power, but only by a battle. He sustained his usurpation by means of Thracian mercenaries, and sent the children of all he suspected as hostages to Naxos. He veiled his despotic power under the forms of the constitution, and even submitted himself to the judgment of the Areopagus on the charge of murder. He kept up his popularity by generosity and affability, by mingling freely with the citizens, by opening to them his gardens, by adorning the city with beautiful edifices, and by a liberal patronage of arts and letters. He founded a public library, and collected the Homeric poems in a single volume. He ruled beneficently, as tyrants often have, — like Cæsar, like Richelieu, like Napoleon, — identifying his own glory with the welfare of the State. He died after a successful reign of thirty-three years, B.C. 527, and his two sons, Hippias and Hipparchus, succeeded him in the government, ruling, like their father, at first wisely but despotically, cultivating art and letters and friendship of great men. But sensual passions led to outrages which resulted in the assassination of Hipparchus. Hippias, having punished the conspirators, changed the spirit of the government, imposed arbitrary taxes, surrounded himself with an armed guard, and ruled tyrannically and cruelly. After four years of despotic government, Athens was liberated, chiefly by aid of the Lacedæmonians, now at the highest of their power. Hippias retired to the court of Persia, and planned and guided the attack of Darius on Greece—a traitor of the most infamous kind, since he combined tyranny at home with the coldest treachery to his country. His accursed family were doomed to perpetual banishment, and never succeeded in securing a pardon. Their power had lasted fifty years, and had been fatal to the liberties of Athens.

Cleisthenes. The increase of the Senate.

The Lacedæmonians did not retire until their king Cleomenes formed a close friendship with Isagoras, the leader of the aristocratic party—and no people were prouder of their birth than the old Athenian nobles. Opposed to him was Cleisthenes, of the noble family of the Alcmæonids, who had been banished in the time of Megacles, for the murder of Cylon, who had been treacherously enticed from the sanctuary at the altar of Athena. Cleisthenes gained the ear of the people, and prevailed over Isagoras, and effected another change in the constitution, by which it became still more democratic. He remodeled the basis of citizenship, heretofore confined to the four Ionic tribes; and divided the whole country into demes, or parishes, each of which managed its local affairs. All freemen were enrolled in the demes, and became members of the tribes, now ten in number, instead of the old four Ionian tribes. He increased the members of the senate from four to five hundred, fifty members being elected from each tribe. To this body was committed the chief functions of executive government. It sat in permanence, and was divided into ten sections, one for each tribe, and each section or committee, called *prytany*, had the presidency of the senate and ecclesia during its term. Each prytany of fifty members was subdivided into committees of ten, each of which held the presidency for seven days, and out of these a chairman was chosen by lot every day, to preside in the senate and assembly, and to keep the keys of the Acropolis and treasury, and public seal. Nothing shows jealousy of power more than the brief term of office which the president exercised.

The ecclesia.

The ecclesia, or assembly of the people, was the arena for the debate of all public measures. The archons were chosen according to the regulations of Solon, but were stripped of their power, which was transferred to the senate and ecclesia. The generals were elected by the people annually, one from each tribe. They were called strategi, and had also the direction of foreign affairs. It was as first strategus that Pericles governed—"prime minister of the people."

Ostracism.

In order to guard against the ascendency of tyrants—the great evil of the ancient States, Cleisthenes devised the institution of *ostracism*, by which a suspected or obnoxious citizen could be removed from the city for ten years, though practically abridged to five. It simply involved an exclusion from political power, without casting a stigma on the character. It was virtually a retirement, during which his property and rights remained intact, and attended with no disgrace. The citizens, after the senate had decreed the vote was needful, were required to write a name in an oyster shell, and he who had less than six thousand votes was obliged to withdraw within ten days from the city. The wisdom of this measure is proved in the fact that no tyrannical usurpation occurred at Athens after that of Pisistratus. This revolution which Cleisthenes effected was purely democratic, to which the aristocrats did not submit without a struggle. The aristocrats called to their aid the Spartans, but without other effect than creating that long rivalry which existed between democracy and oligarchy in Greece, in which Sparta and Athens were the representatives.

About this time began the dominion of Athens over the islands of the Ægean and the system of colonizing conquered States, This was the period which immediately preceded the Persian wars, when Athens reached the climax of political glory.

Bœotia.

Next in importance to the States which have been briefly mentioned was Bœotia, which contained fourteen cities, united in a confederacy, of which Thebes took the lead. They were governed by magistrates, called bœtarchs, elected annually. In these cities aristocratic institutions prevailed. The people were chiefly of Æolian descent, with a strong mixture of the Dorian element, and were dull and heavy, owing, probably, to the easy facilities of support, in consequence of the richness of the soil.

Phocis.

At the west of Bœotia, Phocis, with its small territory, gained great consideration from the possession of the Delphic oracle; but its people thus far, of Achæan origin, played no important part in the politics of Greece.

Thessaly.

North of the isthmus lay the extensive plains of Thessaly, inclosed by lofty mountains. Nature favored this State more than any other in Greece for political pre-eminence, but inhabitants of Æolian origin were any thing but famous. At first they were governed by kings, but subsequently an aristocratic government prevailed. They were represented in the Amphictyonic Council.

Macedonia.

The history of Macedonia is obscure till the time of the Persian wars; but its kings claimed an Heraclid origin. The Doric dialect predominated in a rude form.

Epirus.

Epirus, west of Thessaly and Macedonia, was inhabited by various tribes, under their own princes, until the kings of Molossus, claiming descent from Achilles, founded the dynasty which was so powerful under Pyrrus.

There is but little interest connected with the States of Greece, before the Persian wars, except Sparta, Athens, and Corinth; and hence a very brief notice is all that is needed.

Grecian colonies. The Ionian cities in Asia Minor.

But the Grecian colonies are of more importance. They were numerous in the islands of the Ægean Sea, in Epirus, and in Asia Minor, and even extended into Italy, Sicily, and Gaul. They were said to be planted as early as the Trojan war by the heroes who lived to return—by Agamemnon on the coast of Asia; by the sons of Theseus in Thrace; by Ialmenus on the Euxine; by Diomed and others in Italy. But colonization, to any extent, did not take place until the Æolians invaded Bœotia, and the Dorians, the Peloponnesus. The Achæans, driven from their homes by the Dorians, sought new seats in the East, under chieftains who claimed descent from Agamemnon and other heroes who went to the siege of Troy. They settled, first, on the Isle of Lesbos, where they founded six cities. Others made settlements on the mainland, from the Hermes to Mount Ida. But the greatest migration was made by the Ionians, who, dislodged by Achæans, went first to Attica, and thence to the Cyclades and the coasts of Asia, afterward called Ionia. Twelve independent States were gradually formed of divers elements, and assumed the Ionian name. Among those twelve cities, or States, were Sarnos, Chios, Miletus, Ephesus, Colophon, and Phocæa. The purest Ionian blood was found at Miletus, the seat of Neleus. These cities were probably inhabited by other races before the Ionians came. To these another was subsequently added—Smyrna, which still retains its ancient name. The southwest corner of the Asiatic peninsula, about the same time, was colonized by a body of Dorians, accompanied by conquered Achæans, the chief seat of which was Halicarnassus. Crete, Rhodes, Cos, and Cnidus, were colonized also by the same people; but Rhodes is the parent of the Greek colonies on the south coast of Asia Minor. A century afterward, Cyprus was founded, and then Sicily was colonized, and then the south of Italy. They were successively colonized by different Grecian tribes, Achæan or Æolian, Dorian, and Ionian. But all the colonists had to contend with races previously established, Iberians, Phœnicians, Sicanians; and Sicels. Among the Greek cities in Sicily, Syracuse, founded by Dorians, was the most important, and became, in turn, the founder of other cities. Sybaris and Croton, in the south of Italy, were of Achæan origin. The Greeks even penetrated to the northern part of Africa, and founded Cyrene; while, on the Euxine, along the north coast of Asia Minor, Cyzicus and Sinope arose. These migrations were generally undertaken with the approbation and encouragement of the mother States. There was no colonial jealousy, and no dependence. The colonists, straitened for room at home, carried the benedictions of their fathers, and were emancipated from their control. Sometimes the colony became more powerful than the parent State, but both colonies and parent States were bound together by strong ties of religion, language, customs, and interests. The colonists uniformly became conquerors where they settled, but ever retained their connection with the mother country. And they grew more rapidly than the States from which they came, and their institutions were more democratic. The Asiatic colonies especially, made great advances in civilization by their contact with the East. Music, poetry, and art were cultivated with great enthusiasm. The Ionians took the lead, and their principal city, Miletus, is said to have planted no less than eighty colonies. The greatness of Ephesus was of a later date, owing, in part, to the splendid temple of Artemis, to which Asiatics as well as Greeks made contributions. One of the most remarkable of the Greek colonies was Cyrene, on the coast of Africa, which was of peculiar beauty, and was famous for eight hundred years.

Political importance of the colonies.

So the Greeks, although they occupied a small territory, yet, by their numerous colonies in all those parts watered by the Mediterranean, formed, if not politically, at least socially, a powerful empire, and exercised a vast influence on the civilized world. From Cyprus to Marseilles—from the Crimea to Cyrene, numerous States spoke the same language, and practiced the same rites, which were observed in Athens and Sparta. Hence the great extent of country in Asia and Europe to which the Greek language was familiar, and still more the arts which made Athens the centre of a new civilization. Some of the most noted philosophers and artists of antiquity were born in these colonies. The power of Hellas was not a centralized empire, like Persia, or even Rome, but a domain in the heart and mind of the world. It was Hellas which worked out, in its various States and colonies, great problems of government, as well as social life. Hellas was the parent of arts, of poetry, of philosophy, and of all æsthetic culture—the pattern of new forms of life, and new modes of cultivation. It is this Grecian civilization which appeared in full development as early as five hundred years before the Christian era, which we now propose, in a short chapter, to present—the era which immediately preceded the Persian wars.

CHAPTER XVI
GRECIAN CIVILIZATION BEFORE
THE PERSIAN WARS

Early civilization. We understand by civilization the progress which nations have made in art, literature, material strength, social culture, and political institutions, by which habits are softened, the mind enlarged, the soul elevated, and a wise government, by laws established, protecting the weak, punishing the wicked, and developing wealth and national resources.

Such a civilization did exist to a remarkable degree among the Greeks, which was not only the admiration of their own times, but a wonder to all succeeding ages, since it was established by the unaided powers of man, and affected the relations of all the nations of Europe and Asia which fell under its influence.

It is this which we propose briefly to present in this chapter, not the highest developments of Grecian culture and genius, but such as existed in the period immediately preceding the Persian wars.

Legislation.

One important feature in the civilization of Greece was the progress made in legislation by Lycurmis and Solon, But as this has been alluded to, we pass on to consider first those institutions which were more national and universal.

The Amphictyonic Council.

The peculiar situations of the various States, independent of each other, warlike, encroaching, and ambitious, led naturally to numerous wars, which would have been civil wars had all these petty States been united under a common government. But incessant wars, growing out of endless causes of irritation, would have soon ruined these States, and they could have had no proper development. Something was needed to restrain passion and heal dissensions without a resort to arms, ever attended by dire calamities. And something was needed to unite these various States, in which the same language was spoken, and the same religion and customs prevailed. This union was partially effected by the Amphictyonic Council. It was a congress, composed of deputies from the different States, and deliberating according to rules established from time immemorial. Its meetings were held in two different places, and were convened twice a year, once in the spring, at Delphi, the other in the autumn, near the pass of Thermopylæ. Delphi was probably the original place of meeting, and was, therefore, in one important sense, the capital of Greece. Originally, this council or congress was composed of deputies from twelve States, or tribes—Thessalians, Bœotians, Dorians, Ionians, Perrhæbians, Magnetes, Locrians, Octæans, Phthiots, Achæans, Melians, and Phocians. These tribes assembled together before authentic history commences, before the return of the Heracleids. There were other States which were not represented in this league—Arcadia, Elis, Æolia, and Acarnania; but the league was sufficiently powerful to make its decisions respected by the greater part of Greece. Each tribe, whether powerful or weak, had two votes in the assembly. Beside those members who had the exclusive power of voting, there were others, and more numerous, who had the privilege of deliberation. The object of the council was more for religious purposes than political, although, on rare occasions and national crises, subjects of a political nature were discussed. The council laid down the rules of war, by which each State that was represented was guaranteed against complete subjection, and the supplies of war were protected. There was no confederacy against foreign powers. The functions of the league were confined to matters purely domestic; the object of the league was the protection of temples against sacrilege. But the council had no common army to execute its decrees, which were often disregarded. In particular, the protection of the Delphic oracle, it acted with dignity and effect, whose responses were universally respected.

The Delphic oracle.

As the Delphic oracle was the object which engrossed the most important duties of the council, and the responses of this oracle in early times was a sacred law, the deliberations of the league had considerable influence, and were often directed to political purposes. But the immediate management of the oracle was in the hands of the citizens of Delphi. In process of time the responses of the oracle, by the mouth of a woman, which were thus controlled by the Delphians, lost much of their prestige, in consequence of the presents or bribery by which favorable responses were gained.

The Olympic games.

More powerful than this council, as an institution, were the Olympic games, solemnized every four years, in which all the states of Greece took part. These games lasted four days, and were of engrossing interest. They were supposed to be founded by Hercules, and were of very ancient date.

During these celebrations there was a universal truce, and also during the time it was necessary for the people to assemble and retire to their homes. Elis, in whose territory Olympia was situated, had the whole regulation of the festival, the immediate object of which were various trials of strength and skill. They included chariot races, foot races, horse races, wrestling, boxing, and leaping. They were open to all, even to the poorest Greeks; no accidents of birth or condition affected these honorable contests. The palm of honor was given to the men who had real merit. A simple garland of leaves was the prize, but this was sufficient to call out all the energies and ambition of the whole nation. There were, however, incidental advantages to successful combatants. At Athens, the citizen who gained a prize was rewarded by five hundred drachmas, and was entitled to a seat at the table of the magistrates, and had a conspicuous part on the field of battle. The victors had statues erected to them, and called forth the praises of the poets, and thus these primitive sports incidentally gave an impulse to art and poetry. In later times, poets and historians recited their compositions, and were rewarded with the garland of leaves. The victors of these games thus acquired a social pre-eminence, and were held in especial honor, like those heroes in the Middle Ages who obtained the honor of tournaments and tilts, and, in modern times, those who receive decoration at the hands of kings.

The Pythian games.

The celebrity of the Olympic games, which drew spectators from Asia as well as all the States of Greece, led to similar institutions or festivals in other places. The Pythian games, in honor of Apollo, were celebrated near Delphi every third Olympic year; and various musical contests, exercises in poetry, exhibitions of works of art were added to gymnastic exercises and chariot and horse races. The sacrifices, processions, and other solemnities, resemble those at Olympia in honor of Zeus. They lasted as long as the Olympic games, down to A.D. 394. Wherever the worship of Apollo was introduced, there were imitations of these Pythian games in all the States of Greece.

The Nemæan and Ithmian games.

The Nemæan and Ithmian games were celebrated each twice in every Olympiad, the former on the plain of Nemæa, in Argolis; the latter in the Corinthian Isthmus, under the presidency of Corinth. These also claimed a high antiquity, and at these were celebrated the same feats of strength as at Olympia. But the Olympic festival was the representation of all the rest, and transcended all the rest in national importance. It was viewed with so much interest, that the Greeks measured time itself by them. It was Olympiads, and not years, by which the date of all events was determined. The Romans reckoned their years from the foundation of their city; modern Christian nations, by the birth of Christ; Mohammedans, by the flight of the prophet to Medina; and the Greeks, from the first recorded Olympiad, B.C. 776.

Effect of these festivals.

It was in these festivals, at which no foreigner, however eminent, was allowed to contend for prizes, that the Greeks buried their quarrels, and incited each other to heroism. The places in which they were celebrated became marts of commerce like the mediæval fairs of Germany; and the vast assemblage of spectators favored that communication of news, and inventions, and improvements which has been produced by our modern exhibitions. These games answered all the purposes of our races, our industrial exhibitions, and our anniversaries, religious, political, educational, and literary, and thus had a most decided influence on the development of Grecian thought and enterprise. The exhibition of sculpture and painting alone made them attractive and intellectual, while the athletic exercises amused ordinary minds. They were not demoralizing, like the sports of the amphitheatre, or a modern bull-fight, or even fashionable races. They were more like tournaments in the martial ages of Europe, but superior to them vastly, since no woman was allowed to be present at the Olympic games under pain of death.

Changes in government. Erection of temples. Legal equality and political rights.

It has already been shown that the form of government in the States of Ancient Greece, in the Homeric ages, was monarchical. In two or three hundred years after the Trojan war, the authority of kings had greatly diminished. The great immigration and convulsions destroyed the line of the ancient royal houses. The abolition of royalty was in substance rather than name. First, it was divided among several persons, then it was made elective, first for life, afterward for a definite period. The nobles or chieftains gained increasing power with the decline of royalty, and the government became, in many States, aristocratic. But the nobles abused their power by making an oligarchy, which is a perverted aristocracy. This aroused hatred and opposition on the part of the people, especially in the maritime cities, where the increase of wealth by commerce and the arts raised up a body of powerful citizens. Then followed popular revolutions under leaders or demagogues. These leaders in turn became tyrants, and their exactions gave rise to more hatred than that produced by the government of powerful families. They gained power by stratagem, and perverted it by violence. But to amuse the people whom they oppressed, or to please them, they built temples, theatres, and other public buildings, in which a liberal patronage was extended to the arts. Thus Athens and Corinth, before the Persian wars, were beautiful cities, from the lavish expenditure of the public treasury by the tyrants or despots who had gained ascendency. In the mean time, those who were most eminent for wealth, or power, or virtue, were persecuted, for fear they would effect a revolution. But the parties which the tyrants had trampled upon were rather exasperated than ruined, and they seized every opportunity to rally the people under their standard, and effect an overthrow of the tyrants. Sparta, whose constitution remained aristocratic, generally was ready to assist any State in throwing off the yoke of the usurpers. In some States, like Athens, every change favored the rise of the people, who gradually obtained the ascendency. They instituted the principle of legal equality, by which every freeman was supposed to exercise the attributes of sovereignty. But democracy invariably led to the ascendency of factions, and became itself a tyranny. It became jealous of all who were distinguished for birth, or wealth, or talents. It encouraged flatterers and sycophants. It was insatiable in its demands on the property of the rich, and listened to charges which exposed them to exile and their estates to confiscation. It increased the public burdens by unwise expenditures to please the men of the lower classes who possessed political franchise.

Different forms of government.

But different forms of government existed in different States. In Sparta there was an oligarchy of nobles which made royalty a shadow, and which kept the people in slavery and degradation. In Athens the democratic principle prevailed. In Argos kings reigned down to the Persian wars. In Corinth the government went through mutations as at Athens. In all the States and cities experiments in the various forms of government were perpetually made and perpetually failed. They existed for a time, and were in turn supplanted. The most permanent government was that of Sparta; the most unstable was that of Athens. The former promoted a lofty patriotism and public morality and the national virtues; the latter inequalities of wealth, the rise of obscure individuals, and the progress of arts.

Commercial enterprise.

The fall of the ancient monarchies and aristocracies was closely connected with commercial enterprise and the increase of a wealthy class of citizens. In the beginning of the seventh century before Christ, a great improvement in the art of ship-building was made, especially at Corinth. Colonial settlements kept pace with maritime enterprise; and both of these fostered commerce and wealth. The Euxine lost its terrors to navigators, and the Ægean Sea was filled with ships and colonists. The Adriatic Sea was penetrated, and all the seas connected with the Mediterranean. From the mouth of the Po was brought amber, which was highly valued by the ancients. A great number of people were drawn to Egypt, by the liberal offers of its kings, who went there for the pursuit of knowledge and of wealth, and from which they brought back the papyrus as a cheap material for writing. The productions of Greece were exchanged for the rich fabrics which only Asia furnished, and the cities to which these were brought, like Athens and Corinth, rapidly grew rich, like Venice and Genoa in the Middle Ages.

Increase of wealth. Introduction of art.

Wealth of course introduced art. The origin of art may have been in religious ideas—in temples and the statues of the gods—in tombs and monuments of great men. But wealth immeasurably increased the facilities both for architecture and sculpture. Artists in old times, as in these, sought a pecuniary reward—patrons who could afford to buy their productions, and stimulate their genius. Art was cultivated more rapidly in the Asiatic colonies than in the mother country, both on account of their wealth, and the objects of interest around them. The Ionian cities, especially, were distinguished for luxury and refinement. Corinth took the lead in the early patronage of art, as the most wealthy and luxurious of the Grecian cities.

Architecture.

The first great impulse was given to architecture. The Pelasgi had erected Cyclopean structures fifteen hundred years before Christ. The Dorians built temples on the severest principles of beauty, and the Doric column arose, massive and elegant. Long before the Persian wars the temples were numerous and grand, yet simple and harmonious. The temple of Here, at Samos, was begun in the eighth century, B.C., and built in the Doric style, and, soon after, beautiful structures ornamented Athens.

Sculpture.

Sculpture rapidly followed architecture, and passed from the stiffness of ancient times to that beauty which afterward distinguished Phidias and Polynotus. Schools of art, in the sixth century, flourished in all the Grecian cities. We can not enter upon the details, from the use of wood to brass and marble. The temples were filled with groups from celebrated masters, and their deep recesses were peopled with colossal forms. Gold, silver, and ivory were used as well as marble and brass. The statues of heroes adorned every public place. Art, before the Persian wars, did not indeed reach the refinement which it subsequently boasted, but a great progress was made in it, in all its forms. Engraving was also known, and imperfect pictures were painted. But this art, and indeed any of the arts, did not culminate until after the Persian wars.

Literature.

Literature made equal if not greater progress in the early ages of Grecian history. Hesiod lived B.C. 735; and lyric poetry flourished in the sixth and seventh centuries before Christ, especially the elegiac form, or songs for the dead. Epic poetry was of still earlier date, as seen in the Homeric poems. The Æolian and Ionic Greeks of Asia were early noted for celebrated poets. Alcæus and Sappho lived on the Isle of Lesbos, and were surrounded with admirers. Anacreon of Teos was courted by the rulers of Athens.

Philosophy.

Even philosophy was cultivated at this early age. Thales of Miletus flourished in the middle of the seventh century, and Anaximander, born B.C. 610—one of the great original mathematicians of the world, speculated like Thales, on the origin of things. Pythagoras, born in Samos, B.C. 580—a still greater name, grave and majestic, taught the harmony of the spheres long before the Ionian revolt.

But neither art, nor literature, nor philosophy reached their full development till a later era. It is enough for our purpose to say that, before the Persian wars, civilization was by no means contemptible, in all those departments which subsequently made Greece the teacher and the glory of the world.

CHAPTER XVII
THE PERSIAN WAR

We come now to the most important and interesting of Grecian history—the great contest with Persia—the age of heroes and of battle-fields, when military glory was the master passion of a noble race. What inspiration have all ages gained from that noble contest in behalf of liberty!

Condition of the Ionian cities. Invasion of Scythia by Darius.

We have seen how Asiatic cities were colonized by Greeks, among whom the Ionians were pre-eminent. The cities were governed by tyrants, who were sustained in their usurpation by the power of Persia, then the great power of the world. Darius, then king, had absurdly invaded Scythia, with an immense army of six hundred thousand men, to punish the people for their inroad upon Western Asia, subject to his sway, about a century before. He was followed by his allies, the tyrants of the Ionian cities, to whom he intrusted the guardianship of the bridge of boats by which he had crossed the Danube, B.C. 510. As he did not return within the time specified—sixty days—the Greeks were left at liberty to return. A body of Scythians then appeared, who urged the Greeks to destroy the bridge, as Darius was in full retreat, and thus secure the destruction of the Persian army and the recovery of their own liberty. Miltiades, who ruled the Chersonese—the future hero of Marathon, seconded the wise proposal of the Scythians, but Histiæus, tyrant of Miletus, feared that such an act would recoil upon themselves, and favor another inroad of Scythians—a fierce nation of barbarians. The result was that the bridge was not destroyed, but the further end of it was severed from the shore. Night arrived, and the Persian hosts appeared upon the banks of the river, but finding no trace of it, Darius ordered an Egyptian who had a trumpet-voice to summon to his aid Histiæus, the Milesian. He came forward with a fleet and restored the bridge, and Darius and his army were saved, and the opportunity was lost to the Ionians for emancipating themselves from the Persians. The bridge was preserved, not from honorable fidelity to fulfill a trust, but selfish regard in the despot of Miletus to maintain his power. For this service he was rewarded with a principality on the Strymon. Exciting, however, the suspicion of Darius, by his intrigues, he was carried captive to the Persian court, but with every mark of honor. Darius left his brother Artaphernes as governor of all the cities in Western Asia Minor.

Revolt of the Ionian cities from Persia. Defeat of the Ionian cities.

A few years after this unsuccessful invasion of Scythia by Darius, a political conflict broke out in Naxos, an island of the Cyclades, B.C. 502, which had not submitted to the Persian yoke, and the oligarchy, which ruled the island, were expelled. They applied for aid to Aristagoras, the tyrant of Miletus, the largest of the Ionian cities, who persuaded the Persian satrap to send an expedition against the island. The expedition failed, which ruined the credit of Aristagoras, son-in-law to Histiæus, who was himself incensed at his detention in Susa, and who sent a trusty slave with a message urging the Ionians to revolt. Aristagoras, as a means of success, conciliated popular favor throughout Asiatic Greece, by putting down the various tyrants—the instruments of Persian ascendency. The flames of revolt were kindled, the despots were expelled, the revolted towns were put in a state of defense, and Aristagoras visited Sparta to invoke its aid, inflaming the mind of the king with the untold wealth of Asia, which would become his spoil. Sparta was then at war with her neighbors, and unwilling to become involved in so uncertain a contest. Rejected at Sparta, Aristagoras proceeded to Athens, then the second power in Greece, and was favorably received, for the Athenians had a powerful sympathy with the revolted Ionians; they agreed to send a fleet of twenty ships. When Aristagoras returned, the Persians had commenced the siege of Miletus. The twenty ships soon crossed the Ægean, and were joined by five Eretrian ships coming to the succor of Miletus. An unsuccessful attempt of Aristagoras on Sardis disgusted the Athenians, who abandoned the alliance. But the accidental burning of the city, including the temple of the goddess Cybele, encouraged the revolters, and incensed the Persians. Other Greek cities on the coast took part in the revolt, including the island of Cyprus. The revolt now assumed a serious character. The Persians rallied their allies, among whom were the Phœnicians. An armament of Persians and Phœnicians sailed against Cyprus, and a victory on the land gave the Persians the control of the island. A large army of Persians and their allies collected at Sardis, and, under different divisions reconquered all their principal Ionian cities, except Miletus; but the Ionian fleet kept its ascendency at sea. Aristagoras as the Persians advanced, lost courage and fled to Myrkinus, where he shortly afterward perished.

Histiæus.

Meanwhile Histiæus presented himself at the gates of Miletus, having procured the consent of Darius to proceed thither to quell the revolt. He was, however, suspected by the satrap, Artaphernes, and fled to Chios, whose people he gained over, and who carried him back to Miletus. On his arrival, he found the citizens averse to his reception, and was obliged to return to Chios, and then to Lesbos, where he abandoned himself to piracy.

Want of union among the Ionian cities. Their signal defeat.

A vast Persian host, however, had been concentrated near Miletus, and with the assistance of the Phœnicians, invested the city by sea and land. The entire force of the confederated cities abandoned the Milesians to their fate, and took to their ships, three hundred and fifty-three in number, with a view of fighting the Phœnicians, who had six hundred ships. But there was a want of union among the Ionian commanders, and the sailors abandoned themselves to disorder and carelessness; upon which Dionysius, of Phocæa, which furnished but three ships, rebuked the Ionians for their neglect of discipline. His rebuke was not thrown away, and the Ionians having their comfortable tents on shore, submitted themselves to the nautical labors imposed by Dionysius. At last, after seven days of work, the Ionian sailors broke out in open mutiny, and refused longer to be under the discipline of a man whose State furnished the smallest number of ships. They left their ships, and resumed their pleasures on the shore, unwilling to endure the discipline so necessary in so great a crisis. Their camp became a scene of disunion and mistrust. The Samians, in particular, were discontented, and on the day of battle, which was to decide the fortunes of Ionia, they deserted with sixty ships, and other Ionians followed their example. The ships of Chios, one hundred in number, fought with great fidelity and resolution, and Dionysius captured, with his three ships, three of the Phœnicians'. But these exceptional examples of bravery did not compensate the treachery and cowardice of the rest, and the consequence was a complete defeat of the Ionians at Lade. Dionysius, seeing the ruin of the Ionian camp, did not return to his own city, and set sail for the Phœnician coast, doing all he could as a pirate.

Attack of Miletus. Complete conquest of the Ionian Greeks.

This victory of Lade enabled the Persians to attack Miletus by sea as well as land; the siege was prosecuted with vigor, and the city shortly fell. The adult male population was slain, while the women and children were sent as slaves to Susa. The Milesian territory was devastated and stripped of its inhabitants. The other States hastened to make their submission, and the revolt was crushed, B.C. 496, five years after its commencement. The Persian forces reconquered all the Asiatic Greeks, insular and continental, and the Athenian Miltiades escaped with difficulty from his command in the Chersonese, to his native city. All the threats which were made by the Persians were realized. The most beautiful virgins were distributed among the Persian nobles; the cities were destroyed; and Samos alone remained, as a reward for desertion at the battle of Lade.

Artaphernes organizes the Government. Darius prepares for the invasion of Greece.

The reconquest of Ionia being completed, the satrap proceeded to organize the future government, the inhabitants now being composed of a great number of Persians. Meanwhile, Darius made preparations for the complete conquest of Greece. The wisdom of the advice of Miltiades, to destroy the bridge over the Danube, when Darius and his army would have been annihilated by the Scythians, was now apparent. Mardonius was sent with a large army into Ionia, who deposed the despots in the various cities, whom Artaphernes had reinstated, and left the people to govern themselves, subject to the Persian dominion and tribute. He did not remain long in Ionia, but passed with his fleet to the Hellespont, and joined his land forces. He transported his army to Europe, and began his march through Thrace. Thence marched into Macedonia, and subdued a part of its inhabitants. He then sent his fleet around Mount Athos, with a view of joining it with his army at the Gulf of Therma. But a storm overtook his fleet near Athos, and destroyed three hundred ships, and drowned twenty thousand men. This disaster compelled a retreat, and he recrossed the Hellespont with the shame of failure. He was employed no more by the Persian king.

His immense preparations.

Darius, incited by the traitor Hippias, made new preparation for the invasion of Greece. He sent his heralds in every direction, demanding the customary token of submission—earth and water. Many of the continental cities sent in their submission, including the Thebans, Thessalians, and the island of Ægina, which was on bad terms with Athens. The heralds of Darius were put to death at Athens and Sparta, which can only be explained from the fiercest resentment and rage. These two powers made common cause, and armed all the other States over which they had influence, to resist the Persian domination. Hellas, headed by Sparta, now resolved to put forth all its energies, and embarked, in desperate hostility. A war which Sparta had been waging for several years against Argos crippled that ancient State, and she was no longer the leading power. The only rival which Sparta feared was weakened, and full scope was given, for the prosecution of the Persian war. Ægina, which had submitted to Darius, was visited by Cleomenes, king of Sparta, and hostages were sent to Athens for the neutrality of that island. Athens and Sparta suspended their political jealousies, and acted in concert to resist the common danger.

His vast army.

By the spring of 490 B.C. the preparations of Darius were completed, and a vast army collected on a plain upon the Cilician shore. A fleet of six hundred ships convoyed it to the rendezvous at Samos. The exiled tyrant Hippias was present to guide the forces to the attack of Attica. The Mede Datis, and Artaphernes, son of the satrap of Sardis, nephew to Darius, were the Persian generals. They had orders from Darius to bring the inhabitants of Athens as slaves to his presence.

The Persian fleet.

The Persian fleet, fearing a similar disaster as happened near Mount Athos, struck directly across the Ægean, from Samos to Eubœa, attacking on the way the intermediate islands. Naxos thus was invaded and easily subdued. From Naxos, Datis sent his fleet round the other Cyclades Islands, demanding reinforcements and hostages from all he visited, and reached the southern extremity of Eubœa in safety. Etruria was first subdued, unable to resist. After halting a few days at this city, he crossed to Attica, and landed in the bay of Marathon, on the eastern coast. The despot Hippias, son of Pisistratus, twenty years after his expulsion from Athens, pointed out the way.

Political change at Athens. Miltiades, and other generals.

But a great change had taken place at Athens since his expulsion. The city was now under democratic rule, in its best estate. The ten tribes had become identified with the government and institutions of the city. The senate of the areopagus, renovated by the annual archons, was in sympathy with the people. Great men had arisen under the amazing stimulus of liberty, among whom Miltiades, Themistocles, and Aristides were the most distinguished. Miltiades, after an absence of six years in the Chersonesus of Thrace, returned to the city full of patriotic ardor. He was brought to trial before the popular assembly on the charge of having misgoverned the Chersonese; but he was honorably acquitted, and was chosen one of the ten generals of the republic annually elected. He was not, however, a politician of the democratic stamp, like Themistocles and Aristides, being a descendant of an illustrious race, which traced their lineage to the gods; but he was patriotic, brave, and decided. His advice to burn the bridge over the Danube illustrates his character—bold and far-seeing. Moreover, he was peculiarly hostile to Darius, whom he had so grievously offended.

Themistocles.

Themistocles was a man of great native genius and sagacity. He comprehended all the embarrassments and dangers of the political crisis in which his city was placed, and saw at a glance the true course to be pursued. He was also bold and daring. He was not favored by the accidents of birth, and owed very little to education. He had an unbounded passion for glory and for display. He had great tact in the management of party, and was intent on the aggrandizement of his country. His morality was reckless, but his intelligence was great—a sort of Mirabeau: with his passion, his eloquence, and his talents. His unfortunate end—a traitor and an exile—shows how little intellectual pre-eminence will avail, in the long run, without virtue, although such talents as he exhibited will be found useful in a crisis.

Aristides.

Aristides was inferior to both Alcibiades and Themistocles in genius, in resource, in boldness, and in energy; but superior in virtue, in public fidelity, and moral elevation. He pursued a consistent course, was no demagogue, unflinching in the discharge of trusts, just, upright, unspotted. Such a man, of course, in a corrupt society, would be exposed to many enmities and jealousies. But he was, on the whole, appreciated, and died, in a period of war and revolution, a poor man, with unbounded means of becoming rich—one of the few examples which our world affords of a man who believed in virtue, in God, and a judgment to come, and who preferred the future and spiritual to the present and material—a fool in the eyes of the sordid and bad—a wise man according to the eternal standards.

Athens allies herself with Sparta.

Aristides, Miltiades, and perhaps Themistocles, were elected among the ten generals, by the ten tribes, in the year that Datis led his expedition to Marathon. Each of the ten generals had the supreme command of the army for a day. Great alarm was felt at Athens as tidings reached the city of the advancing and conquering Persians. Couriers were sent in hot haste to the other cities, especially Sparta, and one was found to make the journey to Sparta on foot—one hundred and fifty miles—in forty-eight hours. The Spartans agreed to march, without delay, after the last quarter of the moon, which custom and superstition dictated. This delay was fraught with danger, but was insisted upon by the Spartans.

Prominence of the dangers.

Meanwhile the dangers multiplied and thickened, that not a moment should be lost in bringing the Persians into action. Five of the generals counseled delay. The polemarch, Calimachus, who then had the casting vote, decided for immediate action. Themistocles and Aristides had seconded the advice of Miltiades, to whom the other generals surrendered their days of command—a rare example of patriotic disinterestedness. The Athenians marched at once to Marathon to meet their foes, and were joined by the Platæans, one thousand warriors, from a little city—the whole armed population, which had a great moral effect.

Marshaling of the Grecian forces at Marathon. The battle of Marathon.

The Athenians had only ten thousand hoplites, including the one thousand from Platæa. The Persian army is variously estimated at from one hundred and ten thousand to six hundred thousand. The Greeks were encamped upon the higher ground overlooking the plain which their enemies occupied. The fleet was ranged along the beach. The Greeks advanced to the combat in rapid movement, urged on by the war-cry, which ever animated their charges. The wings of the Persian army were put to flight by the audacity of the charge, but the centre, where the best troops were posted, resisted the attack until Miltiades returned from the pursuit of the retreating soldiers on the wings. The defeat of the Persians was the result. They fled to their ships, and became involved in the marshes. Six thousand four hundred men fell on the Persian side, and only one hundred and ninety-two on the Athenian. The Persians, though defeated, still retained their ships, and sailed toward Cape Sunium, with a view of another descent upon Attica. Miltiades, the victor in the most glorious battle ever till then fought in Greece, penetrated the designs of the Persians, and rapidly retreated to Athens on the very day of battle. Datis arrived at the port of Phalerum to discover that his plans were baffled, and that the Athenians were still ready to oppose him. The energy and promptness of Miltiades had saved the city. Datis, discouraged, set sail, without landing, to the Cyclades.

Results of the battle.

The battle of Marathon, B.C. 490, must be regarded as one of the great decisive battles of the world, and the first which raised the political importance of the Greeks in the eyes of foreign powers. It was fought by Athens twenty years after the expulsion of the tyrants, and as a democratic State. On the Athenians rest the glory forever. It was not important for the number of men who fell on either side, but for giving the first great check to the Persian domination, and preventing their conquest of Europe. And its moral effect was greater than its political. It freed the Greeks from that fear of the Persians which was so fatal and universal, for the tide of Persian conquest had been hitherto uninterrupted. It animated the Greeks with fresh courage, for the bravery of the Athenians had been unexampled, as had been the generalship of Miltiades. Athens was delivered by the almost supernatural bravery of its warriors, and was then prepared to make those sacrifices which were necessary in the more desperate struggles which were to come. And it inspired the people with patriotic ardor, and upheld the new civil constitution. It gave force and dignity to the democracy, and prepared it for future and exalted triumphs. It also gave force to the religious sentiments of the people, for such a victory was regarded as owing to the special favor of the gods.

The Spartans did not arrive until after the battle had been fought, and Datis had returned with his Etrurian prisoners to Asia.

Fame of Miltiades. His subsequent reverses. His death. Jealousies between Aristides and Themistocles.

The victory of Marathon raised the military fame of Miltiades to the most exalted height, and there were no bounds to the enthusiasm of the Athenians. But the victory turned his head, and he lost both prudence and patriotism. He persuaded his countrymen, in the full tide of his popularity, to intrust him with seventy ships, with an adequate force, with powers to direct an expedition according to his pleasure. The armament was cheerfully granted. But he disgracefully failed in an attack on the island of Paros, to gratify a private vindictive animosity. He lost all his *éclat* and was impeached. He appealed, wounded and disabled from a fall he had received, to his previous services. He was found guilty, but escaped the penalty of death, but not of a fine of fifty talents. He did not live to pay it, or redeem his fame, but died of the injury he had received. Thus this great man fell from a pinnacle of glory to the deepest disgrace and ruin—a fate deserved, for he was not true to himself or country. The Athenians were not to blame, but judged him rightly. It was not fickleness, but a change in their opinions, founded on sufficient grounds, from the deep disappointment in finding that their hero was unworthy of their regards. No man who had rendered a favor has a claim to pursue a course of selfishness and unlawful ambition. No services can offset crimes. The Athenians, in their unbounded admiration, had given unbounded trust, and that trust was abused. And as the greatest despots who had mounted to power had earned their success by early services, so had they abused their power by imposing fetters, and the Athenians, just escaped from the tyranny of these despots, felt a natural jealousy and a deep repugnance, in spite of their previous admiration. The Athenians, in their treatment of Miltiades, were neither ungrateful nor fickle, but acted from a high sense of public morality, and in a stern regard to justice, without which the new constitution would soon have been subverted. On the death of Miltiades Themistocles and Aristides became the two leading men of Athens, and their rivalries composed the domestic history of the city, until the renewed and vast preparations of the Persians caused all dissensions to be suspended for the public good.

Not altogether on personal grounds.

But the jealousies and rivalries of these great men were not altogether personal. They were both patriotic, but each had different views respecting the course which Athens should adopt in the greatness of the dangers which impended. The policy of Aristides was to strengthen the army—that of

Themistocles, the navy. Both foresaw the national dangers, but Themistocles felt that the hopes of Greece rested on ships rather than armies to resist the Persians. And his policy was adopted. As the world can not have two suns, so Athens could not be prospered by the presence of two such great men, each advocating different views. One or the other must succumb to the general good, and Aristides was banished by the power of ostracism.

Renewed preparations of Darius. His death.

The wrath of Darius—a man of great force of character, but haughty and self-sufficient, was tremendous when he learned the defeat of Datis, and his retreat into Asia. He resolved to bring the whole force of the Persian empire together to subdue the Athenians, from whom he had suffered so great a disgrace. Three years were spent in active preparations for a new expedition which should be overwhelming. All the allies of Persia were called upon for men and supplies. Nor was he deterred by a revolt of Egypt, which broke out about this time, and he was on the point of carrying two gigantic enterprises—one for the reconquest of Egypt, and the other for the conquest of Greece—when he died, after a reign of thirty-six years, B.C. 485.

Xerxes. His enormous preparations. His bridges over the Hellespont.

He was succeeded by his son Xerxes, who was animated by the animosities, but not the genius of his father. Though beautiful and tall, he was faint-hearted, vain, blinded by a sense of power, and enslaved by women. Yet he continued the preparations which Darius projected. Egypt was first subdued by his generals, and he then turned his undivided attention to Greece. He convoked the dignitaries of his empire—the princes and governors of provinces, and announced his resolution to bridge over the Hellespont and march to the conquest of Europe. Artabanus, his uncle, dissuaded him from the enterprise, setting forth especially the probability that the Greeks, if victorious at sea, would destroy the bridge, and thus prevent his safe return. Mardonius advised differently, urging ambition and revenge, motives not lost on the Persian monarch. For four years the preparations went forward from all parts of the empire, including even the islands in the Ægean. In the autumn of 481 B.C., the largest army this world has ever seen assembled at Sardis. Besides this, a powerful fleet of one thousand two hundred and seven ships of war, besides transports, was collected at the Hellespont. Large magazines of provisions were formed along the coast of Asia Minor. A double bridge of boats, extending from Abydos to Sestos—a mile in length across the Hellespont, was constructed by Phœnicians and Egyptians; but this was destroyed by a storm. Xerxes, in a transport of fury, caused the heads of the engineers to be cut off, and the sea itself scourged with three hundred lashes. This insane wrath being expended, the monarch caused the work to be at once reconstructed, this time by the aid of Greek engineers. Two bridges were built side by side upon more than six hundred large ships, moored with strong anchors, with their heads toward the Ægean. Over each bridge were sketched six vast cables, which held the ships together, and over these were laid planks of wood, upon which a causeway was formed of wood and earth, with a high palisade on each side. To facilitate his march, Xerxes also constructed a canal across the isthmus which connects Mount Athos with the main land, on which were employed Phœnician engineers. The men employed in digging the canal worked under the whip. Bridges were also thrown across the river Strymon.

His advance. He crosses the Hellespont. His review of his army.

These works were completed while Xerxes wintered at Sardis. From that city he dispatched heralds to all the cities of Greece, except Sparta and Athens, to demand the usual tokens of submission—earth and water. He also sent orders to the maritime cities of Thrace and Macedonia to prepare dinner for himself and hosts, as they passed through. Greece was struck with consternation as the news reached the various cities of the vast forces which were on the march to subdue them. The army proceeded from Sardis, in the spring, in two grand columns, between which was the king and guards and select troops—all native Persians, ten thousand foot and ten thousand horse. From Sardis the hosts of Xerxes proceeded to Abydos, through Ilium, where his two bridges across the Hellespont awaited him. From a marble throne the proud and vainglorious monarch saw his vast army defile over the bridges, perfumed with frankincense and strewed with myrtle boughs. One bridge was devoted to the troops, the other to the beasts and baggage. The first to cross were the ten thousand household troops, called Immortals, wearing garlands on their heads; then followed Xerxes himself in his gilded chariot, and then the rest of the army. It occupied seven days for the vast hosts to cross the bridge. Xerxes then directed his march to Doriscus, in Thrace, near the mouth of the Hebrus, where he joined his fleet. There he took a general review, and never, probably, was so great an army marshaled before or since, and composed of so many various nations. There were assembled nations from the Indus, from the Persian Gulf, the Red Sea, the Levant, the Ægean and the Euxine—Egyptian, Ethiopian, and Lybian. Forty-six nations were represented—all that were tributary to Persia. From the estimates made by Herodotus, there were one million seven hundred thousand foot, eighty thousand horse, besides a large number of chariots. With the men who manned the fleet and those he pressed into his service on the march, the aggregate of his forces was two million six hundred and forty thousand. Scarcely an inferior number attended the soldiers as slaves, sutlers, and other persons, swelling the amount of the males to five million two hundred and eighty-three thousand two hundred and twenty—the whole available force of the Eastern world—Asia against Europe: as in mediæval times it was Europe against Asia. It is, however, impossible for us to believe in so large a force, since it could not have been supplied with provisions. But with every deduction, it was still the largest army the world ever saw.

The magnitude of his forces.

After the grand enumeration of forces, Xerxes passed in his chariot to survey separately each body of contingents, to which he put questions. He then embarked in a gilded galley, and sailed past the prows of the twelve hundred ships moored four hundred feet from the shore. That such a vast force could be resisted was not even supposed to be conceivable by the blinded monarch. But Demaratus, the exiled king of Sparta, told him he would be resisted unto death, a statement which was received with derision.

Progress of the Persians.

After the review, the grand army pursued its course westward in three divisions and roads along Thrace, levying enormous contributions on all the Grecian towns, which submitted as the Persian monarch marched along, for how could they resist? The mere provisioning this great host for a single day impoverished the country. But there was no help, for to mortal eyes the success of Xerxes was certain. At Acanthus, Xerxes separated from his fleet, which was directed to sail round Mount Athos, while he pursued his march through Pæonia and Crestonia, and rejoin him at Therma, on the Thermaic Gulf, in Macedonia, within sight of Mount Olympus.

Preparations of the Athenians. Sparta commands the land forces and Athens the naval.

Meanwhile, the Athenians, fully alive to their danger, strained every nerve to make preparations to resist the enemy; fortunately, there was in the treasury a large sum derived from the Lamian mines, and this they applied, on the urgent representations of Themistocles, to building ships and refitting their navy. A Panhellenic congress, under the presidency of Athens and Sparta, assembled at the Isthmus of Corinth.—the first great league since the Trojan war. The representatives of the various States buried their dissensions, the most prominent of which were between Athens and Ægina. In reconciling these feuds, Themistocles took a pre-eminent part. Indeed, there was need, for the political existence of Hellas was threatened, and despair was seen in most every city. Even the Delphic oracle gave out replies discouraging and terrible; intimating, however, that the safety of Athens lay in the wooden wall, which, with extraordinary tact, was interpreted by

Themistocles to mean that the true defense lay in the navy. Salamis was the place designated by the oracle for the retreat, which was now imperative, and thither the Athenians fled, with their wives and children, guarded by their fleet. It was decided by the congress that Sparta should command the land forces, and Athens the united navy of the Greeks; but many States, in deadly fear of the Persians, persisted in neutrality, among which were Argos, Cretes, Corcyra. The chief glory of the defense lay with Sparta and Athens. The united army was sent into Thessaly to defend the defile of Tempe, but discovering that they were unable to do this, since another pass over Mount Olympus was open in the summer, they retreated to the isthmus of Corinth, and left all Greece north of Mount Citheron and the Megarid territory without defense. Had the Greeks been able to maintain the passes of Olympus and Ossa, all the northern States would probably have joined in the confederation against Persia; but, as they were left defenseless, we can not wonder that they submitted, including even the Achæans, Borotians, and Dorians.

The pass of Thermopylæ.

The Pass of Thermopylæ was now fixed upon as the most convenient place of resistance, next to the vale of Tempe. Here the main land was separated from the island of Eubœa by a narrow strait two miles wide. On the northern part of the island, near the town of Histiæa, the coast was called Artemisium, and here the fleet was mustered, to co-operate with the land forces, and oppose, in a narrow strait, the progress of the Persian fleet. The defile of Thermopylæ itself, at the south of Thessaly, was between Mount Œta and an impassable morass on the Maliac Gulf. Nature had thus provided a double position of defense—a narrow defile on the land, and a narrow strait on the water, through which the army and the fleet must need pass if they would co-operate.

Interruption of military preparations by the Olympic games.

While the congress resolved to avail themselves of the double position, by sea and land, the Olympic games, and the great Dorian, of the Carneia, were at hand. These could not be dispensed with, even in the most extraordinary crisis to which the nation could be exposed. While, therefore, the Greeks assembled to keep the national festivals, probably from religious and superstitious motives, auguring no good if they were disregarded, Leonidas, king of Sparta, with three hundred Spartans, two thousand one hundred and twenty Arcadians, four hundred Corinthians, two hundred men from Philius, and eighty from Mycenæ—in all three thousand one hundred hoplites, besides Helots and light troops, was sent to defend the pass against the Persian hosts. On the march through Bœotia one thousand men from Thebes and Thespiæ joined them, though on the point of submission to Xerxes. The Athenians sent their whole force on board their ships, joined by the Platæans.

Leonidas defends the pass of Thermopylæ.

It was in the summer of 480 B.C. when Xerxes reached Therma, about which time the Greeks arrived at their allotted posts. Leonidas took his position in the middle of the Pass—a mile in length, with two narrow openings. He then repaired the old wall built across the Pass by the Phocians, and awaited the coming of the enemy, for it was supposed his force was sufficient to hold it till the games were over. It was also thought that this narrow pass was the only means of access possible to the invading army; but it was soon discovered that there was also a narrow mountain path from the Phocian territory to Thermopylæ. The Phocians agreed to guard this path, and leave the defense of the main pass to the Peloponnesian troops. But Leonidas painfully felt that his men were insufficient in number, and found it necessary to send envoys to the different States for immediate re-enforcements.

The Greek fleet. Disaster to the Persian fleet.

The Greek fleet, assembled at Artemisium, was composed of two hundred and seventy-one triremes and nine penteconters, commanded by Themistocles, but furnished by the different States. A disaster happened to the Greeks very early; three triremes were captured by the Persians, which caused great discouragement, and in a panic the Greeks abandoned their strong naval position, and sailed up the Eubœan Strait to Chalcis. This was a great misfortune, since the rear of the army of Leonidas was no longer protected by the fleet. But a destructive storm dispersed the fleet of the Persians at this imminent crisis, so that it was impossible to lend aid to their army now arrived at Thermopylæ. Four hundred ships of war, together with a vast number of transports, were thus destroyed. The storm lasted three days. After this disaster to the Persians, the Greek fleet returned to Artemisium. Xerxes encamped within sight of Thermopylæ four days, without making an attack, on account of the dangers to which his fleet were exposed. On the fifth day he became wroth at the impudence and boldness of the petty force which quietly remained to dispute his passage, for the Spartans amused themselves with athletic sports and combing their hair. Nor was it altogether presumption on the part of the Greeks, for there were four or five thousand heavily-armed men, the bravest in the land, to defend a passage scarcely wider than a carriage-road—with a wall and other defenses in front.

Attack on the Greeks by the Persians.

The first attack on the Greeks was made by the Medea—the bravest of the Persian army, but their arrows and short spears were of little avail against the phalanx which opposed, armed with long spears, and protected by shields. For two days the attack continued, and was constantly repulsed, for only a small detachment of Greeks fought at a time. Even the "Immortals"—the chosen band of Xerxes—were repulsed with a great loss, to the agony and shame of Xerxes.

Leonidas defends the pass, but is slain. Heroic death of the three hundred Spartans.

On the third day, a Malian revealed to the Persian king the fact that a narrow path, leading over the mountains, was defended only by Phocians, and that this path led to the rear of the Spartans. A strong detachment of Persians was sent in the night to secure this path, and the Phocian guardians fled. The Persians descended the path, and attacked the Greeks in their rear. Leonidas soon became apprised of his danger, but in time to send away his army. It was now clear that Thermopylæ could no longer be defended, but the heroic and self-sacrificing general resolved to remain, and sell his life as dearly as possible, and retard, if he could not resist, the march of the enemy. Three hundred Spartans, with seven hundred Thespians and four hundred Thebans joined him, while the rest retired to fight another day. It required all the efforts of the Persian generals, assisted by the whip, to force the men to attack this devoted band. The Greeks fought with the most desperate bravery, till their spears were broken, and no weapons remained but their swords and daggers. At last, exhausted, they died, surrounded by vast forces, after having made the most heroic defence in the history of the war. Only one man, Aristodemus, returned to his home of all the three hundred Spartans, but only to receive scorn and infamy. The Theban band alone yielded to the Persians, but only at the last hour.

The dismay and indignation of Xerxes.

Nothing could exceed the blended anger and admiration of Xerxes as he beheld this memorable resistance. He now saw, for the first time, the difficulty of subduing such a people as the Greeks, resolved to resist unto death. His mind was perplexed, and he did not know what course to adopt. Had he accepted the advice of Demaratus, to make war on the southern coast of Laconia, and thus distract the Spartans and prevent their co-operation with Athens, he would have probably succeeded.

Naval battle of Artemisium.

But he followed other councils. Meanwhile, the Persian fleet rallied after the storm, and was still formidable, in spite of losses. The Greeks were disposed to retire and leave the strait open to the enemy. The Eubœans, seeing the evil which would happen to them if their island was unprotected, sent to Themistocles a present of thirty talents, if he would keep his position. This money he spent in bribing the different commanders who wished to retire, and it was resolved to remain. The Persians, confident of an easy victory, sent round the island of Eubœa a detachment of two hundred ships, to cut off all hopes of escape to the ships which they expected to capture. A deserter revealed the intelligence to Themistocles, and it was resolved to fight the Persians, thus weakened, at once, but at the close of the day, so that the battle would not be decisive. The battle of Artemisium was a sort of skirmish, to accustom the Greeks to the Phœnician mode of fighting. It was, however, successful, and thirty ships of the Persians were taken or disabled.

Themistocles sails for Salamis.

But the Greeks derived a greater succor than ships and men. Another storm overtook the Persians, damaged their fleet, and destroyed the squadron sent round the island of Eubœa. Another sea-fight was the result, since the Greeks were not only aided by the storm, but new re-enforcements; but this second fight was indecisive. Themistocles now felt he could not hold the strait against superior numbers, and the disaster of Thermopylæ being also now known, he resolved to retreat farther into Greece, and sailed for Salamis.

Despair of the Greeks. Themistocles revives courage by his "wooden wall."

At this period the Greeks generally were filled with consternation and disappointment. Neither the Pass of Thermopylæ, nor the strait which connected the Malicas Gulf with the Ægean, had been successfully defended. The army of Xerxes was advancing through Phocis and Bœotia to the Isthmus of Corinth, while the navy sailed unobstructed through the Eubœan Sea. On the part of the Greeks there had been no preparations commensurate with the greatness of the crisis, while, had they rallied to Thermopylæ, instead of wasting time at the festivals, they would have saved the pass, and the army of Xerxes, strained for provisions, would have been compelled to retreat. The, Lacedæmonians, aroused by the death of their king, at last made vigorous efforts to fortify the Isthmus of Corinth, too late, however, to defend Bœotia and Attica. The situation of Athens was now hopeless, and it was seen what a fatal mistake had been made not to defend, with the whole force of Greece, the Pass of Thermopylæ. There was no help from the Spartans, for they had all flocked to the Isthmus of Corinth, as the last chance of protecting the Peloponnesus. In despair, the Athenians resolved to abandon Athens, with their families, and take shelter at Salamis. Themistocles alone was undismayed, and sought to encourage his countrymen that the "wooden wall" would still be their salvation. The Athenians, if dismayed, did not lose their energies. The recall of the exiles was decreed by Themistocles' suggestion. With incredible efforts the whole population of Attica was removed to Salamis, and the hopes of all were centered in the ships. Xerxes took possession of the deserted city, but found but five hundred captives. He ravaged the country, and a detachment of Persians even penetrated to Delphi, to rob the shrine, but were defeated. Athens was, however, sacked.

The hostile fleets at Salamis.

The combined fleet of the Greeks now numbered three hundred and sixty-six ships, more than half of which were Athenian. Many wished to retreat to the Isthmus of Corinth, and co-operate with the Spartans. Dissensions came near wrecking the last hopes of Greece, and Themistocles only prevailed by threatening to withdraw the Athenian ships unless a battle were at once fought. He resorted to stratagem to compel the fleet to remain together, with no outlet of escape if conquered. Aristides came in the night from Ægina, and informed the Greeks that their whole fleet was surrounded by the Persians—just what Themistocles desired. There was nothing then left but to fight with desperation, for on the issue of the battle depended the fortunes of Greece. Both fleets were stationed in the strait between the bay of Eleusis and the Saronic Gulf, on the west of the island of Salamis.

Self-confidence of Xerxes. Battle of Salamis and retreat of Xerxes.

Xerxes, seated upon a throne upon one of the declivities of Mount Ægaleos, surveyed the armaments and the coming battle. Both parties fought with bravery; but the space was too narrow for the Persians to engage their whole fleet, and they had not the discipline of the Greeks, schooled by severe experience. The Persian fleet became unmanageable, and the victory was gained by the Greeks. Two hundred ships fell into the hands of the victors. But a sufficient number remained to the Persians to renew the battle with better hopes. Xerxes, however, was intimidated, and in a transport of rage, disappointment, and fear, gave the order to retreat. He distrusted the fidelity of the allies, and feared for his own personal safety; he feared that the victors would sail to the Hellespont, and destroy the bridges. Themistocles, on the retreat of the Persians, employed his fleet in levying fines and contributions upon the islands which had supported the Persians, while Xerxes made his way back to the Hellespont, and crossed to Asia, leaving Mardonius in Thessaly, with a large army, to pursue the conquest on land.

The important results.

Thus Greece was saved by the battle of Salamis, and the distinguished services of Themistocles, which can not be too highly estimated. The terrific cloud was dispersed, the Greeks abandoned themselves to joy. Unparalleled honors were bestowed upon the victor, especially in Sparta, and his influence, like that of Alcibiades, after the battle of Marathon, was unbounded. No man ever merited greater reward.

Mardonius left in command of the Persians. He ravishes Attica and Bœotia.

Though the Persians now abandoned all hopes of any farther maritime attack, yet still great success was anticipated from the immense army which Mardonius commanded. The Greeks in the northern parts still adhered to him, and Thessaly was prostrate at his feet. He sent Alexander, of Macedon, to Athens to offer honorable terms of peace, which were nobly rejected, and he was sent back with this message: "Tell Mardonius that as long as the sun shall continue in his present path we will never contract alliance with a foe who has shown no reverence to our gods and heroes, and who has burned their statues and houses." The league was renewed with Sparta for mutual defense and offense, in spite of seductive offers from Mardonius; but the Spartans displayed both indifference and selfishness to any interests outside the Peloponnesus. They fortified the Isthmus of Corinth, but left Attica undefended. Mardonius accordingly marched to Athens, and again the city was the spoil of the Persians. The Athenians again retreated to Salamis, with bitter feelings against Sparta for her selfishness and ingratitude. Again Mardonius sought to conciliate the Athenians, and again his overtures were rejected with wrath and defiance. The Athenians, distressed, sent envoys to Sparta to remonstrate against her slackness and selfishness, not without effect, for, at last, a large Spartan force was collected under Pausanias. Meanwhile Mardonius ravaged Attica and Bœotia, and then fortified his camp near Platæa, ten furlongs square. Platæa was a plain favorable to the action of the cavalry, not far from Thebes; but his army was discouraged after so many disasters—in modern military language, demoralized—while Artabazus, the second in command, was filled with jealousy. Nor could much be hoped from the Grecian allies, who secretly were hostile to the invaders. The Thebans and Bœotians appeared to be zealous, but were governed by fear merely of a superior power, and hence were unreliable. It can not be supposed that the Thebans, who sided with the Persians, by compulsion, preferred their cause to that of their countrymen, great as may have been national jealousy and rivalries.

The Greeks assemble against the Persians at Platæa. Preparations for battle.

The total number of Lacedæmonians, Corinthians, Athenians, and other Greeks, assembled to meet the Persian army, B.C. 479, was thirty-eight thousand seven hundred men, heavily armed, and seventy-one thousand three hundred light armed, without defensive armor; but most of these were simply in attendance on the hoplites. The Persians, about three hundred thousand in number, occupied the line of the river Asopus, on a plain; the Greeks stationed themselves on the mountain declivity near Erythæ. The Persian cavalry charged, to dislodge the Greeks, unwilling to contend on the plain; but the ground was unfavorable for cavalry operations, and after a brief success, was driven back, while the general, Masistias, who commanded it, was slain. His death, and the repulse of the cavalry, so much encouraged Pausanias, the Spartan general, that he quitted his ground on the mountain declivity, and took position on the plain beneath. The Lacedæmonians composed the right wing; the Athenians, the left; and various other allies, the centre. Mardonius then slightly changed his position, crossing the Asopus, nearer his own camp, and took post on the left wing, opposite the right wing of the Greeks, commanded by Pausanias. Both armies then offered sacrifices to the gods, but Mardonius was able to give constant annoyance to the Greeks by his cavalry, and the Thebans gave great assistance. Ten days were thus spent by the two armies, without coming into general action, until Mardonius, on becoming impatient, against the advice of Artabazus, second in command, resolved to commence the attack. The Greeks were forewarned of his intention, by Alexander of Macedon, who came secretly to the Greek camp at night—a proof that he, as well as others, were impatient of the Persian yoke. The Lacedæmonians, posted in the right wing, against the Persians, changed places with the Athenians, who were more accustomed to Persian warfare; but this manœuvre being detected, Mardonius made a corresponding change in his own army—upon which Pausanias led back again his troops to the right wing, and a second movement of Mardonius placed the armies in the original position.

Battle of Platæa.

A vigorous attack of the Persian cavalry now followed, which so annoyed the Greeks, that Pausanias in the night resolved to change once again his position, and retreated to the hilly ground, north of Platæa, about twenty furlongs distant, not without confusion and mistrust on the part of the Athenians. Mardonias, astonished at this movement, pursued, and a general engagement followed. Both armies fought with desperate courage, but discipline was on the side of the Greeks, and Mardonius was slain, fighting gallantly with his guard. Artabazus, with the forty thousand Persians under his immediate command, had not taken part, and now gave orders to retreat, and retired from Greece. The main body, however, of the defeated Persians retired to their fortified camp. This was attacked by the Lacedæmonians, and carried with immense slaughter, so that only three thousand men survived out of the army of Mardonius, save the forty thousand which Artabazus—a more able captain—had led away. The defeat of the Persians was complete, and the spoils which fell to the victors was immense—gold and silver, arms, carpets, clothing, horses, camels, and even the rich tent of Xerxes himself, left with Mardonius. The booty was distributed among the different contingents of the army. The real victors were the Lacedæmonians, Athenians, and Tegeans; the Corinthians did not reach the field till the battle was ended, and thus missed their share of the spoil.

Chastisement of Thebes.

There was one ally of the Persians which Pausanias resolved to punish— the city of Thebes when a merited chastisement was inflicted, and the customary solemnities were observed, and honors decreed for the greatest and most decisive victory which the Greeks had ever gained. A confederacy was held at Platæa, in which a permanent league was made between the leading Grecian States, not to separate until the common foe was driven back to Asia.

Battle of Mycale.

While these great events were transpiring in Bœotia, the fleet of the Greeks, after the battle of Salamis, undertook to rescue Samos from the Persians, and secure the independence of the Ionian cities in Asia. The Persian fleet, now disheartened, abandoned Samos and retired to Mycale, in Ionia. The Greek fleet followed, but the Persians abandoned or dismissed their fleet, and joined their forces with those of Tigranes, who, with an army of sixty thousand men, guarded Ionia. The Greeks disembarked, and prepared to attack the enemy just as the news reached them of the battle of Platæa. This attack was successful, partly in consequence of the revolt of the Ionians in the Persian camp, although the Persians fought with great bravery. The battle of Mycale was as complete as that of Platæa and Marathon, and the remnants of the Persian army retired to Sardis. The Ionian cities were thus, for the time, delivered of the Persians, as well as Greece itself chiefly by means of the Athenians and Corinthians. The Spartans, with inconceivable narrowness, were reluctant to receive the continental Ionians as allies, and proposed to transport them across the Ægean into Western Greece, which proposal was most honorably rejected by the Athenians. In every thing, except the defense of Greece Proper, and especially the Peloponnesus, the Spartans showed themselves inferior to the Athenians in magnanimity and enlarged views. After the capture of Sestos, B.C. 478, which relieved the Thracian Chersonese from the Persians, the fleet of Athens returned home. The capture of this city concludes the narration of Herodotus, which ended virtually the Persian war, although hostilities were continued in Asia. The battle of Marathon had given the first effective resistance to Persian conquests, and created confidence among the Greeks. The battle of Salamis had destroyed the power of Persia on the sea, and prevented any co-operation of land and naval forces. The battle of Platæa freed Greece altogether of the invaders. The battle of Mycale rescued the Ionian cities.

Rivalry between Athens and Sparta.

Athens had, on the whole, most distinguished herself in this great and glorious contest, and now stood forth as the guardian of Hellenic interests on the sea and the leader of the Ionian race. Sparta continued to take the lead of the military States, to which Athens had generously submitted. But a serious rivalry now was seen between these leading States, chiefly through the jealousy of Sparta, which ultimately proved fatal to that supremacy which the Greeks might have maintained overall the powers of the world. Sparta wished that Athens might remain unfortified, in common with all the cities of Northern Greece, while the isthmus should be the centre of all the works of defense. But Athens, under the sagacious and crafty management of Themistocles, amused the Spartans by delays, while the whole population were employed upon restoring its fortifications.

Disgrace and death of Pausanias.

Although the war against the Persians was virtually concluded by the capture of Sestos, an expedition was fitted out by Sparta, under Pausanias, the hero of Platæa, to prosecute hostilities on the shores of Asia. After liberating most of the cities of Cyprus, and wresting Byzantium from the Persians, which thus left the Euxine free to Athenian ships, from which the Greeks derived their chief supplies of foreign corn, Pausanias, giddy with his victories, unaccountably began a treasonably correspondence with Xerxes, whose daughter he wished to marry, promising to bring all Greece again under his sway. He was recalled to Sparta, before this correspondence was known, having given offense by adopting the Persian dress, and surrounding himself with Persian and Median guards. When his treason was at last detected, he attempted to raise a rebellion among the Helots, but failed, and died miserably by hunger in the temple in which he had taken sanctuary.

Fall of Themistocles. Cimon Death of Themistocles..

A fall scarcely less melancholy came to the illustrious Themistocles. In spite of his great services, his popularity began to decline. He was hated by the Spartans for the part he took in the fortification of the city, who brought all their influence against him. He gave umbrage to the citizens by his personal vanity, continually boasting of his services. He erected a private chapel in honor of Artemis. He prostituted his great influence for arbitrary and corrupt purposes. He accepted bribes without scruple, to the detriment of the State, and in violation of justice and right. And as the Persians could offer the highest bribes, he was suspected of secretly favoring their interests. The old rivalries between him and Aristides were renewed; and as Aristides was no longer opposed to the policy which Athens adopted, of giving its supreme attention to naval defenses, and, moreover, constantly had gained the respect of the city by his integrity and patriotism, especially by his admirable management at Delos, where he cemented the confederacy of the maritime States, his influence was perhaps greater than that of Themistocles, stained with the imputation of *Medism*. Cimon, the son of Miltiades, also became a strong opponent. Though acquitted of accepting bribes from Persia, Themistocles was banished by a vote of ostracism, as Aristides had been before—a kind of exile which was not dishonorable, but resorted to from regard to public interests, and to which men who became unpopular were often subjected, whatever may have been their services or merits. He retired to Argos, and while there the treason of Pausanias was discovered. Themistocles was involved in it, since the designs of Pausanias were known by him. Joint envoys from Sparta and Athens were sent to arrest him, which, when known, he fled to Corcyra, and thence to Admetus, king of the Molossians. The Epirotic prince shielded him in spite of his former hostility, and furnished him with guides to Pydna, across the mountains, from which he succeeded in reaching Ephesus, and then repaired to the Persian court. At Athens he was proclaimed a traitor, and his property, amounting to one hundred talents, accumulated by the war, was confiscated. In Persia, he represented himself as a deserter, and subsequently acquired influence with Artaxerxes, and devoted his talents to laying out schemes for the subjugation of Greece. He received the large sum of fifty talents yearly, and died at sixty-five years of age, with a blighted reputation, such as no previous services could redeem from infamy.

Death of Aristides.

Aristides died four years after the ostracism of Themistocles, universally respected, and he died so poor as not to have enough for his funeral expenses. Nor did any of his descendants ever become rich.

Death of Xerxes.

Xerxes himself, the Ahasuerus of the Scriptures, who commanded the largest expedition ever recorded in human annals, reached Sardis, eight months after he had left it, disgusted with active enterprise, and buried himself amid the intrigues of his court and seraglio, in Susa, as recorded in the book of Esther. He was not deficient in generous impulses, but deficient in all those qualities which make men victorious in war. He died fifteen years after, the victim of a conspiracy, in his palace, B.C. 465—six years after Themistocles had sought his protection.

CHAPTER XVIII
THE AGE OF PERICLES

Rivalry between the Grecian States.

With the defeat of the Persian armies, Athens and Sparta became, respectively, the leaders of two great parties in Greece. Athens advocated maritime interests and democratic institutions; Sparta, was the champion of the continental and oligarchal powers. The one was Ionian, and organized the league of Delos, under the management of Aristides; the other was Dorian, and chief of the Peloponnesian confederacy. The rivalries between these leading States involved a strife between those ideas and interests of which each was the recognized representative. Those States which previously had been severed from each other by geographical position and diversity of interests, now rallied under the guidance either of Athens or Sparta. The intrigues of Themistocles and Pausanias had prevented that Panhellenic union, so necessary for the full development of political power, and which was for a time promoted by the Persian war. Athens, in particular, gradually came to regard herself as a pre-eminent power, to which the other States were to be tributary. Her empire, based on maritime supremacy, became a tyranny to which it was hard for the old allies to submit.

Pre-eminently between Athens and Sparta.

But the rivalry between Sparta and Athens was still more marked. Sparta had thus far taken the lead among the Grecian States, and Athens had submitted to it in the Persian invasion. But the consciousness of new powers, which naval warfare developed, the *éclat* of the battles of Marathon and Salamis, and the confederacy of Delos, changed the relative position of the two States. Moreover, to Athens the highest glory of resisting the Persians was due, while her patriotic and enlarged spirit favorably contrasted with the narrow and selfish policy of Sparta.

Opposition by Sparta to the fortifications of Athens.

And this policy was seen in nothing more signally than in the oppositions he made to the new fortifications of Athens, so that Themistocles was obliged to go to Sparta, and cover up by deceit and falsehood the fact that the Athenians were really repairing their walls, which they had an undoubted right to do, but which Ægina beheld with fear and Sparta with jealousy. And this unreasonable meanness and injustice on the part of Sparta, again reacted on the Athenians, and created great bitterness and acrimony.

The city nevertheless fortified. The Peireus. Increase of the navy. Confederacy of Delos.

But in spite of the opposition of Sparta, the new fortifications arose, to which all citizens, rich and poor, lent their aid, and on a scale which was not unworthy of the grandeur of a future capital. The circuit of the walls was fifty stadia or seven miles, and they were of sufficient strength and height to protect the city against external enemies. And when they were completed Themistocles—a man of great foresight and genius, persuaded the citizens to fortify also their harbor, as a means of securing the ascendency of the city in future maritime conflicts. He foresaw that the political ascendency of Athens was based on those "wooden walls" which the Delphic oracle had declared to be her hope in the Persian invasion. The victory at Salamis had confirmed the wisdom of the prediction, and given to Athens an imperishable glory. Themistocles persuaded his countrymen that the open roadstead of Phalerum was insecure, and induced them to inclose the more spacious harbors of Peireus and Munychia, by a wall as long as that which encircled Athens itself,—so thick and high that all assault should be hopeless, while within its fortifications the combined fleets of Greece could safely be anchored, and to which the citizens of Athens could also retire in extreme danger. Peireus accordingly was inclosed at vast expense and labor by a wall fourteen feet in thickness, which served not merely for a harbor, but a dock-yard and arsenal. Thither resorted metics or resident foreigners, and much of the trade of Athens was in their hands, since they were less frequently employed in foreign service. They became a thrifty population of traders and handy craftsmen identified with the prosperity of Athens. These various works, absorbed much of the Athenian force and capital, yet enough remained to build annually twenty new triremes—equivalent to our modern ships of the line. Athens now became the acknowledged head and leader of the allied States, instead of Sparta, whose authority as a presiding State was now openly renunciated by the Athenians. The Panhellenic union under Sparta was now broken forever, and two rival States disputed the supremacy,—the maritime States adhering to Athens, and the land States, which furnished the larger part of the army at Platæa, adhering to Sparta. It was then that the confederacy of Delos was formed, under the presidency of Athens, which Aristides directed. His assessment was so just and equitable that no jealousies were excited, and the four hundred and sixty talents which were collected from the maritime States were kept at Delos for the common benefit of the league, managed by a board of Athenian officers. It was a common fear which led to this great contribution, for the Phœnician fleet might at any time reappear, and, co-operating with a Persian land force, destroy the liberties of Greece. Although Athens reaped the chief benefit of this league, it was essentially national. It was afterward indeed turned to aggrandize Athens, but, when it was originally made, was a means of common defense against a power as yet unconquered though repulsed.

Confederacy of Delos.

During all the time that the fortifications of Athens and the Peireus were being made, Themistocles was the ruling spirit at Athens, while Aristides commanded the fleet and organized the confederacy of Delos. It was thus several years before he became false to his Countrymen, and the change was only gradually wrought in his character, owing chiefly to his extravagant habits and the arrogance which so often attends success.

Change in the Athenian constitution.

During this period, a change was also made in the civil constitution of Athens. All citizens were rendered admissible to office. The State became still more democratic. The archons were withdrawn from military duties, and confined to civil functions. The stategi or generals gained greater power with the extending political relations, and upon them was placed the duty of superintending foreign affairs. Athens became more democratical and more military at the same time.

The political growth of Athens.

From this time, 479 B.C., we date the commencement of the Athenian empire. It gradually was cemented by circumstances rather than a long-sighted and calculating ambition. At the head of the confederacy of Delos, opportunities were constantly presented of centralizing power, while its rapid increase of population and wealth favored the schemes which political leaders advanced for its aggrandizement. The first ten years of the Athenian hegemony or headship were years of active warfare against the Persians. The capture of Eion, on the Strymon, with its Persian garrison, by Cimonon, led to the settlement of Amphipolis by the Athenians; and the fall of the cities which the Persians had occupied in Thrace and in the various islands of the Ægean increased the power of Athens.

The Confederate States.

The confederate States at last grew weary of personal military service, and prevailed upon the Athenians to provide ships and men in their place, for which they imposed upon themselves a suitable money-payment. They thus gradually sunk to the condition of tributary allies, unwarlike and averse to privation, while the Athenians, stimulated by new and expanding ambition, became more and more enterprising and powerful.

Unpopularity of Athens.

But with the growth of Athens was also the increase of jealousies. Athens became unpopular, not only because she made the different maritime States her tributaries, but because she embarked in war against them to secure a still greater aggrandizement. Naxos revolted, but was conquered, B.C. 467. The confederate State was stripped of its navy, and its fortifications were razed to the ground. Next year the island of Thasos likewise seceded from the alliance, and was subdued with difficulty, and came near involving Athens in a war with Sparta. The Thasians invoked the aid of Sparta, which was promised though not fulfilled, which imbittered the relations between the two leading Grecian States.

Expeditions against Persia.

During this period, from the formation of the league at Delos, and the fall of Thasos, about thirteen years, Athens was occupied in maintaining expeditions against Persia, being left free from embarrassments in Attica. The towns of Platæa and Thespiæ were restored and repeopled under Athenian influence.

Sparta. Rebellion of the Helots. Cimon opposed to Pericles. Alliance of different states with Athens.

The jealousy of Sparta, in view of the growing power of Athens, at last gave vent in giving aid to Thebes, against the old policy of the State, to enable that city to maintain supremacy over the lesser Bœotian towns. The Spartans even aided in enlarging her circuit and improving her fortifications, which aid made Thebes a vehement partisan of Sparta. Soon after, a terrible earthquake happened in Sparta, 464 B.C., which calamity was seized upon by the Helots as a fitting occasion for revolt. Defeated, but not subdued, the insurgents retreated to Ithome, the ancient citadel of their Messenian ancestors, and there intrenched themselves. The Spartans spent two years in an unsuccessful siege, and were forced to appeal to their allies for assistance. But even the increased force made no impression on the fortified hill, so ignorant were the Greeks, at this period, of the art of attacking walls. And when the Athenians, under Cimon, still numbered among the allies of Sparta, were not more successful, their impatience degenerated to mistrust and suspicion, and summarily dismissed the Athenian contingent. This ungracious and jealous treatment exasperated the Athenians, whose feelings were worked upon by Pericles who had opposed the policy of sending troops at all to Laconia. Cimon here was antagonistic to Pericles, and wished to cement the more complete union of Greece against Persia, and maintain the union with Sparta. Cimon, moreover, disliked the democratic policy of Pericles. But the Athenians rallied under Pericles, and Cimon lost his influence, which had been paramount since the disgrace of Themistocles. A formal resolution was passed at Athens to renounce the alliance with Sparta against the Persians, and to seek alliance with Argos, which had been neutral during the Persian invasion, but which had regained something of its ancient prestige and power by the conquest of Mycenæ and other small towns. The Thessalians became members of this new alliance which was intended to be antagonistic to Sparta. Megara, shortly after, renounced the protection of the Peloponnesian capital, and was enrolled among the allies of Athens,—a great acquisition to Athenian power, since this city secured the passes of Mount Gerania, so that Attica was protected from invasion by the Isthmus of Corinth. But the alliance of Megara and Athens gave deep umbrage to Corinth as well as Sparta, and a war with Corinth was the result, in which Ægina was involved as the ally of Sparta and Corinth.

Defeat of Athens on the land and victory on the sea.

The Athenians were at first defeated on the land; but this defeat was more than overbalanced by a naval victory over the Dorian seamen, off the island of Ægina, by which the naval force of *Ægina* hitherto great, was forever prostrated. The Athenians captured seventy ships and commenced the siege of the city itself. Sparta would have come to the rescue, but was preoccupied in suppressing the insurrection of the Helots. Corinth sent three hundred hoplites to Ægina and attacked Megara. But the Athenians prevailed both at Ægina and Megara, which was a great blow to Corinth.

Pericles begins his career. Cimon banished.

Fearing, however, a renewed attack from Corinth and the Peloponnesian States, now full of rivalry and enmity, the Athenians, under the leadership of Pericles, resolved to connect their city with the harbor of Peireus by a long wall—a stupendous undertaking at that time. It excited the greatest alarm among the enemies of Athens, and was a subject of contention among different parties in the city. The party which Cimon, now ostracised, had headed, wished to cement the various Grecian States in a grand alliance against the Persians, and dreaded to see this long wall arise as a standing menace against the united power of the Peloponnesus. Moreover, the aristocrats of Athens disliked a closer amalgamation with the maritime people of the Peireus, as well as the burdens and taxes which this undertaking involved. These fortifications doubtless increased the power of Athens, but weakened the unity of Hellenic patriotism; and increased those jealousies which ultimately proved the political ruin of Greece.

Hostilities between Sparta and Athens.

Under the influence of these rivalries and jealousies the Lacedæmonians, although the Helots were not subdued, undertook a hostile expedition out of the Peloponnesus, with eleven thousand five hundred men, ostensibly to protect Doris against the Phœcians, but really to prevent the further aggrandizement of Athens, and this was supposed to be most easily effected by strengthening Thebes and securing the obedience of the Bœotian cities. But there was yet another design, to prevent the building of the long walls, to which the aristocratical party of Athens was opposed, but which Pericles, with long-sighted views, defended.

Ascendency of Pericles. His character and accomplishments.

This extraordinary man, with whom the glory and greatness of Athens are so intimately associated, now had the ascendency over all his rivals. He is considered the ablest of all the statesmen which Greece produced. He was of illustrious descent, and spent the early part of his life in retirement and study, and when he emerged from obscurity his rise was rapid, until he gained the control of his countrymen, which he retained until his death. He took the side of the democracy, and, in one sense, was a demagogue, as well as a statesman, since he appealed to popular passions and interests. He was very eloquent, and was the idol of the party which was dominant in the State. His rank and fortune enabled him to avail himself of every mode of culture and self-improvement known in his day. He loved music, philosophy, poetry, and art. The great Anaxagoras gave a noble direction to his studies, so that he became imbued with the sublimest ideas of Grecian wisdom. And his eloquence is said to have been of the most lofty kind. His manners partook of the same exalted and dignified bearing as his philosophy. He never lost his temper, and maintained the severest self-control. His voice was sweet, and his figure was graceful and commanding. He early distinguished himself as a soldier, and so gained upon his countrymen that, when Themistocles and Aristides were dead, and Cimon engaged in military expeditions, he supplanted all who had gone before him in popular favor. All his sympathies were with the democratic party, while his manners and habits and tastes and associations were those of the aristocracy. His political career lasted forty years from the year 469 B.C. He was unremitting in his public duties, and was never seen in the streets unless on his way to the assembly or senate. He was not fond of convivial pleasures, and was, though affable, reserved and dignified. He won the favor of the people by a series of measures which provided the poor with amusement and means of subsistence. He caused those who served in the courts to be paid for their attendance and services. He weakened the power of the court of the Areopagus, which was opposed to popular measures.

Assured of his own popularity, he even contrived to secure the pardon of Cimon, his great rival, when publicly impeached.

The union of the Peireus with Athens.

Pericles was thus the leading citizen of his country, when he advocated the junction of the Peireus with Athens by the long walls which have been alluded to, and when the Spartan army in Bœotia threatened to sustain the oligarchal party in the city. The Athenians, in view of this danger, took decisive measures. They took the field at once against their old allies, the Lacedæmonians. The unfortunate battle of Tanagra was decided in favor of the Spartans, chiefly through the desertion of the Thessalian horse.

Magnanimity of Cimon.

Cimon, though ostracised, appeared in the field of battle, and requested permission to fight in the ranks. Though the request was refused, he used all his influence with his friends to fight with bravery and fidelity to his country's cause, which noble conduct allayed the existing jealousies, and through the influence of Pericles, his banishment of ten years was revoked. He returned to Athens, reconciled with the party which had defeated him, and so great was the admiration of his magnanimity that all parties generously united in the common cause. Another battle with the enemy was fought in Bœotia, this time attended with success, the result of which was the complete ascendency of the Athenians over all Bœotia. They became masters of Thebes and all the neighboring towns, and reversed all the acts of the Spartans, and established democratic governments, and forced the aristocratical leaders into exile. Phocis and Locris were added to the list of dependent allies, and the victory cemented their power from the Corinthian Gulf to the strait of Thermopylæ.

Completion of the long walls.

Then followed the completion of the long walls, B.C. 455, and the conquest of Ægina. Athens was now mistress of the sea, and her admiral displayed his strength by sailing round the Peloponnesus, and taking possession of many cities in the Gulf of Corinth. But the Athenians were unsuccessful in an expedition into Thessaly, and sustained many losses in Egypt in the great warfare with Persia.

Death of Cimon.

After the success of the Lacedæmonians at Tanagra they made no expeditions out of the Peloponnesus for several years, and allowed Bœotia and Phocis to be absorbed in the Athenian empire. They even extended the truce with Athens for five years longer, and this was promoted by Cimon, who wished to resume offensive operations against the Persians. Cimon was allowed to equip a fleet of two hundred triremes and set sail to Cyprus, where he died. The expedition failed under his successor, and this closed all further aggressive war with the Persians.

Pericles without rivals.

The death of Cimon, whose interest it was to fight the Persians, and thus by the spoils and honors of war keep up his influence at home, left Pericles without rivals, and with opportunities to develop his policy of internal improvements, and the development of national resources, to enable Athens to maintain her ascendency over the States of Greece. So he gladly concluded peace with the Persians, by the terms of which they were excluded from the coasts of Asia Minor and the islands of the Ægean; while Athens stipulated to make no further aggression on Cyprus, Phœnicia, Cilicia, and Egypt.

Aggrandizement of Athens.

Athens, at peace with all her enemies, with a large empire of tributary allies, a great fleet, and large accumulations of treasure, sought now to make herself supreme in Greece. The fund of the confederacy of Delos was transferred to the Acropolis. New allies sought her alliance. It is said the tributary cities amounted to one thousand. She was not only mistress of the sea, but she was the equal of Sparta on the land. Beside this political power, a vast treasure was accumulated in the Acropolis. Such rapid aggrandizement was bitterly felt by Corinth, Sicyon, and Sparta, and the feeling of enmity expanded until it exploded in the Peloponnesian war.

Change in the constitution by Pericles. Increase of democratic power. The dikasts. Ascendency of the democratic power.

It was while Athena was at this height of power and renown that further changes were made in the constitution by Pericles. Great authority was still in the hands of the court of the Areopagus, which was composed exclusively of ex-archons, sitting for life, and hence of very aristocratic sentiments. It was indeed a judicial body, but its functions were mixed; it decided all disputes, inquired into crimes, and inflicted punishments. And it was enabled to enforce its own mandates, which were without appeal, and led to great injustice and oppression. The magistrates, serving without pay, were generally wealthy, and though their offices were eligible to all the citizens, still, practically, only the rich became magistrates, as is the case with the British House of Commons. Hence, magistrates possessing large powers, and the senate sitting for life, all belonging to the wealthy class, were animated by aristocratic sympathies. But a rapidly increasing democracy succeeded in securing the selection of archons by lot, in place of election. This threw more popular elements into the court of Areopagus. The innovations which Pericles effected, of causing the jury courts, or Dikasteries, to be regularly paid, again threw into public life the poorer citizens. But the great change which he effected was in transferring to the numerous dikasts, selected from the citizens, a new judicial power, heretofore exercised by the magistrates, and the senate of the Areopagus. The magistrate, instead of deciding causes and inflicting punishment beyond the imposition of a small fine, was constrained to impanel a jury to try the cause. In fact, the ten dikasts became the leading judicial tribunals, and as these were composed, each, of five hundred citizens, judgments were virtually made by the people, instead of the old court. The pay of each man serving as a juror was determined and punctually paid. The importance of this revolution will be seen when these dikasts thus became the exclusive assemblies, of course popular, in which all cases, civil and criminal, were tried. The magistrates were thus deprived of the judicial functions which they once enjoyed, and were confined to purely administrative matters. The commanding functions of the archon were destroyed, and he only retained power to hear complaints, and fix the day of trial, and preside over the dikastic assembly. The senate of the Areopagus, which had exercised an inquisitorial power over the lives and habits of the citizens, and supervised the meetings of the assembly—a power uncertain but immense, and sustained by ancient customs,—now became a mere nominal tribunal. And this change was called for, since the members of the court were open to bribery and corruption, and had abused their powers, little short of paternal despotism. And when the great public improvements, the growth of a new population, the rising importance of the Penæus, the introduction of nautical people, and the active duties of Athens as the head of the Delian confederacy—all, together, gave force to the democratic elements of society, the old and conservative court became stricter, and more oppressive, instead of more popular and conciliatory.

Other political changes effected by Pericles.

But beside this great change in the constitution, Pericles effected others also. Under his influence, a general power of supervision, over the magistrates and the assembly, was intrusted to seven men called Nomophylakes, or Law Guardians, changed every year, who sat with the president in the senate and assembly, and interposed when any step was taken contrary to existing laws. Other changes were also effected with a view to the enforcement of laws, upon which we can not enter. It is enough to say that it was by means of Pericles that the magistrates were stripped of judicial power, and the Areopagus of all its jurisdiction, except in cases of homicide, and numerous and paid and popular dikasts were substituted to decide judicial cases, and repeal and enact laws; this, says Grote, was the consummation of the Athenian democracy. And thus it remained until the time of Demosthenes.

Improvements of Athens.

But the influence of Pericles is still more memorable from the impulse he gave to the improvements of Athens and his patronage of art and letters. He conceived the idea of investing his city with intellectual glory, which is more permanent than any conquests of territory. And since he could not make Athens the centre of political power, owing to the jealousies of other States, he resolved to make her the great attraction to all scholars, artists, and strangers. And his countrymen were prepared to second his glorious objects, and were in a condition to do so, enriched by commerce, rendered independent by successes over the Persians, and jealous Grecian rivals, and stimulated by the poets and philosophers who flourished in that glorious age. The age of Pericles is justly regarded as the epoch of the highest creation genius ever exhibited, and gave to Athens an intellectual supremacy which no military genius could have secured.

The public buildings.

The Persian war despoiled and depopulated Athens. The city was rebuilt on a more extensive plan, and the streets were made more regular. The long walls to the Peiræus were completed—a double wall, as it were, with a space between them large enough to secure the communication between the city and the port, in case an enemy should gain a footing in the wide space between the Peiræan and Thaleric walls. The port itself was ornamented with beautiful public buildings, of which the Agora was the most considerable. The theatre, called the Odeon, was erected in Athens for musical and poetical contests. The Acropolis, with its temples, was rebuilt, and the splendid Propylæa, of Doric architecture, formed a magnificent approach to them. The temple of Athenæ—the famous Parthenon—was built of white marble, and adorned with sculptures in the pediments and frieze by the greatest artists of antiquity, while Phidias constructed the statue of the goddess of ivory and gold. No Doric temple ever equaled the severe proportions and chaste beauty of the Parthenon, and its ruins still are one of the wonders of the world. The Odeon and Parthenon were finished during the first seven years of the administration of Pericles, and many other temples were constructed in various parts of Attica. The genius of Phidias is seen in the numerous sculptures which ornamented the city, and the general impulse he gave to art. Other great artists labored in generous competition,—sculptors, painters, and architects,—to make Athens the most beautiful city in the world.

Impulse given to literature. The drama.

"It was under the administration of Pericles that Greek literature reached its culminating height in the Attic drama, a form of poetry which Aristotle justly considers as the most perfect; and it shone with undiminished splendor to the close of the century. It was this branch of literature which peculiarly marked the age of Pericles—the period between the Persian and Peloponnesian wars. The first regular comedies were produced by Epicharmus, who was born in Cos, B.C. 540, and exhibited at Syracuse. Comedy arose before tragedy, and was at first at the celebration of Dionysus by rustic revelers in the season of the vintage, in the form of songs and dances. But these were not so appropriate in cities, and the songs of the revelers were gradually molded into the regular choral dithyramb, while the performers still preserved the wild dress and gestures of the satyrs—half goat and half man—who accompanied Dionysus." The prevalence of tales of crime and fate and suffering naturally impressed spectators with tragic sentiments, and tragedy was thus born and separated from comedy. Both forms received their earliest development in the Dorian States, and were particularly cultivated by the Megarians. "Thespis, a native of Icaria, first gave to tragedy its dramatic character, in the time of Pisistratus, B.C. 535. He introduced the dialogue, relieved by choral performances, and the recitation of mythological and heroic adventures. He traveled about Attica in a wagon, which served him for a stage; but the art soon found its way to Athens, where dramatic contests for prizes were established in connection with the festivals of Dionysus. These became State institutions. Chœrilus, B.C. 523, and Phrynichus followed Thespis, and these ventured from the regions of mythology to contemporaneous history."

Æschylus. Sophocles.

It was at this time that Æschylus, the father of tragedy, exhibited his dramas at Athens, B.C. 500. He added a second actor, and made the choral odes subordinate to the action. The actors now made use of masks, and wore lofty head-dresses and magnificent robes. Scenes were painted according to the rules of perspective, and an elaborate mechanism was introduced upon the stage. New figures were invented for the dancers of the chorus. Sophocles still further improved tragedy by adding the third actor, and snatched from Æschylus the tragic prize. He was not equal to Æschylus in the boldness and originality of his characters, or the loftiness of his sentiments, or the colossal grandeur of his figures; but in the harmony of his composition, and the grace and vigor displayed in all the parts—the severe unity, the classic elegance of his style, and the charm of his expressions he is his superior. These two men carried tragedy to a degree of perfection never afterward attained in Greece. It was not merely a spectacle to the people, but was applied to moral and religious purposes. The heroes of Æschylus are raised above the sphere of real life, and often they are the sport of destiny, or victims of a struggle between superior beings. The characters of Sophocles are rarely removed beyond the sphere of mortal sympathy, and they are made to rebuke injustice and give impressive warnings.

Comedy.

Comedy also made a great stride during the administration of Pericles; but it was not till his great ascendency was at its height that Aristophanes was born, B.C. 444. The comedians of the time were allowed great license, which they carried even into politics, and which was directed against Pericles himself.

Power of the stage.

The Athenian stage at this epoch was the chief means by which national life and liberty were sustained. It answered the functions of the press and the pulpit in our day, and quickened the perceptions of the people. The great audiences which assembled at the theatres were kindled into patriotic glow, and were moved by the noble thoughts, and withering sarcasm, and inexhaustible wit of the poets. "The gods and goddesses who swept majestically over the tragic stage were the objects of religious and national faith, real beings, whose actions and sufferings claimed their deepest sympathy, and whose heroic fortitude served for an example, or their terrific fate for a warning. So, too, in the old comedy, the persons, habits, manners, principles held up to ridicule were all familiar to the audience in their daily lives; and the poet might exhibit in a humorous light objects which to attack seriously would have been a treason or a sacrilege, and might recommend measures which he could only have proposed in the popular assembly with a halter round his neck." This susceptibility of the people to grand impressions, and the toleration of rulers, alike show a great degree of popular intelligence and a great practical liberty in social life.

The historians and philosophers.

The age of Pericles was also adorned by great historians and philosophers. Herodotus and Thucydides have never been surpassed as historians, while the Sophists who succeeded the more earnest philosophers of a previous age, gave to Athenian youth a severe intellectual training. Rhetoric, mathematics and natural history supplanted speculation, led to the practice of eloquence as an art, and gave to society polish and culture. The Sophists can not indeed be compared with those great men who preceded or succeeded them in philosophical wisdom, but their influence in educating the Grecian mind, and creating polished men of society, can not be disproved. Politics became a profession in the democratic State, which demanded the highest culture, and an extensive acquaintance with the principles of moral and political science. This was the age of lectures, when students voluntarily assembled to learn from the great masters of thought that knowledge which would enable them to rise in a State where the common mind was well instructed.

Athens declines in moral power.

But it must also be admitted that while the age of Pericles furnished an extraordinary stimulus to the people, in art, in literature, in political science, and in popular institutions, the great teachers of the day inculcated a selfish morality, and sought an æsthetic enjoyment irrespective of high moral improvement, and the inevitable result was the rapid degeneracy of Athens, and the decline even in political influence, and strength, as was seen in the superior power of Sparta in the great contest to which the two leading States of Greece were hurried by their jealousies and animosities. The prosperity was delusive and outside; for no intellectual triumph, no glories of art, no fascinations of literature, can balance the moral forces which are generated in self-denial and lofty public virtue.

Aspasia.

It was while the power and glory of Pericles were at their height that he formed that memorable attachment to Aspasia, a Milesian woman, which furnished a fruitful subject for the attacks of the comic poets. She was the most brilliant and intellectual woman of the age, and her house was the resort of the literary men and philosophers and artists of Athens until the death of Pericles. He formed as close a union with her as the law allowed, and her influence in creating a sympathy with intellectual excellence can not be questioned. But she was charged with pandering to the vices of Pericles, and corrupting society by her example and influence.

Latter days of Pericles. Policy of Pericles.

The latter years of Pericles were marked by the outbreak of that great war with Sparta, which crippled the power of Athens and tarnished her glories. He also was afflicted by the death of his children by the plague which devastated Athens in the early part of the Peloponnesian war, to which attention is now directed. The probity of Pericles is attested by the fact that during his long administration he added nothing to his patrimonial estate. His policy was ambitious, and if it could have been carried out, it would have been wise. He sought first to develop the resources of his country—the true aim of all enlightened statesmen—and then to make Athens the centre of Grecian civilization and political power, to which all other Stales would be secondary and subservient. But the rivalries of the Grecian States and inextinguishable jealousies would not allow this. He made Athens, indeed, the centre of cultivated life; he could not make it the centre of national unity. In attempting this he failed, and a disastrous war was the consequence.

Pericles lived long enough to see the commencement of the contest which ultimately resulted in the political ruin of Athens, and which we now present.

CHAPTER XIX
THE PELOPONNESIAN WAR

Causes of the war.

The great and disastrous war between the two leading States of Greece broke out about two years and a half before the death of Pericles, but the causes of the war can be traced to a period shortly after the Persians were driven out of the Ionian cities. It arose primarily from the rapid growth and power of Athens, when, as the leader of the maritime States, it excited the envy of Sparta and other republics. A thirty years' truce was made between Athens and Sparta, B.C. 445, after the revolution in Bœotia, when the ascendency of Pericles was undisputed, which forced his rival, Thucydides, a kinsman of Cimon, to go into temporary exile. The continuance of the truce is identical with the palmy days of Athens, and the glory of Pericles, during which the vast improvements to the city were made, and art and literature flourished to a degree unprecedented in the history of the ancient world.

War between Corcyra and Corinth. Both parties appealed to Athens. Athens decides in favor of Corcyra.

After the conquest of Samos the jealousy of Sparta reached a point which made it obvious that the truce could not much longer be maintained, though both powers shrunk from open hostilities, foreseeing the calamities which would result. The storm burst out in an unexpected quarter. The city of Epidamnus had been founded by colonists from Corcyra, on the eastern side of the Adriatic. It was, however, the prey of domestic factions, and in a domestic revolution a part of the inhabitants became exiles. These appealed to the neighboring barbarians, who invested the city by sea and land. The city, in distress, invoked the aid of Corcyra, the parent State, which aid being disregarded, the city transferred its allegiance to Corinth. The Corinthians, indulging a hatred of Corcyra, took the distressed city under their protection. This led to a war between Corcyra and Corinth, in which the Corinthians were defeated. But Corinth, burning to revenge the disaster, fitted out a still larger force against Corcyra. The Corcyræans, in alarm, then sent envoys to Athens to come to their assistance. The Corinthians also sent ambassadors to frustrate their proposal. Two assemblies were held in Athens in reference to the subject. The delegates of Corcyra argued that peace could not long be maintained with Sparta, and that in the coming contest the Corcyræans would prove useful allies. The envoys of Corinth, on the other hand, maintained that Athens could not lend aid to Corcyra without violating the treaty with Corinth. The Athenians decided to assist Corcyra, and ten ships were sent, under the command of Lacedæmonieus, the son of Cimon. This was considered a breach of faith by the Corinthians, and a war resulted between Corinth and Athens. The Corinthians then invited the Lacedæmonians to join them and make common cause against an aggressive and powerful enemy, that aimed at the supremacy of Greece. In spite of the influence of Athenian envoys in Sparta, who attempted to justify the course their countrymen had taken, the feeling against Athens was bitter and universally hostile. Instant hostilities were demanded in defense of the allies of Sparta, and war was decided upon.

Thus commenced the Peloponnesian war, which led to such disastrous consequences, and which was thus brought about by the Corinthians, B.C. 433, sixteen years before the conclusion of the truce.

Intrigues of Sparta.

To Athens the coming war was any thing but agreeable. It had no hopes of gain, and the certainty of prodigious loss. But the Spartans were not then prepared for the contest, and hostilities did not immediately commence. They contented themselves, at first, with sending envoys to Athens to multiply demands and enlarge the grounds of quarrel. The offensive was plainly with Sparta. The first requisition which Sparta made was the expulsion of the Alcmæonidæ from Athens, to which family Pericles belonged—a mere political manœuvre to get rid of so commanding a statesman. The enemies of Pericles, especially the comic actors at Athens, seized this occasion to make public attacks upon him, and it was then that the persecution of Aspasia took place, as well as that against Anaxagoras, the philosopher, the teacher, and friend of Pericles. He was also accused of peculation in complicity with Phidias. But he was acquitted of the various charges made by his enemies. Nor could his services be well dispensed with in the great crisis of public affairs, even had he been guilty, as was exceedingly doubtful.

Pericles urges the Athenians to support a war. Imperious demands of Sparta. Preparations for war. Wealth of Athens.

The reluctance on the part of the Athenians to go to war was very great, but Pericles strenuously urged his countrymen to resent the outrageous demands of Sparta, which were nothing less than the virtual extinction of the Athenian empire. He showed that the Spartans, though all-powerful on the Peloponnesus, had no means of carrying on an aggressive war at a distance, neither leaders nor money, nor habits of concert with allies; while Athens was mistress of the sea, and was impregnable in defense; that great calamities would indeed happen in Attica, but even if overrun by Spartan armies, there were other territories and islands from which a support could be derived. "Mourn not for the loss of land," said the orator, "but reserve your mourning for the men that acquire land." His eloquence and patriotism prevailed with a majority of the assembly, and answer was made to Sparta that the Athenians were prepared to discuss all grounds of complaint pursuant to the truce, by arbitration, but that they would yield nothing to authoritative command. This closed the negotiations, which Pericles foresaw would be vain and useless, since the Spartans were obstinately bent on war. The first imperious blow was struck by the Thebans—allies of Sparta. They surprised Platæa in the night. The gates were opened by the oligarchal party; a party of Thebans were admitted into the agora; but the people rallied, and the party was overwhelmed. Meanwhile another detachment of Thebans arrived in the morning, and, discovering what had happened, they laid waste the Platæan territory without the walls. The Platæans retaliated by slaughtering their prisoners. Messengers left the city, on the entrance of the Thebans, to carry the news to Athens, and the Athenians issued orders to seize all the Bœotians who could be found in Attica, and sent re-enforcements to Platæa. This aggression of the Thebans silenced the opponents of Pericles, who now saw that the war had actually begun, and that active preparations should be made. Athens immediately sent messengers to her allies, tributary as well as free, and contributions flowed in from all parts of the Athenian empire. Athens had soon three hundred triremes fit for service, twelve hundred horsemen, sixteen hundred bowmen, and twenty-nine thousand hoplites. The Acropolis was filled with the treasure which had long been accumulating, not less than six thousand talents—about $7,000,000 of our money—an immense sum at that time, when gold and silver were worth twenty or thirty times as much as at present. Moreover, the various temples were rich in votive offerings, in deposits, plate, and sacred vessels, while the great statue of the goddess, lately set up in the Parthenon by Phidias, composed of gold and ivory, was itself valued at four hundred talents. The contributions of allies swelled the resources of Athens to one thousand talents, or over $11,000,000.

Immense array of forces against Athens.

Sparta, on the other hand, had but few ships, no funds, and no powers of combination, and it would seem that success would be on the side of Athens, with her unrivaled maritime skill, and the unanimity of the citizens. Pericles did not promise successful engagements on the land, but a successful resistance, and the maintenance of the empire. His policy was purely defensive. But if Sparta was weak in money and ships, she was rich in allies. The entire strength of the Peloponnesus was brought out, assisted by Megarians, Bœotians, Phocians, Locrians, and other States. Corinth, Megara, Sicyon, Elis, and other maritime cities furnished ships while Bœotians, Phocians, and Locrians furnished cavalry. Not even to resist the Persian hosts was so large a land force collected, as was now assembled to destroy the supremacy of Athens. And this great force was animated with savage hopes, while the Athenians were not without desponding anticipations, for there was little hope of resisting the Spartans and their allies on the field. The Spartans, moreover, resolved, by means of their allies, to send a fleet able to cope with that of Athens, and even were so transported with enmity and jealousy as to lay schemes for invoking the aid of Persia.

Invasion of Attica. Defensive policy of Pericles.

The invasion of Attica was the primary object of Sparta and her allies; and at the appointed time the Lacedæmonian forces were mustered on the Isthmus of Corinth, under the command of Archidamus. Envoys were sent to Athens to summon a surrender, but Pericles would not receive them, nor allow them to enter the city, upon which the Lacedæmonian army commenced its march to Attica. It required all the eloquence and tact of Pericles to induce the proprietors of Attica to submit to the devastation of their cultivated territory, and fly with their families and movable property to Athens or the neighboring islands, without making an effort to resist the invaders. But this was the policy of Pericles. He knew he could not contend with superior forces on the land. It was hard for the people to submit to the cruel necessity of seeing their farms devastated without opposition. But they made the sacrifice, and intrenched themselves behind the fortifications of Athens. Then was seen the wisdom of the long walls which connected Athens with the Piræus.

Retreat of the Lacedæmonians.

Meanwhile the Spartan forces—sixty thousand hoplites, advanced through Attica, burning and plundering every thing on their way, and reached Acharnæ, within seven miles of Athens. The Athenians, pent up behind their walls, and seeing the destruction of their property, were eager to go forth and fight, but were dissuaded by Pericles. Then came to him the trying hour. He was denounced as the cause of the existing sufferings, and was reviled as a coward. But nothing disturbed his equanimity, and he refused even to convene the assembly. As one of the ten generals he had this power; but it was a remarkable thing that the people should have respected the democratic constitution so far as to submit, when their assembly would have been justified by the exigency of the crisis. But while the Athenians remained inactive behind their walls, the cavalry was sent out on skirmishing expeditions, and a large fleet was sent to the Peloponnesus with orders to devastate the country in retaliation. The Spartans, after having spent thirty or forty days in Attica, retired for want of provisions. Ægina was also invaded, and the inhabitants were expelled and sent to the Peloponnesus. Megara was soon after invaded by an army under Pericles himself, and its territory was devastated—a retribution well deserved, for both Megara and Ægina had been zealous in kindling the war.

Athens sets aside 1,000 talents for future contingencies.

Expecting a prolonged struggle, the Athenians now made arrangements for putting Attica in permanent defense, both by sea and land, and set apart one thousand talents, out of the treasure of the Acropolis, which was not to be used except in certain dangers previously prescribed, and a law was passed making it a capital offense for any citizen to propose its use for any other purpose.

Results of the first year of the war.

The first year of the war closed without decisive successes on either side. The Athenians made a more powerful resistance than was anticipated. It was supposed they could not hold out against the superior forces of their enemies more than a year. They had the misfortune to see their territory wasted, and their treasures spent in a war which they would gladly have avoided. But, on the other hand, they inflicted nearly equal damages upon the Peloponnesus, and still remained masters of the sea. Pericles pronounced a funeral oration on those who had fallen and stimulated his countrymen to continued resistance, and excited their patriotic sentiments. Thus far the anticipations of the statesman and orator had been more than realized.

The Spartans again invade Attica.

The second year of the war opened with another invasion of Attica by the Spartans and their allies. They inflicted even more injury than in the preceding year, but they found the territory deserted, all the population having retired within the defenses of Athens.

The plague at Athens.

But a new and unforeseen calamity now fell upon the Athenians, and against which they could not guard. A great pestilence broke out in the city, which had already overrun Western Asia. Its progress was rapid and destructive, and the overcrowded city was but too favorable for its ravages. Thucydides has left a graphic and mournful account of this pestilence, analogous to the plague of modern times. The victims generally perished on the seventh or ninth day, and no treatment was efficacious. The sufferings and miseries of the people were intense, and the calamity by many was regarded as resulting from the anger of the gods. The pestilence demoralized the population, who lost courage and fortitude. The sick were left to take care of themselves. The utmost lawlessness prevailed. The bonds of law and morality were relaxed, and the thoughtless people abandoned themselves to every species of folly and excess, seeking, in their despair, to seize some brief moments of joy before the hand of destiny should fall upon them. For three years did this calamity desolate Athens, and the loss of life was deplorable, both in the army and among private citizens. Pericles lost both his children and his sister; four thousand four hundred hoplites died, and a greater part of the horsemen.

Naval expedition against Sparta. Death of Pericles.

And yet, amid the devastation which the pestilence inflicted, Pericles led another expedition against the coasts of the Peloponnesus. But the soldiers carried infection with them, and a greater part of them died of the disease at the siege or blockade of Potidæa. The Athenians were nearly distracted by the double ravages of pestilence and war, and became incensed against Pericles, and sent messengers to Sparta to negotiate peace. But the Spartans turned a deaf ear, which added to the bitterness against their heroic leader, whose fortitude and firmness were never more effectively manifested. He was accused, and condemned to pay a fine, and excluded from re-election. Though he was restored to power and confidence, his affliction bore heavily upon his exalted nature, and he died, B.C. 430, in the early period of the war. He had, indeed, many enemies, and was hunted down by the comic writers, whose trade it was to deride all political characters, yet his wisdom, patriotism, eloquence, and great services are indisputable, and he died, leaving on the whole, the greatest name which had ever ennobled the Athenians.

Sparta invokes the aid of the Persians.

The war, of course, languished during the prevalence of the epidemic, and much injury was done to Athenian commerce by Peloponnesian privateers, who put to death all their prisoners. It was then that Sparta sent envoys to Persia to solicit money and troops against Athens, which shows that no warfare is so bitter as civil strife, and that no expedients are too disgraceful not to be made use of, in order to gratify malignant passions. But the envoys were seized in Thrace by the allies of Athens, and delivered up to the Athenians, and by them were put to death.

Results of the second year of the war.

In January, B.C. 429, Potidæa surrendered to the Athenian generals, upon favorable terms, after enduring all the miseries of famine. The fall of this city cost Athens two thousand talents. The Lacedæmonians, after two years, had accomplished nothing. They had not even relieved Potidæa.

Siege of Platæa.

On the third year, the Lacedæmonians, instead of ravaging Attica, marched to the attack of Platæa. The inhabitants resolved to withstand the whole force of the enemies. Archidemus, the Lacedæmonian general, commenced the siege, defended only by four hundred native citizens and eighty Athenians. So unskilled were the Greeks in the attack of fortified cities, that the besiegers made no progress, and were obliged to resort to blockade. A wall of circumvallation was built around the city, which was now left to the operations of famine.

Naval defeat of the Spartans.

At the same time the siege was pressed, an Athenian armament was sent to Thrace, which was defeated; but in the western part of Greece the Athenian arms were more successful. The Spartans and their allies suffered a repulse at Stratus, and their fleet was defeated by Phormio, the Athenian admiral. Nothing could exceed the rage of the Lacedæmonians at these two disasters. They collected a still larger fleet, and were again defeated with severe loss near Naupactus, by inferior forces. But the defeated Lacedæmonians, under the persuasion of the Megarians, undertook the bold enterprise of surprising the Piræus, during the absence of the Athenian fleet; but the courage of the assailants failed at the critical hour, and the port of Athens was saved. The Athenians then had the precaution to extend a chain across the mouth of the harbor, to guard against such surprises in the future.

Results of the third campaign.

Athens, during the summer, had secured the alliance of the Odrysians, a barbarous but powerful nation in Thrace. Their king, Sitalces, with an army of fifteen thousand men, attacked Perdiccas, the king of Macedonia, and overran his country, and only retired from the severity of the season and the want of Athenian co-operation. Such were the chief enterprises and events of the third campaign, and Athens was still powerful and unhumbled.

Renewed invasion of Athens. Revolt and subjugation of Mitylene.

The fourth year of the war was marked by a renewed invasion of Attica, without any other results than such as had happened before. But it was a more serious calamity to the Athenians to learn that Mitylene and most of Lesbos had revolted—one of the most powerful of the Athenian allies. Nothing was left to Athens but to subjugate the city. A large force was sent for this purpose, but the inhabitants of Mitylene appealed to the Spartans for aid, and prepared for a vigorous resistance. But the treasures of Athens were now nearly consumed, and the Athenians were obliged to resort to contributions to force the siege, which they did with vigor. The Lacedæmonians promised succor, and the Mitylenæans held out till their provisions were exhausted, when they surrendered to the Athenians. The Lacedæmonians advanced to relieve their allies, but were too late. The Athenian admiral pursued them, and they returned to the Peloponnesus without having done any thing. Paches, the Athenian general, sent home one thousand Mitylenæan prisoners, while it was decreed to slaughter the whole remaining population—about six thousand—able to carry arms, and makes slaves of the women and children. This severe measure was prompted by Cleon. But the Athenians repented, and a second decree of the assembly, through the influence of Diodotus, prevented the barbarous revenge; but the Athenians put to death the prisoners which Paches had sent, razed the fortifications of Mitylene, took possession of all her ships of war, and confiscated all the land of the island except that which belonged to one town that had been faithful. So severe was ancient warfare, even among the most civilized of the Greeks.

Surrender of Platæa.

The surrender of Platæa to the Lacedæmonians took place not long after; but not until one-half of the garrison had sallied from the city, scaled the wall of circumvallation, and escaped safely to Athens. The Platæans were sentenced to death by the Spartan judges, and barbarously slain. The captured women were sold as slaves, and the town and territory were handed over to the Thebans.

Cruelties of the Athenians at Corcyra.

Scenes not less bloody took place in the western part of Greece, in the island of Corcyra, before which a naval battle was fought between the Lacedæmonians and the Athenians. The island had been governed by oligarchies, under the protection of Sparta, but the retirement of the Lacedæmonian fleet enabled the Athenian general to wreak his vengeance on the party which had held supremacy, which was exterminated in the most cruel manner, which produced a profound sensation, and furnished Thucydides a theme for the most profound reflections on the acerbity and ferocity of the political parties, which, it seems, then divided Greece, and were among the exciting causes of the war itself—the struggle between the advocates of democratic and aristocratic institutions.

Nicias. He continues the policy of Pericles. Opposed by Alcibiades and Cleon.

A new character now appears upon the stage at Athens—Nicias—one of the ten generals who, in rank and wealth, was the equal of Pericles. He belonged to the oligarchal party, and succeeded Cimon and Thucydides in the control of it. But he was moderate in his conduct, and so won the esteem of his countrymen, that he retained power until his death, although opposed to the party which had the ascendency. He was incorruptible as to pecuniary gains, and adopted the conservative views of Pericles, avoiding new acquisitions at a distance, or creating new enemies. He surrounded himself, not as Pericles did, with philosophers, but religions men, avoided all scandals, and employed his large fortune in securing popularity. Pericles disdained to win the people by such means, cultivated art, and patronized the wits who surrounded Aspasia. Nicias was zealous in the worship of the gods, was careful to make no enemies, and conciliated the poor by presents. Yet he increased his private fortune, so far as he could, by honorable means, and united thrift and sagacity with honesty and piety. He was not a man of commanding genius, but his character was above reproach, and was never assailed by the comic writers. He was the great opponent of Alcibiades, the oracle of the democracy—one of those memorable demagogues who made use of the people to forward his ambitious projects. He was also the opponent of Cleon, whose office it was to supervise official men for the public conduct—a man of great eloquence, but fault-finding and denunciatory.

The fifth year of the war.

The fifth year of the war was not signalized by the usual invasion of Attica, which gave the Athenians leisure to send an expedition under Nicias against the island of Melos, inhabited by ancient colonists from Sparta. Demosthenes, another general, was sent around the Peloponnesus to attack Acarnania, and he ravaged the whole territory of Leueas. He also attacked Ætolia, but was completely beaten, and obliged to retire with loss; but this defeat was counterbalanced by a great victory, the next year, over the enemy at Olpæ, when the Lacedæmonian general was slain. He returned in triumph to Athens with considerable spoil. The attention of the Athenians was now directed to Delos, the island sacred to Apollo, and a complete purification of the island was made, and the old Delian festivals renewed with peculiar splendor.

The sixth year of the war. Undecisive nature of the conflict. Great defeat of the Lacedæmonians at Pylus. Sparta seeks peace. Peace prevented by Cleon.

The war had now lasted six years, without any grand or decisive results on either side. The expeditions of both parties were of the nature of raids — destructive, cruel, irritating, but without bringing any grand triumphs. Though the seventh year was marked by the usual enterprise on the part of the Lacedæmonians — the invasion of Attica — Corcyra promised to be the principal scene of military operations. Both an Athenian and Spartan fleet was sent thither. But an unforeseen incident gave a new character to the war. In the course of the voyage to Corcyra, Demosthenes, the Athenian general, stopped at Pylus, with the intention of erecting a fort on the uninhabited promontory, since it protected the spacious basin now known as the bay of Navarino, and was itself easily defended. Eurymedon, the admiral, insisted on going directly to Corcyra, but the fleet was driven by a storm into the very harbor which Demosthenes proposed to defend. The place was accordingly fortified by Demosthenes, where he himself remained with a garrison, while the fleet proceeded to Corcyra. Intelligence of this insult to Sparta — the attempt to plant a hostile fort on its territory — induced the Lacedæmonians to send their fleet to Pylus, instead of Corcyra. Forty-three triremes, under Thrasymelidas, and a powerful land force, advanced to attack Demosthenes, intrenched with his small army on the rocky promontory. When the news of this new diversion reached the Athenian fleet at Corcyra, it returned to Pylus, to succor Demosthenes. Here a naval battle took place, in which the Lacedæmonians were defeated. This defeat jeopardized the situation of the Spartan army which had occupied the island of Shacteria, cut off from supplies from the main land, as well as the existence of the fleet. So great was this exigency, that the ephors came from Sparta to consult on operations. They took a desponding view, and sent a herald to the Athenian generals to propose an armistice, in order to allow time for envoys to go to Athens and treat for peace. But Athens demanded now her own terms, elated by the success. Cleon, the organ of the popular mind, excited and sanguine, gave utterance to the feelings of the people, and insisted on the restoration of all the territory they had lost during the war. The Lacedæmonian envoys, unable to resist a vehement speaker like Cleon, which required qualities they did not possess, and which could only be acquired from skill in managing popular assemblies, to which they were unused, returned to Pylus. And it was the object of Cleon to prevent a hearing of the envoys by a select committee (what they desired) for fear that Nicias and other conservative politicians would accede to their proposals. Thus the best opportunity that could be presented for making an honorable peace and reuniting Greece was lost by the arts of a demagogue, who inflamed and shared the popular passions. Had Pericles been alive, the treaty would probably have been made, but Nicias had not sufficient influence to secure it.

Renewed hostilities. Surrender of Sphacteria. Triumph of the Athenians. Who refuse all overtures of peace.

War therefore recommenced, with fresh irritation. The Athenian fleet blockaded the island where the Spartan hoplites were posted, and found in the attempt, which they thought so easy, unexpected obstacles. Provisions clandestinely continually reached the besieged. Week after week passed without the expected surrender. Demosthenes, baffled for want of provisions and water for his own fleet, sent urgently to Athens for re-enforcements, which caused infinite mortification. The people now began to regret that they had listened to Cleon, and not to the voice of wisdom. Cleon himself was sent with the re-enforcements demanded, against his will, although he was not one of the ten generals. The island of Sphacteria now contained the bravest of the Lacedæmonian troops—from the first families of Sparta—a prey which Cleon and Demosthenes were eager to grasp. They attacked the island with a force double of that of the defenders, altogether ten thousand men, eight hundred of whom were hoplites. The besieged could not resist this overwhelming force, and retreated to their last redoubt, but were surrounded and taken prisoners. This surrender caused astonishment throughout Greece, since it was supposed the Spartan hoplites would die, as they did at Thermopylæ, rather than allow themselves to be taken alive, and this calamity diminished greatly the lustre of the Spartan arms. A modern army, surrounded with an overwhelming force, against which all resistance was madness, would have done the same as the Spartans. But it was a sad blow to them. Cleon, within twenty days of his departure, arrived at Athens with his three hundred Lacedæmonian prisoners, amid universal shouts of joy, for it was the most triumphant success which the Athenians had yet obtained. The war was prosecuted with renewed vigor, and the Lacedæmonians again made advances for peace, but without effect. The flushed victors would hear of no terms but what were disgraceful to the Spartans. The chances were now most favorable to Athens. Nicias invaded the Corinthian territory with eighty triremes, two thousand hoplites, and two hundred horsemen, to say nothing of the large number which supported these, and committed the same ravages that the Spartans and their allies had inflicted upon Attica.

Among other events, the Athenians this year captured the Persian ambassador, Artaphernes, on his way to Sparta. He was brought to Athens, and his dispatches were translated and made public. He was sent back to Ephesus, with Athenian envoys, to the great king, to counteract the influence of the Spartans, but Artaerxes had died when they reached Susa.

Situation of Athens in eighth year of the war.

The capture of Sphacteria, and the surrender of the whole Lacedæmonian fleet, not only placed Athens, on the opening of the eighth year of the war, in a situation more commanding than she had previously enjoyed, but stimulated her to renewed operations on a grander scale, not merely against Sparta, but to recover the ascendency in Bœotia, which was held before the thirty years' truce. The Lacedæmonians, in concert with the revolted Chalcidic allies of Athens in Thrace, and Perdiccas, king of Macedonia, also made great preparations for more decisive measures. The war had dragged out seven years, and nothing was accomplished which seriously weakened either of the contending parties.

Despair of the Lacedæmonians, and slaughter of the Helots.

The first movement was made by the Athenians on the Laconian coast. The island of Cythera was captured by an expedition led by Nicias, of sixty triremes and two thousand hoplites, beside other forces, and the coast was ravaged. Then Thyrea, an Æginetan settlement, between Laconia and Argolis, fell into the hands of the Athenians, and all the Æginetans were either killed in the assault, or put to death as prisoners. These successive disasters alarmed the Lacedæmonians, and they now began to fear repeated assaults on their own territory, with a discontented population of Helots. This fear prompted an act of cruelty and treachery which had no parallel in the history of the war. Two thousand of the bravest Helots were entrapped, as if especial honors were to be bestowed upon them, and barbarously slain. None but the five ephors knew the bloody details. There was even no public examination of this savage inhumanity, which shows that Sparta was governed, as Venice was in the Middle Ages, by a small but exceedingly powerful oligarchy.

After this cruelty was consummated, envoys came from Perdiccas and the Chalcidians of Thrace, invoking aid against Athens. It was joyfully granted, and Brasidas, at the request of Perdiccas and the Chalcidians, was sent with a large force of Peloponnesian hoplites.

Attack of Megara.

Meanwhile the Athenians formed plans to attack Megara, whose inhabitants had stimulated the war, and had been the greatest sufferers by it. A force was sent under Hippocrates and Demosthenes to surprise the place, and also Nisæa. The long walls of Megara, similar to those of Athens, were taken by surprise, and the Athenians found themselves at the gates of the city, which came near falling into their hands by treachery. Baffled for the moment, the Athenians attacked Clisæa, which lay behind it, and succeeded.

Relieved by Brasidas.

But Brasidas, the Lacedæmonian general, learning that the long walls had fallen into the hands of the Athenians, got together a large force of six thousand hoplites and six hundred cavalry, and relieved Megara, and the Athenians were obliged to retire. Ultimately the Megarians regained possession of the long walls, and instituted an oligarchal government.

Occupation of Delium by the Athenians.

The Athenians, disappointed in getting possession of Megara, which failed by one of those accidents ever recurring in war, organized a large force for the attack of Bœotia, on three sides, under Hippocrates and Demosthenes. The attack was first made at Siphae, by Demosthenes, on the Corinthian Gulf, but failed. In spite of this failure by sea, Hippocrates marched with a land force to Delium, with seven thousand hoplites, and twenty-five thousand other troops, and occupied the place, which was a temple consecrated to Apollo, and strongly fortified it. When the work of fortification was completed, the army prepared to return to Athens.

Battle of Delium.

Forces from all parts of Bœotia rallied, and met the Athenians. Among the forces of the Bœotians was the famous Theban band of three hundred select warriors, accustomed to fight in pairs, each man attached to his companion by peculiar ties of friendship. At Delium was fought the great battle of the war, in which the Athenians were routed, and the general, Hippocrates, with a thousand hoplites, were slain. The victors refused the Athenians the sacred right of burying their dead, unless they retired altogether from Delium—the post they had fortified on Bœotian territory. To this the Athenians refused to submit, the consequence of which was the siege and capture of Delium.

Among the hoplites who fought in this unfortunate battle, which was a great discouragement to the Athenian cause, was the philosopher Socrates. The famous Alcibiades also served in the cavalry, and helped to protect Socrates in his retreat, after having bravely fought.

Disasters of the Athenians in Thrace. Successes of Brasidas.

The disasters of the Athenians in Thrace were yet more considerable. Brasidas, with a large force, including seventeen hundred hoplites, rapidly marched through Thrace and Thessaly, and arrived in Macedonia safely, and attacked Acanthus, an ally of Athens. It fell into his hands, as well as Stageirus, and he was thus enabled to lay plans for the acquisition of Amphipolis, which was founded by Athenian colonists. He soon became master of the surrounding territory. He then offered favorable terms of capitulation to the citizens of the town, which were accepted, and the city surrendered—the most important of all the foreign possessions of Athens. The bridge over the Strymon was also opened, by which all the eastern allies of Athena were approachable by land. This great reverse sent dismay into the hearts of the Athenians, greater than had before been felt. The bloody victory at Delium, and the conquests of Brasidas, more than balanced the capture of Sphacteria. Sparta, under the victorious banner of Brasidas, a general of great probity, good faith, and moderation, now proclaimed herself liberator of Greece. Athens, discouraged and baffled, lost all the prestige she had gained.

Loss of Amphipolis.

But Amphipolis was lost by the negligence of the Athenian commanders. Encles and Thucydides, the historian, to whom the defense of the place was intrusted, had means ample to prevent the capture had they employed ordinary precaution. The Athenians, indignant, banished Thucydides for twenty years, and probably Eucles also—a just sentence, since they did not keep the bridge over the Strymon properly guarded, nor retained the Athenian squadron at Eion. The banishment of Thucydides gave him leisure to write the history on which his great fame rests—the most able and philosophical of all the historical works of antiquity.

Truce of one year.

Brasidas, after the fall of Amphipolis, extended his military operations with success. He took Torone, Lecythus, and other places, and then went into winter quarters. The campaign had been disastrous to the Athenians, and a truce of one year was agreed upon by the belligerent parties—Athens of the one party, and Sparta, Corinth, Sicyon, Epidaurus, and Megara, of the other.

Its conditions.

The conditions of this truce stipulated that Delphi might be visited by all Greeks, without distinction; that all violations of the property of the Delphian god should be promptly punished; that the Athenian garrisons at Pylus, Cythera, Nisæa, and Methana, should remain unmolested; that the Lacedæmonians should be free to use the sea for trading purposes; and that neither side should receive deserters from the other—important to both parties, since Athens feared the revolt of subject allies, and Sparta the desertion of Helots.

But two days had elapsed after the treaty was made before Scione in Thrace revolted to Brasidas—a great cause of exasperation to the Athenians, although the revolt took place before the treaty was known. Mendes, a neighboring town, also revolted. Brasidas sent the inhabitants a garrison to protect themselves, and departed with his forces for an expedition into the interior of Macedonia, but was soon compelled to retreat before the Illyrians.

Both Cleon and Brasidas opposed to the truce.

An Athenian force, under Nicias and Nicostratus, however, proceeded to Thrace to recover the revolted cities. Everywhere else the truce was observed. It was intended to give terms for more complete negotiations. This was the policy of Nicias. But Cleon and his party, the democracy, was opposed to peace, and wished to prosecute the war vigorously in Thrace. Brasidas, on his part, was equally in favor of continued hostilities. And this was the great question of the day in Greece.

Death of Cleon and of Brasidas.

The war party triumphed, and Cleon, by no means an able general, was sent with an expedition to recover Amphipolis, B.C. 422. He succeeded in taking Torone, but Amphipolis, built on a hill in the peninsula formed by the river Strymon, as it passes from the Strymonic Gulf to Lake Kerkernilis, was a strongly fortified place in which Brasidas intrenched. He was obliged to remain inactive at Eion, at the mouth of the river, three miles distant from Amphipolis, which excited great discontent in his army, but which was the wiser course, until his auxiliaries arrived. But the murmur of the hoplites compelled him to some sort of action, and while he was reconnoitering, he was attacked by Brasidas. Cleon was killed, and his army totally defeated. Brasidas, the ablest general of the day, however, was also mortally wounded, and carried from the field. This unsuccessful battle compelled the Athenians to return home, deeply disgusted with their generals. But they embarked in the enterprise reluctantly, and with no faith in their leader, and this was one cause of their defeat. The death of Brasidas, however, converted the defeat into a substantial victory, since there remained no Spartan with sufficient ability to secure the confidence of the allies. Brasidas, when he died, was the first man in Greece, and universally admired for his valor, intelligence, probity, and magnanimity.

Consequences of the battle of Amphipolis. The peace of Nicias.

The battle of Amphipolis was decisive; it led to a peace between the contending parties. It is called the peace of Nicias, made in March, B.C. 421. By the provisions of this treaty of peace, which was made for fifty years, Amphipolis was restored to the Athenians, all persons had full liberty to visit the public temples of Greece, the Athenians restored the captive Spartans, and the various towns taken during the war were restored on both sides. This peace was concluded after a ten years' war, when the resources of both parties were exhausted. It was a war of ambition and jealousy, without sufficient reasons, and its consequences were disastrous to the general welfare of Greece. In some respects it must be considered, not merely as a war between Sparta and Athens to gain supremacy, but a war between the partisans of aristocratic and democratic institutions throughout the various States.

Causes of the war still continued.

The peace made by Nicias between Athens and Sparta for fifty years was not of long continuance. It was a truce rather than a treaty, since neither party was overthrown—but merely crippled—like Rome and Carthage after the first Punic war. The same causes which provoked the contest still remained—an unextinguishable jealousy between States nearly equal in power, and the desire of ascendency at any cost. But we do not perceive in either party that persistent and self-sacrificing spirit which marked the Romans in their conquest of Italy. The Romans abandoned every thing which interfered with their aggressive policy: the Grecian States were diverted from political aggrandizement by other objects of pursuit—pleasure, art, wealth.

Alcibiades.

There was needed only a commanding demagogue, popular, brilliant, and unprincipled, to embroil Greece once more in war, and such a man was Alcibiades, who appeared upon the stage at the death of Cleon. And hostilities were easily kindled, since the allies on both sides were averse to the treaty which had been made, and the conditions of the peace were not fulfilled. Athens returned the captive Spartans she had held since the battle of Sphacteria, but Amphipolis was not restored, from the continued enmity of the Thracian cities. Both parties were full of intrigues, and new combinations were constantly being formed. Argos became the centre of a new Peloponnesian alliance. A change of ephors at Sparta favored hostile measures, and an alliance was made between the Bœotians and Lacedæmonians. The Athenians, on their side, captured Scione, and put to death the prisoners.

Character of Alcibiades.

It was in this unsettled state of things, when all the late contending States were insincere and vacillating, that Alcibiades stood forth as a party leader. He was thirty-one years of age, belonged to an ancient and powerful family, possessed vast wealth, had great personal beauty and attractive manners, but above all, was unboundedly ambitious, and grossly immoral—the most insolent, unprincipled, licentious, and selfish man that had thus far scandalized and adorned Athenian society. The only redeeming feature in his character was his friendship for Socrates, who, it seems, fascinated him by his talk, and sought to improve his morals. He had those brilliant qualities, and luxurious habits, and ostentatious prodigality, which so often dazzle superficial people, especially young men of fashion and wealth, but more even than they, the idolatrous rabble. So great was his popularity and social prestige, that no injured person ever dared to bring him to trial, and he even rescued his own wife from the hands of the law when she sought to procure a divorce—a proof that even in democratic Athens all bowed down to the insolence of wealth and high social position.

His intellectual training under Socrates.

Alcibiades, though luxurious and profligate, saw that a severe intellectual training was necessary to him if he would take rank as a politician, for a politician who can not make a speech stands a poor chance of popular favor. So he sought the instructions of Socrates, Prodicus, Protagoras, and others—not for love of learning, but as means of success, although it may be supposed that the intellectual excitement, which the discourse, cross-examination, and ironical sallies of Socrates produced, was not without its force on so bright a mind.

His abandoned habits.

Alcibiades commenced his public life with a sullied reputation, and with numerous enemies created by his unbearable insolence, but with a flexibility of character which enabled him to adapt himself to whatever habits circumstances required. He inspired no confidence, and his extravagant mode of life was sure to end in ruin, unless he reimbursed himself out of the public funds; and yet he fascinated the people who mistrusted and hated him. The great comic poet, Aristophanes, said of him to the Athenians: "You ought not to keep a lion's whelp in your city at all, but if you choose to keep him, you must submit to his behavior."

His intrigues.

Alcibiades, in commencing his political life, departed from his family traditions; for he was a relative of Pericles, and became a partisan of the oligarchal party. But he soon changed his polities, on receiving a repulse from the Spartans, who despised him, and he became a violent democrat. His first memorable effort was to bring Argos, then in league with Sparta, into alliance with Athens, in which he was successful. He then cheated the Lacedæmonian envoys who were sent to protest against the alliance and make other terms, and put them in a false position, and made them appear deceitful, and thus arrayed against them the wrath of the Athenians. As Alcibiades had prevailed upon these envoys, by false promises and advice, to act a part different from what they were sent to perform, Nicias was sent to Sparta to clear up embarrassments, but failed in his object, upon which

Athens concluded an alliance with Argos, Elis, and Mantinea, which only tended to complicate existing difficulties.

His extravagance at the Olympic games.

Shortly after this alliance was concluded, the Olympic games were celebrated with unusual interest, from which the Athenians had been excluded during the war. Here Alcibiades appeared with seven chariots, each with four horses, when the richest Greeks had hitherto possessed but one, and gained two prizes. He celebrated his success by a magnificent banquet more stately and expensive than those given by kings. But while the Athenians thus appeared at the ninetieth Olympiad, the Lacedæmonians were excluded by the Eleians, who controlled the festival, from an alleged violation of the Olympic truce, but really from the intrigues of Alcibiades.

Renewal of hostilities.

The subsequent attack of Argos and Athens on Epidaurus proved that the peace between Athens and Sparta existed only in name. It was distinctly violated by the attack of Argos by the Lacedæmonians, Bœotians, and Corinthians, and the battle of Mantinea opened again the war. This was decided in favor of the Lacedæmonians, with a great loss to the Athenians and their allies, including both their generals, Laches and Nicostratus.

Effect of the battle of Mantinea.

The moral effect of the battle of Mantinea, B.C. 418, was overwhelming throughout Greece, and re-established the military prestige of Sparta. It was lost by the withdrawal of three thousand Eleians before the battle, illustrating the remark of Pericles that numerous and equal allies could never be kept in harmonious co-operation. One effect of the battle was a renewed alliance between Sparta and Argos, and the re-establishment of an oligarchal government in the latter city. Mantinea submitted to Sparta, and the Achaian towns were obliged to submit to a remodeling of their political institutions, according to the views of Sparta. The people of Argos, however, took the first occasion which was presented for regaining their power, assisted by an Athenian force under Alcibiades, and Argos once again became an ally of Athens.

Siege of Melos.

The next important operation of the war was the siege and conquest of Melos, a Dorian island, by the Athenians, B.C. 416. The inhabitants were killed, and the women and children were sold as slaves, and an Athenian colony was settled on the island. But this massacre, exceeding even the customary cruelty of war in those times, raised a general indignation among the allies of Sparta.

The invasion of Sicily.

But an expedition of far greater importance was now undertaken by the Athenians—the most gigantic effort which they ever made, but which terminated disastrously, and led to the ruin and subjugation of their proud and warlike city, as a political power. This was the invasion of Sicily and siege of Syracuse.

Before we present this unfortunate expedition, some brief notice is necessary of the Grecian colonies in Sicily.

The Grecian colonies in Sicily. Syracuse.

In the eighth century before Christ Sicily was inhabited by two distinct races of barbarians—the Sikels and Sikans—besides Phœnician colonies, for purposes of trade. The Sikans were an Iberian tribe, and were immigrants of an earlier date than the Sikels, by whom they were invaded. The earliest Grecian colony was (B.C. 735) at Naxos, on the eastern coast of the island, between the Straits of Messina and Mount Ætna, founded by Theocles, a Chalcidian mariner, who was cast by storms upon the coast, and built a fort on a hill called Taurus, to defend himself against the Sikels, who were in possession of the larger half of the island. Other colonists followed, chiefly from the Peloponnesus. In the year following that Naxos was founded, a body of settlers from Corinth landed on the islet Ortygia, expelled the Sikel inhabitants, and laid the foundation of Syracuse. Successive settlements were made forty-five years after at Gela, in the southwestern part of the island. Other settlements continued to be made, not only from Greece, but from the colonies themselves; so that the old inhabitants were gradually Hellenized and merged with Greek colonists, while the Greeks, in their turn, adopted many of the habits and customs of the Sikels and Sikans. The various races lived on terms of amity, for the native population was not numerous enough to become formidable to the Grecian colonists.

Agrigentum and Gela. The reign of Gelo. His power in Sicily. His successor Hiero. Grandeur of Syracuse.

Five hundred years before Christ the most powerful Grecian cities in Sicily were Agrigentum and Gela, on the south side of the island. The former, within a few years of its foundation, B.C. 570, fell under the dominion of one of its rich citizens, Phalasaris, who proved a cruel despot, but after a reign of sixteen years he was killed in an insurrection, and an oligarchal government was established, such as then existed in most of the Grecian cities. Syracuse was governed in this way by the descendants of the original settlers. Gela was, on the other hand, ruled by a despot called Gelo, the most powerful man on the island. He got possession of Syracuse, B.C. 485, and transferred the seat of his power to this city, by bringing thither the leading people and making slaves of the rest. Under Gelo Syracuse became the first city on the island, to which other towns were tributary. When the Greeks confederated against Xerxes, they sent to solicit his aid as the imperial leader of Sicily, and he could command, according to Herodotus, twenty thousand hoplites, two hundred triremes, two thousand cavalry, two thousand archers, and two thousand light-armed horse. So great was then the power of this despot, who now sought to expel the Carthaginians and unite all the Hellenic colonies in Sicily under his sway. But the aid was not given, probably on account of a Carthaginian invasion simultaneous with the expedition of the Persian king. The Carthaginians, according to the historian, arrived at Panormus B.C. 480, with a fleet of three thousand ships and a land force of three hundred thousand men, besides chariots and horses, under Hamilcar—a mercenary army, composed of various African nations. Gelo marched against him with fifty thousand foot and five thousand horse, and gained a complete victory, so that one hundred and fifty thousand, on the side of the Carthaginians, were slain, together with their general. The number of the combatants is doubtless exaggerated, but we may believe that the force was very great. Gelo was now supreme in Sicily, and the victory of Himera, which he had gained, enabled him to distribute a large body of prisoners, as slaves, in all the Grecian colonies. It appears that he was much respected, but he died shortly after his victory, leaving an infant son to the guardianship of two of his brothers, Polyzelus and Hiero, who became the supreme governors of the island. A victory gained by Hiero over the tyrant of Agrigentum gave him the same supremacy which Gelo had enjoyed. On his death, B.C. 467, the succession was disputed between his brother, Thrasybulus, and his nephew, the son of Gelo; but Thrasybulus contrived to make away with his nephew, and reigned alone, cruelly and despotically, until a revolution took place, which resulted in his expulsion and the fall of the Gelonian dynasty. Popular governments were now established in all the Sicilian cities, but these were distracted by disputes and confusions. Syracuse became isolated from the other cities, and a government whose powers were limited by the city. The expulsion of the Gelonian dynasty left the Grecian cities to reorganize free and constitutional governments; but Syracuse maintained a proud pre-eminence, and her power was increased from time to time by conquests in the interior over the old population. Agrigentum was next in power, and scarcely inferior in wealth. The temple of Zeus, in this city, was one of the most magnificent in the world. The population was large, and many were the rich men who kept chariots and competed at the Olympic games. In these Sicilian cities the intellectual improvement kept pace with the material, and the little town of Elea supported the two greatest speculative philosophers of Greece—Parmenides and Zeno. Empedocles, of Agrigentum, was scarcely less famous.

The Dorian cities of Sicily make war on the Ionian.

Such was the state of the Sicilian cities on the outbreak of the Peloponnesian war. Being generally of Dorian origin, they sympathized with Sparta, and great expectations were formed by the Lacedæmonians of assistance from their Sicilian allies. The cities of Sicily could not behold the contest between Athens and Sparta without being drawn into the quarrel, and the result was that the Dorian cities made war on the Ionian cities, which, of course, sympathized with Athens. As these cities were weaker than the Dorian, they solicited aid from Athens, and an expedition was sent to Sicily under Laches, B.C. 426. Another one, under Polydorus, followed, but without decisive results. The next year still another and larger expedition, under Eurymedon and Sophocles, arrived in Sicily, while Athens was jubilant by the possession of the Spartan prisoners, and the possession of Pylus and Cythera. The Sicilian cities now fearing that their domestic strife would endanger their independence and make them subject to Athens, the most ambitious and powerful State in Greece, made a common league with each other. Eurymedon acceded to the peace and returned to Athens, much to the displeasure of the war party, which embraced most of the people, and he and his colleague were banished.

Intervention of Athens. Opposed by Nicias, but favored by Alcibiades.

But wars between the Sicilian cities again led to the intervention of Athens. Egesta especially sent envoys for help in her struggle against Selinus, which was assisted by Syracuse. Alcibiades warmly seconded these envoys, and inflamed the people with his ambitious projects. He, more than any other man, was the cause of the great Sicilian expedition which proved the ruin of his country. He was opposed by Nicias, who foretold all the miserable consequences of so distant an expedition, when so little could be gained and so much would be jeopardized, and when, on the first reverse, the enemies of Athens would rally against her. He particularly cautioned his countrymen not only against the expedition, but against intrusting the command of it to an unprincipled and selfish man who squandered his own patrimony in chariot races and other extravagances, and would be wasteful of the public property—a man without the experience which became a leader in so great an enterprise. Alcibiades, in reply, justified his extravagance at the Olympic games, where he contested with seven chariots, as a means to impress Sparta with the wealth and power of Athens, after a ten years' war. He inflamed the ambition of the assembly, held out specious hopes of a glorious conquest which would add to Athenian power, and make her not merely pre-eminent, but dominant in Greece. The assembly, eager for war and glory, sided with the youthful and magnificent demagogue, and disregarded the counsels of the old patriot, whose wisdom and experience were second to none in the city.

Athenian expedition against Syracuse.

Consequently the expedition was fitted out for the attack of Syracuse— the largest and most powerful which Athens ever sent against an enemy; for all classes, maddened by military glory, or tempted by love of gain, eagerly embarked in the enterprise. Nicias, finding he could not prevent the expedition, demanded more than he thought the people would be willing to grant. He proposed a gigantic force. But in proposing this force, he hoped he might thus discourage the Athenians altogether by the very greatness of the armament which he deemed necessary. But so popular was the enterprise, that the large force he suggested was voted. Alcibiades had flattered the people that their city was mistress of the sea, and entitled to dominion over all the islands, and could easily prevail over any naval enemy.

Self-confidence of the Athenians.

Three years had now elapsed since the peace of Nicias, and Athens had ample means. The treasury was full, and triremes had accumulated in the harbor. The confidence of the Athenians was as unbounded as was that of Xerxes when he crossed the Hellespont, and hence there had been great zeal and forwardness in preparation.

Unfavorable auguries.

When the expedition was at last ready, an event occurred which filled the city with gloom and anxious forebodings. The half statues of the god Hermes were distributed in great numbers in Athens in the most conspicuous situations, beside the doors of private houses and temples, and in the agora, so that the people were accustomed to regard the god as domiciled among them for their protection. In one night, at the end of May, B.C. 415, these statues were nearly all mutilated. The heads, necks, and busts were all destroyed, leaving the lower part of them—mere quadrangular pillars, without arms, or legs, or body—alone standing. The sacrilege sent universal dismay into the city, and was regarded as a most depressing omen, and was done, doubtless, with a view of ruining Alcibiades and frustrating the expedition. But all efforts were vain to discover the guilty parties.

Alcibiades accused of divulging the Eleusinian mysteries.

And this was not the only means adopted to break down the power of a man whom the more discerning perceived was the evil genius of Athens. Alcibiades was publicly accused of having profaned and divulged the Eleusinian mysteries. The charge was denied by Alcibiades, who demanded an immediate trial. It was eluded by his enemies, who preferred to have the charge hanging over his head, in case of the failure of the enterprise which he had projected.

Sailing of the Athenian fleet.

So the fleet sailed from Piræus amid mingled sentiments of anxiety and popular enthusiasm. It consisted of one hundred triremes, with a large body of hoplites. It made straight for Corcyra, where the contingents of the allies were assembled, which nearly doubled its force. The Syracusans were well informed as to its destination, and made great exertions to meet this great armament, under Nicias, Alcibiades, and Lamachus. The latter commander recommended an immediate attack of Syracuse, as unprepared and dismayed.

Escape of Alcibiades to Sparta.

Alcibiades wished first to open negotiations with the Sikels, of the interior, to detach them from the aid of Syracuse. His plan was followed, but before he could carry it into operation he was summoned home to take his trial. Fearing the result of the accusations against him, for, in his absence, the popular feeling had changed respecting him—fear and reason had triumphed over the power of his personal fascination—Alcibiades made his escape to the Peloponnesus.

Nicias commands the expedition. Rebellion and treason of Alcibiades.

The master spirit of the expedition was now removed, and its operations were languid and undecided, for Nicias had no heart in it. The delays which occurred gave the Syracusans time to prepare, and more confidence in their means of defense. So that when the forces of the Athenians were landed in the great harbor, they found a powerful army ready to resist them. In spite of a victory which Nicias gained near Olympeion, the Syracusans were not dejected, and the Athenian fleet was obliged to seek winter quarters at Catana, and also send for additional re-enforcements. Nicias unwisely delayed, but his inexcusable apathy afforded the enemy leisure to enlarge their fortifications. The Syracusans constructed an entirely new wall around the inner and outer city, and which also extended across the whole space from the outer sea to the great harbor, so that it would be difficult for the Athenians, in the coming siege, to draw lines of circumvallation around the city. Syracuse also sent envoys to Corinth and Sparta for aid, while Alcibiades, filled now with intense hatred of Athens, encouraged the Lacedæmonians to send a force to the Sicilian capital. He admitted that it was the design of Athens first to conquer the Sicilian Greeks, and then the Italian Greeks; then to make an attempt on Carthage, and then, if that was successful, to bring together all the forces of the subjected States and attack the Peloponnesus itself, and create a great empire, of which Athens was to be the capital. Such an avowal was doubtless the aim of the ambitious Alcibiades when he first stimulated the enterprise, which, if successful, would have made him the most powerful man in Greece; but he was thwarted by his enemies at home, and so he turned all his energies against his native State. His address made a powerful effect on the Lacedæmonians, who, impelled by hatred and jealousy, now resolved to make use of the services of the traitor, and send an auxiliary force to Syracuse.

Situation of Syracuse. Inaction of Nicias. Athenian fleet inclosed by the Syracusans. Retreat of Athenians.

That city then consisted of two parts—an inner and an outer city. The outer city was defended on two sides by the sea, and a sea wall. On the land side a long wall extended from the sea to the fortified high land of Achradina, so that the city could only be taken by a wall of circumvallation, so as to cut off supplies by land; at the same time it was blockaded by sea. But the delay of Nicias had enabled the Syracusans to construct a new wall, covering both the outer and inner city, and extending from the great port to the high land near the bay of Magnesi, so that any attack, except from a single point, was difficult, unless the wall of circumvallation was made much larger than was originally intended. Amid incredible difficulties the Athenians constructed their works, and in an assault from the cliff of Epipolæ, where they were intrenched, their general, Lamachus, was slain. But the Athenians had gained an advantage, and the siege was being successfully prosecuted. It was then that the Lacedæmonians arrived under Gylippus, who was unable to render succor. But Nicias, despising him, allowed him to land at Himera, from whence he marched across Sicily to Syracuse. A Corinthian fleet, under Gorgylus, arrived only just in time to prevent the city from capitulating, and Gylippus entered Syracuse unopposed. The inaction of Nicias, who could have prevented this, is unaccountable. But the arrival of Gylippus turned the scale, and he immediately prosecuted vigorous and aggressive measures. He surprised an Athenian fort, and began to construct a third counter-wall on the north side of the Athenian circle. The Athenians, now shut up within their lines, were obliged to accept battle, and were defeated, and even forced to seek shelter within their fortified lines. Under this discouragement, Nicias sent to Athens for another armament, and the Athenians responded to his call. But Sparta also resolved to send re-enforcements, and invade Attica besides. Sicilian forces also marched in aid of Syracuse. The result of all these gathering forces, in which the whole strength of Greece was employed, was the total defeat of the Athenian fleet in the Great Harbor, in spite of the powerful fleet which had sailed from Athens under Demosthenes. The Syracusans pursued their advantage by blocking up the harbor, and inclosing the whole Athenian fleet. The Athenians resolved then to force their way out, which led to another general engagement, in which the Athenians were totally defeated. Nicias once again attempted to force his way out, with the remainder of his defeated fleet, but the armament was too much discouraged to obey, and the Athenians sought to retreat by land. But all the roads were blockaded. The miserable army, nevertheless, began its hopeless march completely demoralized, and compelled to abandon the sick and wounded. The retreating army was harassed on every side, no progress could be made, and the discouraged army sought in the night to retreat by a different route. The rear division, under Demosthenes, was overtaken and forced to surrender, and were carried captives to Syracuse—some six thousand in number. The next day, the first division, under Nicias, also was overtaken and made prisoners. No less than forty thousand who had started from the Athenian camp, six days before, were either killed or made prisoners, with the two generals who commanded them. The prisoners at first were subjected to the most cruel and inhuman treatment, and then sold as slaves. Both Nicias and Demosthenes were put to death, B.C. 413.

Mismanagement of Nicias.

Such was the disastrous close of the Sicilian expedition. Our limits prevent an extended notice. We can only give the barren outline. But never in Grecian history had so large a force been arrayed against a foreign power, and never was ruin more complete. The enterprise was started at the instance of Alcibiades. It was he who brought this disaster on his country. But it would have been better to have left the expedition to his management. Nicias was a lofty and religious man, but was no general. He grossly mismanaged from first to last. The confidence of the Athenians was misplaced; and he, after having spent his life in inculcating a conservative policy, which was the wiser, yet became the unwilling instrument of untold and unparalleled calamities. His fault was over-confidence. He was personally brave, religious, incorruptible, munificent, affable—in all respects honorable and respectable, but he had no military genius.

Exhaustion of Athens.

The Lacedæmonians, at the suggestion of Alcibiades, had permanently occupied Decelea—a fortified post within fifteen miles of Athens, and instead of spending a few weeks in ravaging Attica, now intrenched themselves, and issued out in excursions until they had destroyed all that was valuable in the neighborhood of Athens. The great calamities which the Athenians had suffered prevented them from expelling the invaders, and the city itself was now in the condition of a post besieged. All the accumulations in her treasury were exhausted, and she was compelled to dismiss even her Thracian mercenaries. They were sent back to their own country under Dotrephes; but after inflicting great atrocities in Bœotia, were driven back by the Thebans.

The Athenian navy hopelessly crippled.

The Athenian navy was now so crippled that it could no longer maintain the supremacy of the sea. The Corinthians were formidable rivals and enemies. A naval battle at Naupactus, at the mouth of the Corinthian Gulf, between the Athenians and Corinthians, though indecisive, yet really was to the advantage of the latter.

Effects of the disastrous expedition against Syracuse. The Athenians compelled to make use of their reserved fund.

The full effects of the terrible catastrophe at Syracuse were not at first made known to the Athenians, but gradually a settled despair overspread the public mind. The supremacy of Athens in Greece was at an end, and the city itself was endangered. The inhabitants now put forth all the energies that a forlorn hope allowed. The distant garrisons were recalled; all expenses were curtailed; timber was collected for new ships, and Capo Sunium was fortified. But the enemies of Athens were also stimulated to renewed exertions, and subject-allies were induced to revolt. Persia sent envoys to Sparta. The Eubœans and Chians applied to the same power for aid in shaking off the yoke of Athens now broken and defenseless. Although a Peloponnesian fleet was defeated by the Athenians on its way to assist Chios in revolt, yet new dangers multiplied. The infamous Alcibiades crossed with a squadron to Chios, and the Athenians were obliged to make use of their reserved fund of one thousand talents, which Pericles had set aside for the last extremity, in order to equip a fleet, under the command of Strombichides. Alcibiades passed over to Miletus, and induced this city also to revolt. A shameful treaty was made between Sparta and Persia to carry on war against Athens; and the first step in the execution of the treaty was to hand Miletus over to a Persian general. Ionia now became the seat of war, and a victory was gained near Miletus by the Athenians, but this was balanced by the capture of Iasus by the Lacedæmonians. The Athenians rallied at Samos, which remained faithful, and still controlled one hundred and twenty-eight triremes at this island. Alternate successes and defeats happened to the contending parties, with no decided result.

Escape of Alcibiades from Sparta.

The want of success on the coast of Asia led the Lacedæmonians to suspect Alcibiades of treachery. Moreover, his intrigue with the wife of Agis made the king of Sparta his relentless enemy. Agis accordingly procured a decision of the ephors to send out instructions for his death. He was warned in time, and made his escape to the satrap Tissaphernes, who commanded the forces of Persia. He persuaded the Persian not to give a decisive superiority to either of the contending parties, who followed his advice, and kept the Peloponnesian fleet inactive, and bribed the Spartan general. Having now gratified his revenge against Athens and lost the support of Sparta, Alcibiades now looked to his native country as the best field for his unprincipled ambition. "He opened negotiations with the Athenian commanders at Samos, and offered the alliance of Persia as the price of his restoration, but proposed as a further condition the overthrow of the democratic government at Athens."

Popular revolution in Athens.

Then followed the political revolution which Alcibiades had planned, in conjunction with oligarchal conspirators. The rally of the city, threatened with complete ruin, had been energetic and astonishing, and she was now, a year after the disaster at Syracuse, able to carry on a purely defensive system, though with crippled resources. But for this revolution Athens might have secured her independence.

Restless schemes of Alcibiades.

The proposal of Alcibiades to change the constitution was listened to by the rich men, on whom the chief burden of the war had fallen. With the treasures of Persia to help them, they hoped to carry on the war against Sparta without cost to themselves. It was hence resolved at Samos, among the Athenians congregated there, to send a deputation to Athens, under Pisander, to carry out their designs. But they had no other security than the word of Alcibiades, that restless and unpatriotic schemer, that they would secure the assistance of Persia. And it is astonishing that such a man—so faithless—could be believed.

Vain promises of Alcibiades. Aid invoked from Persia. An oligarchy at Athens. Alcibiades cheats the Athenians.

One of the generals of the fleet at Samos, Phrynichus, strongly opposed this movement, and gave good reasons; but the tide of opinion among the oligarchal conspirators ran so violently against him, that Pisander was at once dispatched to Athens. He laid before the public assembly the terms which Alcibiades proposed. The people, eager at any cost to gain the Persian king as an ally, in their extremity listened to the proposal, though unwilling, and voted to relinquish their political power. Pisander made them believe it was a choice between utter ruin and the relinquishment of political privileges, since the Lacedæmonians had an overwhelming force against them. It was while Chios seemed likely to be recovered by the Athenians, and while the Peloponnesian fleet was paralyzed at Rhodes by Persian intrigues, that Pisander returned to Ionia to open negotiations with

Alcibiades and Tissaphernes. But Alcibiades had promised too much, the satrap having no idea of lending aid to Athens, and yet he extricated himself by such exaggerated demands, which he knew the Athenians would never concede to Persia, that negotiations were broken off, and a reconciliation was made between Persia and Sparta. The oligarchal conspirators had, however, gone so far that a retreat was impossible. The democracy of Athens was now subverted. Instead of the Senate of Five Hundred and the assembled people, an oligarchy of Four Hundred sat in the Senate house, and all except five thousand were disfranchised—and these were not convened. The oligarchy was in full power when Pisander returned to Athens. All democratic magistrates had been removed, and no civil functionaries were paid. The Four Hundred had complete control. Thus perished, through the intrigues of Alcibiades, the democracy of Athens. He had organized the unfortunate expedition to Sicily; he had served the bitterest enemies of his country; and now, he had succeeded in overturning the constitution which had lasted one hundred years, during which Athens had won all her glories. Why should the Athenians receive back to their confidence so bad a man? But whom God wishes to destroy, he first makes mad, and Alcibiades, it would seem, was the instrument by which Athens was humiliated and ruined as a political power. The revolution was effected in an hour of despair, and by delusive promises. The character and conduct of the insidious and unscrupulous intriguer were forgotten in his promises. The Athenians were simply cheated.

Athens seeks peace with Sparta. Unprincipled conduct of Alcibiades.

The Four Hundred, installed in power, solemnized their installation by prayer and sacrifice, put to death some political enemies, imprisoned and banished others, and ruled with great rigor and strictness. They then sought to make peace with Sparta, which was declined. The army at Samos heard of these changes with exceeding wrath, especially the cruelties which were inflicted on all citizens who spoke against the new tyranny. A democratic demonstration took place at Samos, by which the Samians and the army were united in the strongest ties, for the Samians had successfully resisted a like revolution on their island. The army at Samos refused to obey any orders from the oligarchy, and constituted a democracy by themselves. Yet the man who had been instrumental in creating this oligarchy, with characteristic versatility and impudence, joined the democracy at Samos. He came to Samos by invitation of the armament, and pledged himself to secure Persian aid, and he was believed and again trusted. He then launched into a new career, and professed to take up again the interests of the democracy at Athens. The envoys of the Four Hundred which were sent to Samos were indignantly sent back, and the general indignation against the oligarchy was intensified. Envoys from Argos also appeared at Samos, offering aid to the Athenian democracy. There was now a strong and organized resistance to the Four Hundred, and their own divisions placed them further in a precarious situation. Theramenes demanded that the Five Thousand, which body had been thus far nominal, should be made a reality. The Four Hundred again solicited aid from Sparta, and constructed a fort for the admission of a Spartan garrison, while a Lacedæmonian fleet hovered near the Piræus.

Subversion of the oligarchy. Restoration of the old constitution.

The long-suppressed energies of the people at length burst forth. A body of soldiers seized the fortress the oligarchy were constructing for a Spartan garrison, and demolished it. The Four Hundred made important concessions, and agreed to renew the public assembly. While these events occurred a naval battle took place near Eretria between the Lacedæmonians and the Athenians, in which the latter were defeated. The victory, if they had pushed their success, would have completed the ruin of Athens, since her home fleet was destroyed, and that at Samos was detained by Alcibiades. When it was seen the hostile fleet did not enter the harbor, the Athenians recovered their dismay and prosecuted their domestic revolution by deposing the Four Hundred and placing the whole government in the hands of the Five Thousand, and this body was soon enlarged to that of universal citizenship. The old constitution was restored, except that part of it which allowed pay to the judges. Most of the oligarchal leaders fled, and a few of them were tried and executed — those who had sought Spartan aid. Thus this selfish movement terminated, after the oligarchy had enjoyed a brief reign of only a few months.

Alternate successes and failures of the belligerents.

While Athens was distracted by changes of government, the war was conducted on the coasts of Asia between the belligerents with alternate success and defeat. Abydos, connected with Miletus by colonial ties, revolted from Athens, and Lampsacus, a neighboring town, followed its example two days afterward. Byzantium also went over to the Lacedæmonians, which enabled them to command the strait. Alcibiades pursued still his double game with Persia and Athens. An Athenian fleet was sent to the Hellespont to contend with the Lacedæmonian squadron, and gained an incomplete victory at Cynossema, whose only effect was to encourage the Athenians. The Persians gave substantial aid to the Lacedæmonians, withheld for a time by the intrigues of Alcibiades, who returned to Samos, but was shortly after seized by Tissaphernes and sent to Sardis, from which he contrived to escape. He partially redeemed his infamy by a victory over the Peloponnesian fleet at Cyzicus, and captured it entirely, which disaster induced the Spartans to make overtures of peace, which were rejected through the influence of Cleophon, the demagogue.

Revival of the hopes of the Athenians.

The Athenian fleet now reigned alone in the Propontis, the Bosphorus, and the Hellespont, and levied toll on all the ships passing through the straits, while Chrysopolis, opposite to Byzantium, was occupied by Alcibiades. Athens now once more became hopeful and energetic. Thrasyllus was sent with a large force to Ionia, and joined his forces with the fleet which Alcibiades commanded at Sestos, but the conjoined forces were unable to retake Abydos, which was relieved by Pharnabazus, the Persian satrap.

Cyrus sent to Phrygia.

The absence of the fleet from Athens encouraged the Lacedæmonians, who retook Pylus, B.C. 409, while the Athenians captured Chalcedon, and the following year Byzantium itself. Such was the state of the contending parties when Cyrus the younger was sent by his father Darius as satrap of Lydia, Phrygia, and Cappadocia, and whose command in Asia Minor was attended by important consequences. Tissaphernes and Pharnabazus were still left in command of the coast.

Union of Cyrus with Lysander.

Cyrus, a man of great ambition and self-control, came to Asia Minor with a fixed purpose of putting down the Athenian power, which for sixty years had humbled the pride of the Persian kings. He formed a hearty and cordial alliance with Lysander, the Spartan admiral, and the most eminent man, after Brasidas, whom the Lacedæmonians had produced during the war. He was a man of severe Spartan discipline and virtue, but ambitious and cruel. He visited Cyrus at Sardis, was welcomed with every mark of favor, and induced Cyrus to grant additional pay to every Spartan seaman.

Return of Alcibiades to Athens. His exploits.

Meanwhile Alcibiades re-entered his native city in triumph, after eight years' exile, and was welcomed by all parties as the only man who had sufficient capacity to restore the fallen fortunes of Athens. His confiscated property was restored, and he was made captain-general with ample powers, while all his treasons were apparently forgotten, which had proved so fatal to his country—the sending of Gylippus to Syracuse, the revolt of Chios and Miletus, and the conspiracy of the Four Hundred. The effect of this treatment, so much better than what he deserved, intoxicated this wayward and unprincipled, but exceedingly able man. His first exploit was to sail to Andros, now under a Lacedæmonian garrison, whose fields he devastated, but was unable to take the town. He then went to Samos, and there learned that all his intrigues with Persia had failed, and that Persia was allied still more strongly with the Lacedæmonians under Lysander.

His reverses. Lysander recalled to Sparta.

This great general, now at Ephesus, pursued a cautious policy, and refused to give battle to the Athenian forces under Alcibiades, who then retired to Phocæa, leaving his fleet under the command of Antiochus, his favorite pilot. Antiochus, in the absence of his general, engaged the Lacedæmonian fleet, but was defeated and slain at Notium. The conduct of Alcibiades produced great disaffection at Athens. He had sailed with a fleet not inferior to that which he commanded at Syracuse, and had made great promises of future achievements, yet in three months he had not gained a single success. He was therefore dismissed from his command, which was given to ten generals, of whom Conon was the most eminent, while he retired to the Chersonese. Lysander, at the same time, was superseded in the command of the Lacedæmonians by Callicratidas, in accordance with Spartan custom, his term being expired.

Vigorous measures of the Lacedæmonians. The battle of Arginusæ.

Callicratidas was not welcomed by Cyrus, and he was also left without funds by Lysander, who returned to the Persians the sums he had received. This conduct so much enraged the Spartan admiral that he sailed with his whole fleet—the largest which had been assembled during the war, one hundred and forty triremes, of which only ten were Lacedæmonian—the rest being furnished by allies—to Lesbos, and liberated the Athenian captives and garrison at Methymna, and seemed animated by that old Panhellenic patriotism which had united the Greeks half a century before against the Persian invaders, declaring that not a single Greek should be reduced to slavery if he could help it. But while he was thus actuated by these noble sentiments, he also prosecuted the war of his country, which had been intrusted to him to conduct. He blocked up the Athenian fleet at Mitylene, which had no provisions to sustain a siege. The Athenians now made prodigious efforts to relieve Conon, and one hundred and ten triremes were sent from the Piræus, and sailed to Samos. Callicratidas, apprised of the approach of the large fleet, went out to meet it. At Arginusæ was fought a great battle, in which the Spartan admiral was killed, and his forces completely defeated. Sixty-nine Lacedæmonian ships were destroyed; the Athenians lost twenty-five, a severe loss to Greece, since, if Callicratidas had gained the victory, he would, according to Grote, have closed the Peloponnesian war, and united the Greeks once more against Persia.

The battle of Arginusæ now gave the Athenians the control of the Asiatic seas, and so discouraged were the Lacedæmonians, that they were induced to make proposals of peace. This is doubted, indeed, by Grote, since no positive results accrued to Athens.

Lysander returns to power.

The Chians and other allies of Sparta, in conjunction with Cyrus, now sent envoys to the ephors, to request the restoration of Lysander to the command of the fleet. They acceded to the request substantially, and Lysander reached Ephesus, B.C. 405, to renovate the Lacedæmonian power and turn the fortunes of war.

Capture of the Athenian fleet. Despair of Athens.

The victorious Athenian fleet was now at Ægospotami, in the Hellespont, opposite Lampsacus, having been inactive for nearly a year. There the fleet was exposed to imminent danger, which was even seen by Alcibiades, in his forts opposite, on the Chersonese. He expostulated with the Athenian admirals, but to no purpose, and urged them to retire to Sestos. As he feared, the Athenian fleet was surprised, at anchor, on this open shore, while the crews were on shore in quest of a meal. One hundred and seventy triremes were thus ingloriously captured, without the loss of a man—the greatest calamity which had happened to Athens since the beginning of the war, and decisive as to its result. The captive generals were slaughtered, together with four thousand Athenian prisoners. Conon, however, made his escape. So disgraceful and unnecessary was this great calamity, that it is supposed the fleet was betrayed by its own commanders; and this supposition is strengthened by its inactivity since the battle of Arginusæ. This crowning disaster happened in September, B.C. 405, and caused a dismay at Athens such as had never before been felt—not even when the Persians were marching through Attica. Nothing was now left to the miserable city but to make what preparation it could for the siege, which everybody foresaw would soon take place. The walls were put in the best defense it was possible, and two of the three ports were blocked up. Not only was Athens deprived of her maritime power, but her very existence was now jeopardized.

Annihilation of the Athenian empire.

Lysander was in no haste to march upon Athens, since he knew that no corn ships could reach the city from the Euxine, and that a famine would soon set in. The Athenian empire was annihilated, and nothing remained but Athens herself! The Athenians now saw that nothing but union between the citizens could give them any hope of success, and they made a solemn pledge in the Acropolis to bury their dissensions and cultivate harmonious feelings.

Surrender of Athens to the Spartans.

In November, Lysander, with two hundred triremes, blockaded the Piræus. The whole force of Sparta, under King Pausanias, went out to meet him, and encamped at the gates of Athens. The citizens bore the calamity with fortitude, and, when they began to die of hunger, sent propositions for capitulation. But no proposition was received which did not include the demolition of the long walls which Pericles had built. As famine pressed, and the condition of the people had become intolerable, Athens was obliged to surrender on the hard conditions that the Piræus should be destroyed, the long walls demolished, all foreign possessions evacuated, all ships surrendered, and, most humiliating of all, that Athens should become the ally of Sparta, and follow her lead upon the sea and upon the land.

Fate of Athens.

Thus fell imperial Athens, after a glorious reign of one hundred years. Lysander entered the city as a conqueror. The ships were surrendered, all but twelve, which the Athenians were allowed to retain; the unfinished ships in the dockyards were burned, the fortifications demolished, and the Piræus dismantled. The constitution of the city was annulled, and a board of thirty was nominated, under the dictation of Lysander, for the government of the city. The conqueror then sailed to Samos, which was easily reduced, and oligarchy was restored on that island, as at Athens.

Close of the war.

The fall of Athens virtually closed the Peloponnesian war, after a bitter struggle between the two leading States of Greece for thirty years. Lysander became the leading man in Greece, and wielded a power greater than any individual Greek before or after him. Sparta, personified in him, became supreme, and ruled over all the islands, and over the Asiatic and Thracian cities. The tyrants whom he placed over Athens exercised their power with extreme rigor—sending to execution all who were obnoxious, seizing as spoil the property of the citizens, and disarming the remaining hoplites in the city. They even forbade intellectual teaching, and shut the mouth of Socrates. Such was Athens, humbled, deprived of her fleet, and rendered powerless, with a Spartan garrison occupying the Acropolis, and discord reigning even among the Thirty Tyrants themselves.

Cause of the fall of Athens. Miserable spirit of the war. Alcibiades the evil genius of Athens. His inglorious death.

In considering the downfall of Athens, we perceive that the unfortunate Sicilian expedition which Alcibiades had stimulated proved the main cause. Her maritime supremacy might have been maintained but for this aggression, which Pericles never would have sanctioned, and which Nicias so earnestly disapproved. After that disaster, the conditions of the State were totally changed, and it was a bitter and desperate struggle to retain the fragments of empire. And the catastrophe proved, ultimately, the political ruin of Greece herself, since there was left no one State sufficiently powerful to resist foreign attacks. The glory of Athens was her navy, and this being destroyed, Greece was open to invasion, and to the corruption brought about by Persian gold. It was Athens which had resisted Persia, and protected the maritime States and islands. When Athens was crippled, the decline of the other States was rapid, for they had all exhausted themselves in the war. And the war itself has few redeeming features. It was a wicked contest carried on by rivalry and jealousy. And it produced, as war generally does, a class of unprincipled men who aggrandize themselves at the expense of their country. Nothing but war would have developed such men as Alcibiades and Lysander, and it is difficult to say which of the two brought the greatest dishonor on their respective States. Both were ambitious, and both hoped to gain an ascendency incompatible with free institutions. To my mind, Alcibiades is the worst man in Grecian history, and not only personally disgraced by the worst vices, but his influence was disastrous on his country. Athens owed her political degradation more to him than any other man. He was insolent, lawless, extravagant, and unscrupulous, from his first appearance in public life. He incited the Sicilian expedition, and caused it to end disastrously by sending Gylippus to Syracuse. He originated the revolt of Chios and Miletus, the fortification of Decelea, and the conspiracy of the Four Hundred. And though he partially redeemed his treason by his three years' services, after his exile, yet his vanity, and intrigues, and prodigality prevented him from accomplishing what he promised. It is true he was a man of great resources, and was never defeated either by sea or land; "and he was the first man in every party he espoused—Athenian, Spartan, or

Persian, oligarchial or democratical, but he never inspired confidence with any party, and all parties successively threw him off." The end of such a man proclaims the avenging Nemesis in this world. He died by the hands of Persian assassins at the instance of both Lysander and Cyrus, who felt that there could be nothing settled so long as this restless schemer lived. And he died, unlamented and unhonored, in spite of his high birth, wealth, talents, and personal accomplishments.

Glory of Lysander.

Lysander was more fortunate; he gained a great ascendency in Sparta, but his ambition proved ruinous to his country, by involving it in those desperate wars which are yet to be presented.

CHAPTER XX
MARCH OF CYRUS AND RETREAT OF
THE TEN THOUSAND GREEKS

Effect of the Peloponnesian war.

The Peloponnesian war being closed, a large body of Grecian soldiers were disbanded, but rendered venal and restless by the excitements and changes of the past thirty years, and ready to embark in any warlike enterprise that promised money and spoil. They were unfitted, as is usually the case, for sober and industrial pursuits. They panted for fresh adventures.

The real ends of Cyrus disguised.

This restless passion which war ever kindles, found vent and direction in the enterprise which Cyrus led from Western Asia to dethrone his brother Artaxerxes from the throne of Persia. Some fourteen thousand Greeks from different States joined his standard—not with a view of a march to Babylon and an attack on the great king, but to conquer and root out the Pisidian mountaineers, who did much mischief from their fastnesses in the southeast of Asia Minor. This was the ostensible object of Cyrus, and he found no difficulty in enlisting Grecian mercenaries, under promise of large rewards. All these Greeks were deceived but one man, to whom alone Cyrus revealed his real purpose. This was Clearchus, a Lacedæmonian general of considerable ability and experience, who had been banished for abuse of authority at Byzantium, which he commanded. He repaired to Sardis and offered his services to Cyrus, who had been sent thither by his father Darius to command the Persian forces. Cyrus accepted the overtures of Clearchus, who secured his confidence so completely that he gave him the large sum of ten thousand darics, which he employed in hiring Grecian mercenaries.

Mercenary Greeks enlist under Cyrus.

Other Greeks of note also joined the army of Cyrus with a view of being employed against the Pisidians. Among them were Aristippus and Menon, of a distinguished family in Thessaly; Proxenus, a Bœotian; Agis, an Arcadian; Socrates, an Achæan, who were employed to collect mercenaries, and who received large sums of money. A considerable body of Lacedæmonians were also taken under pay.

The march of these men to Babylon, and their successful retreat, form one of the most interesting episodes in Grecian history, and it is this march and retreat which I purpose briefly to present.

Character of Cyrus. High estimation in which he held the Greeks.

Cyrus was an extraordinary man. The younger son of the Persian king, he aimed to secure the sovereignty of Persia, which fell to his elder brother, Artaxerxes, on the death of Darius. During his residence at Sardis, as satrap or governor, he perceived and felt the great superiority of the Greeks to his own countrymen, not only intellectually, but as soldiers. He was brave, generous, frank, and ambitious. Had it been his fortune to have achieved the object of his ambition, the whole history of Persia would have been changed, and Alexander would have lived in vain. Perceiving and appreciating the great qualities of the Greeks, and learning how to influence them, he sought, by their aid, to conquer his way to the throne.

He dissembles his designs.

But he dissembled his designs so that they were not suspected, even in Persia. As has been remarked, he communicated them only to the Spartan general, Clearchus. Neither Greek nor Persian divined his object as he collected a great army at Sardis. At first he employed his forces in the siege of Miletus and other enterprises, which provoked no suspicion of his real designs.

He commences his march.

When all was ready, he commenced his march from Sardis, in March, B.C. 401, with about eight thousand Grecian hoplites and one hundred thousand native troops, while a joint Lacedæmonian and Persian fleet coasted around the south of Asia Minor to co-operate with the land forces.

Character of the Greeks who joined his standard.

These Greeks who thus joined his standard under promise of large pay, and were unwittingly about to plunge into unknown perils, were not outcasts and paupers, but were men of position, reputation, and, in some cases, of wealth. About half of them were Arcadians. Young men of good family, ennuied of home, restless and adventurous, formed the greater part, although many of mature age had been induced by liberal offers to leave their wives and children. They simply calculated on a year's campaign in Pisidia, from which they would return to their homes enriched. So they were assured by the Greek commanders at Sardis, and so these commanders believed, for Cyrus stood high in popular estimation for liberality and good faith.

Xenophon.

Among other illustrious Greeks that were thus to be led so far from home was Xenophon, the Athenian historian, who was induced by his friend Proxenus, of Bœotia, to join the expedition. He was of high family, and a pupil of Socrates, but embarked against the wishes and advice of his teacher.

When the siege of Miletus was abandoned, and Cyrus began his march, his object was divined by the satrap Tissaphernes, who hastened to Persia to put the king on his guard.

Cyrus reviews his army. The Greeks perceive that they have been deceived.

At Celenæ, or Kelænæ, a Phrygian city, Cyrus halted and reviewed his army. Grecian re-enforcements here joined him, which swelled the number of Greeks to thirteen thousand men, of whom eleven thousand were hoplites. As this city was on the way to Pisidia, no mistrust existed as to the object of the expedition, not even when the army passed into Lycaonia, since its inhabitants were of the same predatory character as the Pisidians. But when it had crossed Mount Taurus, which bounded Cilicia, and reached Tarsus, the Greeks perceived that they had been cheated, and refused to advance farther. Clearchus attempted to suppress the mutiny by severe measures, but failed. He then resorted to stratagem, and pretended to yield to the wishes of the Greeks, and likewise refused to march, but sent a secret dispatch to Cyrus that all would be well in the end, and requested him to send fresh invitations, that he might answer by fresh refusals. He then, with the characteristic cunning and eloquence of a Greek, made known to his countrymen the extreme peril of making Cyrus their enemy in a hostile country, where retreat was beset with so many dangers, and induced them to proceed. So the army continued its march to Issus, at the extremity of the Issican Gulf, and near the mountains which separate Cilicia from Syria. Here Cyrus was further re-enforced, making the grand total of Greeks in his army fourteen thousand.

Cyrus crosses into Syria. He crosses the Euphrates. Battle of Cunaxa.

He expected to find the passes over the mountains, a day's journey from Issus, defended, but the Persian general Abrocomas fled at his approach, and Cyrus easily crossed into Syria by the pass of Beilan, over Mount Amanus. He then proceeded south to Myriandus, a Phœnician maritime town, where he parted from his fleet. Eight days' march brought his army to Thapsacus, on the Euphrates, where he remained five days to refresh his troops. Here again the Greeks showed a reluctance to proceed, but, on the promise of five minæ a head, nearly one hundred dollars more than a year's pay, they consented to advance. It was here Cyrus crossed the river unobstructed, and continued his march on the left bank for nine days, until he came to the river Araxes, which separates Syria from Arabia. Thus far his army was well supplied with provisions from the numerous villages through which they passed; but now he entered a desert country, entirely without cultivation, where the astonished Greeks beheld for the first time wild asses, antelopes, and ostriches. For eighteen days the army marched without other provisions than what they brought with them, parched with thirst and exhausted by heat. At Pylæ they reached the cultivated territory of Babylonia, and the alluvial plains commenced. Three days' further march brought them to Cunaxa, about seventy miles from Babylon, where the army of Artaxerxes was marshaled to meet them. It was an immense force of more than a million of men, besides six thousand horse-guards and two hundred chariots. But so confident was Cyrus of the vast superiority of the Greeks and their warfare, that he did not hesitate to engage the overwhelming forces of his brother with only ten thousand Greeks and one hundred thousand Asiatics. The battle of Cunaxa was fatal to Cyrus; he was slain and his camp was pillaged. The expedition had failed.

Dismay of the Greeks. They retreat.

Dismay now seized the Greeks, as well it might—a handful of men in the midst of innumerable enemies, and in the very centre of the Persian empire. But such men are not driven to despair. They refused to surrender, and make up their minds to retreat—to find their way back again to Greece, since all aggressive measures was madness.

This retreat, amid so many difficulties, and against such powerful and numerous enemies, is one of the most gallant actions in the history of war, and has made those ten thousand men immortal.

Their forlorn condition.

Ariæus, who commanded the Asiatic forces on the left wing of the army at the battle of Cunaxa, joined the Greeks with what force remained, in retreat, and promised to guide them to the Asiatic coast, not by the route which Cyrus had taken, for this was now impracticable, but by a longer one, up the course of the Tigris, through Armenia, to the Euxine Sea. The Greeks had marched ninety days from Sardis, about fourteen hundred and sixty-four English miles, and rested ninety-six days in various places. Six months had been spent on the expedition, and it would take more than that time to return, considering the new difficulties which it was necessary to surmount.

The condition of the Greeks, to all appearance, was hopeless. How were they to ford rivers and cross mountains, with a hostile cavalry in their rear, without supplies, without a knowledge of roads, without trustworthy guides, through hostile territories?

Deceitful negotiations of the Persians.

The Persians still continued their negotiations, regarding the advance or retreat of the Greeks alike impossible, and curious to learn what motives had brought them so far from home. They replied that they had been deceived, that they had no hostility to the Persian king, that they had been ashamed to desert Cyrus in the midst of danger, and that they now desired only to return home peaceably, but were prepared to repel hostilities.

The Persian king aims at their overthrow.

It was not pleasant to the Persian monarch to have thirteen thousand Grecian veterans, whose prestige was immense, and whose power was really formidable, in the heart of the kingdom. It was not easy to conquer such brave men, reduced to desperation, without immense losses and probable humiliation. So the Persians dissembled. It was their object to get the Greeks out of Babylonia, where they could easily intrench and support themselves, and then attack them at a disadvantage. So Tissaphernes agreed to conduct them home by a different route. They acceded to his proposal, and he led them to the banks of the Tigris, and advanced on its left bank, north to the Great Zab River, about two hundred miles from Babylon. The Persians marched in advance, and the Greeks about three miles in the rear. At the Great Zab they halted three days, and then Tissaphernes enticed the Greek generals to his tent, ostensibly to feast them and renew negotiations. There they were seized, sent prisoners to the Persian court, and treacherously murdered.

The despair of the Greeks.

Utter despair now seized the Greeks. They were deprived of their generals, in the heart of Media, with unscrupulous enemies in the rear, and the mountains of Armenia in their front, whose passes were defended by hostile barbarians, and this in the depth of winter, deprived of guides, and exposed to every kind of hardship, difficulty, and danger. They were apparently in the hands of their enemies, without any probability of escape. They were then summoned to surrender to the Persians, but they resolved to fight their way home, great as were their dangers and insurmountable the difficulties—a most heroic resolution. And their retreat, under these circumstances, to the Euxine, is the most extraordinary march in the whole history of war.

Xenophon rallies the Greeks.

But a great man appeared, in this crisis, to lead them, whose prudence, sagacity, moderation, and courage can never be sufficiently praised, and his successful retreat places him in the ranks of the great generals of the world. Xenophon, the Athenian historian, now appears upon the stage with all those noble qualities which inspired the heroes at the siege of Troy—a man as religious as he was brave and magnanimous, and eloquent even for a Greek. He summoned together the captains, and persuaded them to advance, giving the assurance of the protection of Zeus. He then convened the army, and inspired them by his spirit, with surpassing eloquence, and acquired the ascendency of a Moses by his genius, piety, and wisdom. His military rank was not great, but in such an emergency talents and virtues have more force than rank.

Their retreat to the Tigris. Their perils and hardships.

So, under his leadership, the Greeks crossed the Zab, and resumed their march to the north, harassed by Persian cavalry, and subjected to great privations. The army no longer marched, as was usual, in one undivided hollow square, but in small companies, for they were obliged to cross mountains and ford rivers. So long as they marched on the banks of the Tigris, they found well-stocked villages, from which they obtained supplies; but as they entered the country of the Carducians, they were obliged to leave the Tigris to their left, and cross the high mountains which divided it from Armenia. They were also compelled to burn their baggage, for the roads were nearly impassable, not only on account of the narrow defiles, but from the vast quantities of snow which fell. Their situation was full of peril, and fatigue, and privation. Still they persevered, animated by the example and eloquence of their intrepid leader. At every new pass they were obliged to fight a battle, but the enemies they encountered could not withstand their arms in close combat, and usually fled, contented to harass them by rolling stones down the mountains on their heads, and discharging their long arrows.

The march through Armenia. They reach the Euxine.

The march through Armenia was still more difficult, for the inhabitants were more warlike and hardy, and the passage more difficult. They also were sorely troubled for lack of guides. The sufferings of the Greeks were intense from cold and privation. The beasts of burden perished in the snow, while the soldiers were frost-bitten and famished. It was their good fortune to find villages, after several days' march, where they halted and rested, but assailed all the while by hostile bands. Yet onward they pressed, wearied and hungry, through the country of the Taochi, of the Chalybes, of the Scytheni, of the Marones, of the Colchians, and reached Trapezus (Trebizond) in safety. The sight of the sea filled the Greeks with indescribable joy after so many perils, for the sea was their own element, and they could now pursue their way in ships rather than by perilous marches.

New troubles and dangers.

But the delays were long and dreary. There were no ships to transport the warriors to Byzantium. They were exposed to new troubles from the indifference or hostility of the cities on the Euxine, for so large a force created alarm. And when the most pressing dangers were passed, the license of the men broke out, so that it was difficult to preserve order and prevent them from robbing their friends. They were obliged to resort to marauding expeditions among the Asiatic people, and it was difficult to support themselves. Not being able to get ships, they marched along the coast to Cotyora, exposed to incessant hostilities. It was now the desire of Xenophon to found a new city on the Euxine with the army; but the army was eager to return home, and did not accede to the proposal. Clamors arose against the general who had led them so gloriously from the heart of Media, and his speeches in his defense are among the most eloquent on Grecian record. He remonstrated against the disorders of the army, and had sufficient influence to secure reform, and completely triumphed over faction as he had over danger.

They pass by sea to Sinope. Their courage and faith.

At last ships were provided, and the army passed by sea to Sinope—a Grecian colony—where the men were hospitably received, and fed, and lodged. From thence the army passed by sea to Heracleia, where the soldiers sought to extort money against the opposition of Xenophon and Cherisophus, the latter of whom had nobly seconded the plans of Xenophon, although a Spartan of superior military rank. The army, at this opposition, divided into three factions, but on suffering new disasters, reunited. It made a halt at Calpe, where new disorders broke out. Then Cleander, Spartan governor of Byzantium, arrived with two triremes, who promised to conduct the army, and took command of it, but subsequently threw up his command from the unpropitious sacrifices. Nothing proved the religious character of the Greeks so forcibly as their scrupulous attention to the rites imposed by their pagan faith. They undertook no enterprise of importance without sacrifices to the gods, and if the auguries were unfavorable, they relinquished their most cherished objects.

They reach Byzantium.

From Calpe the army marched to Chalcedon, turning into money the slaves and plunder which it had collected. There it remained seven days.

But nothing could be done without the consent of the Spartan admiral at Byzantium, Anaxibius, since the Lacedæmonians were the masters of Greece both by sea and land. This man was bribed by the Persian satrap Pharnabazus, who commanded the north-western region of Asia Minor, to transport the army to the European side of the Bosphorus. It accordingly crossed to Byzantium, but was not allowed to halt in the city, or even to enter the gates.

But are excluded from the city. They enlist in the service of Sparta.

The wrath of the soldiers was boundless when they were thus excluded from Byzantium. They rushed into the town and took possession, which conduct gave grave apprehension to Xenophon, who mustered and harangued the army, and thus prevented anticipated violence. They at length consented to leave the city, and accepted the services of the Theban Coeratidas, who promised to conduct them to the Delta of Thrace, for purposes of plunder, but he was soon dismissed. After various misfortunes the soldiers at length were taken under the pay of Seuthes, a Thracian prince, who sought the recovery of his principality, but who cheated them out of their pay. A change of policy among the Lacedæmonians led to the conveyance of the Cyrenian army into Asia in order to make war on the satraps. Xenophon accordingly conducted his troops, now reduced to six thousand men, over Mount Ida to Pergamus. He succeeded in capturing the Persian general Asidates, and securing a valuable booty, B.C. 399. The soldiers whom he had led were now incorporated with the Lacedæmonian army in Asia, and Xenophon himself enlisted in the Spartan service. His subsequent fortunes we have not room to present. An exile from Athens, he settled in Scillus, near Olympia, with abundant wealth, but ultimately returned to his native city after the battle of Leuctra.

Moral effect of the expedition.

The impression produced on the Grecian mind by the successful retreat of the Ten Thousand was profound and lasting. Its most obvious effect was to produce contempt for Persian armies and Persian generals, and to show that Persia was only strong by employing Hellenic strength against the Hellenic cause. The real weakness of Persia was thus revealed to the Greeks, and sentiments were fostered which two generations afterward led to the expeditions of Alexander and the subjection of Asia to Grecian rule.

CHAPTER XXI
THE LACEDÆMONIAN EMPIRE

Sparta never lost her power.

I have already shown that Sparta, after a battle with the Argives, B.C. 547, obtained the ascendency in the southern part of the Peloponnesus, and became the leading military State of Greece. This prestige and power were not lost. The severe simplicity of Spartan life, the rigor of political and social institutions, the aristocratic form of government, and above all the military spirit and ambition, gave permanence to all conquests, so that in the Persian wars Sparta took the load of the land forces. The great rival power of Sparta was Athens, but this was founded on maritime skill and enterprise. It was to the navy of Athens, next after the hoplites of Sparta, that the successful resistance to the empire of Persia may be attributed.

Continued glory of Athens also.

After the Persian wars the rivalship between Athens and Sparta is the most prominent feature in Grecian history. The confederacy of Delos gave to Athens supremacy over the sea, and the great commercial prosperity of Athens under Pericles, and the empire gained over the Ionian colonies and the islands of the Ægaean, made Athens, perhaps, the leading State. It was the richest, the most cultivated, and the most influential of the Grecian States, and threatened to absorb gradually all the other States of Greece in her empire.

Consequences of the Peloponnesian war.

This ascendency and rapid growth in wealth and power were beheld with jealous eyes, not only by Sparta, but other States which she controlled, or with which she was in alliance. The consequence was, the Peloponnesian war, which lasted half a generation, and which, after various vicissitudes and fortunes, terminated auspiciously for Sparta, but disastrously to Greece as a united nation. The Persian wars bound all the States together by a powerful Hellenic sentiment of patriotism. The Peloponnesian war dissevered this Panhellenic tie. The disaster at Syracuse was fatal to Athenian supremacy, and even independence. But for this Athens might have remained the great power of Greece. The democratic organization of the government gave great vigor and enterprise to all the ambitious projects of Athens. If Alcibiades had lent his vast talents to the building up of his native State, even then the fortunes of Athens might have been different. But he was a traitor, and threw all his energies on the side of Sparta, until it was too late for Athens to recover the prestige she had won. He partially redeemed his honor, but had he been animated by the spirit of Pericles or Nicias, to say nothing of the self-devotion of Miltiades, he might have raised the power of Athens to a height which nothing could have resisted.

Paramount authority of Sparta after the victories of Lysander.

Lysander completed the war which Brasidas had so nobly carried on, and took possession of Athens, abolished the democratic constitution, demolished the walls, and set up, as his creatures, a set of tyrants, and also a Spartan governor in Athens. Under Lysander, the Lacedæmonian rule was paramount in Greece. At one time, he had more power than any man in Greece ever enjoyed. He undertook to change the government of the allied cities, and there was scarcely a city in Greece where the Spartans had not the ascendency. In most of the Ionian cities, and in all the cities which had taken the side of Athens, there was a Spartan governor, so that when Xenophon returned with his Ten Thousand to Asia Minor, he found he could do nothing without the consent of the Spartan governors. Moreover, the rule of Sparta was hostile to all democratic governments. She sought to establish oligarchal institutions everywhere. Perhaps this difference between Athens and Sparta respecting government was one great cause of tho Peloponnesian war.

Sparta incurs the jealousy of Greece.

But the same envy which had once existed among the Grecian States of the prosperity of Athens, was now turned upon Sparta. Her rule was arrogant and hard and she in turn had to experience the humiliation of revolt from her domination. "The allies of Sparta," says Grote, "especially Corinth and Thebes, not only relented in their hatred of Athens, now she had lost her power, but even sympathized with her suffering exiles, and became disgusted with the self-willed encroachments of Sparta; while the Spartan king, Pausanias, together with some of the ephors, were also jealous of the arbitrary and oppressive conduct of Lysander. He refused to prevent the revival of the democracy. It was in this manner that Athens, rescued from that sanguinary and rapacious *régime* of the Thirty Tyrants, was enabled to reappear as a humble and dependent member of the Spartan alliance—with nothing but the recollection of her former power, yet with her democracy again in vigorous action for internal government."

Her oppressive superiority.

The victory of Ægospotami, which annihilated the Athenian navy, ushered in the supremacy of Sparta, both on the land and sea, and all Greece made submission to the ascendant power. Lysander established in most of the cities an oligarchy of ten citizens, as well as a Spartan harmost, or governor. Everywhere the Lysandrian dekarchy superseded the previous governments, and ruled oppressively, like the Thirty at Athens, with Critias at their head. And no justice could be obtained at Sparta against the bad conduct of the harmosts who now domineered in every city. Sparta had embroiled Greece in war to put down the ascendency of Athens, but exercised a more tyrannical usurpation than Athens ever meditated. The language of Brasidas, who promised every thing, was in striking contrast to the conduct of Lysander, who put his foot on the neck of Greece.

Effect of the tyrannical policy of Sparta.

The rule of the Thirty at Athens came to an end by the noble efforts of Thrasybulus and the Athenian democracy, and the old constitution was restored because the Spartan king was disgusted with the usurpations and arrogance of Lysander, and forbore to interfere. Had Sparta been wise, with this vast accession of power gained by the victories of Lysander, she would have ruled moderately, and reorganized the Grecian world on sound principles, and restored a Panhellenic stability and harmony. She might not have restored, as Brasidas had promised, a universal autonomy, or the complete independence of all the cities, but would have bound together all the States under her presidency, by a just and moderate rule. But Sparta had not this wisdom. She was narrow, hard, and extortionate. She loved her own, as selfish people generally do, but nothing outside her territory with any true magnanimity. And she thus provoked her allies into rebellion, so that her chance was lost, and her dominion short-lived. Athens would have been more enlightened, but she never had the power, as Sparta had, of organizing a general Panhellenic combination. The nearest approach which Athens ever made was the confederacy of Delos, which did not work well, from the jealousy of the cities. But Sparta soon made herself more unpopular than Athens ever was, and her dream of empire was short.

Renewal of the war with Persia.

The first great movement of Sparta, after the establishment of oligarchy in all the cities which yielded to her, was a renewal of the war with Persia. The Asiatic Greek cities had been surrendered to Persia according to treaty, as the price for the assistance which Persia rendered to Sparta in the war with Athens. But the Persian rule, under the satraps, especially of Tissaphernes, who had been rewarded by Artaxerxes with more power than before, became oppressive and intolerable. Nothing but aggravated slavery impended over them. They therefore sent to Sparta for aid to throw off the Persian yoke. The ephors, with nothing more to gain from Persia, and inspired with contempt for the Persian armies—contempt created by the expedition of the Ten Thousand—readily listened to the overtures, and sent a considerable force into Asia, under Thimbron. He had poor success, and was recalled, and Dereyllidas was sent in his stead. He made a truce with Tissaphernes, in order to attack Pharnabazus, against whom he had an old grudge, and with whom Tissaphernes himself happened for the time to be on ill terms. Dereyllidas overrun the satrapy of Pharnabazus, took immense spoil, and took up winter-quarters in Bythinia. Making a truce with Pharnabazus, he crossed over into Europe and fortified the Chersonesus against the Thracians. He then renewed the war both against Pharnabazus and Tissaphernes upon the Mæander, the result of which was an agreement, on the part of the satraps, to exempt the Grecian cities from tribute and political interference, while the Spartan general promised to withdraw from Asia his army, and the Spartan governors from the Grecian cities.

Agesilaus, king of Sparta.

At this point, B.C. 397, Dercyllidas was recalled to Sparta, and King Agesilaus, who had recently arrived with large re-enforcements, superseded him in command of the Lacedæmonian army. Agesilaus was the son of king Archidamus, and half-brother to King Agis. He was about forty when he became king, through the influence of Lysamler, in preference to his nephew, and having been brought up without prospects of the throne, had passed through the unmitigated rigor of the Spartan drill and training. He was distinguished for all the Spartan virtues—obedience to authority, extraordinary courage and energy, simplicity and frugality.

Recall of Agesilaus from the war.

Agesilaus was assisted by large contingents from the allied Greek cities for his war in Asia; but Athens, Corinth, and Thebes stood aloof. Lysander accompanied him as one of the generals, but gave so great offense by his overweening arrogance, that he was sent to command at the Hellespont. The truce between the Spartans and Persians being broken, Agesilaus prosecuted the war vigorously against both Tissaphernes and Pharnabazus. He gained a considerable victory over the Persians near Sardis, invaded Phrygia, and laid waste the satrapy of Pharnabazus. He even surprised the camp of the satrap, and gained immense booty. But in the midst of his victories he was recalled by Sparta, which had need of his services at home. A rebellion of the allies had broken out, which seriously threatened the stability of the Spartan empire.

Discontent of the Grecian States. Alienation of the allies of Sparta.

"The prostration of the power of Athens had removed that common bond of hatred and alarm which attached the allied cities to the headship of Sparta; while her subsequent conduct had given positive offense, and had excited against herself the same fear of unmeasured imperial ambition which had before run so powerfully against Athens. She had appropriated to herself nearly the whole of the Athenian maritime empire, with a tribute of one thousand talents. But while Sparta had gained so much by the war, not one of her allies had received the smallest remuneration. Even the four hundred and seventy talents which Lysander brought home out of the advances made by Cyrus, together with the booty acquired at Decelea, was all detained by the Lacedæmonians. Hence there arose among the allies not only a fear of the grasping dominion, but a hatred of the monopolizing rapacity of Sparta. This was manifested by the Thebans and Corinthians when they refused to join Pausanias in his march against Thrasybulus and the Athenian exiles in Piræus. But the Lacedæmonians were strong enough to despise this alienation of the allies, and even to take revenge on such as incurred their displeasure. Among these were the Elians, whose territory they invaded, but which they retreated from, on the appearance of an earthquake."

The following year the Spartans, under King Agis, again invaded the territory of Elis, enriched by the offerings made to the temple of Olympeia. Immense booty in slaves, cattle, and provisions was the result of this invasion, provoked by the refusal of the Elians to furnish aid in the war against Athens. The Elians were obliged to submit to hard terms of peace, and all the enemies of Sparta were rooted out of the Peloponnesus.

Enrichment of Sparta.

Such was the triumphant position of Sparta at the close of the Peloponnesian war. And a great change had also taken place in her internal affairs. The people had become enriched by successful war, and gold and silver were admitted against the old institution of Lycurgus, which recognized only iron money. The public men were enriched by bribes. The strictness of the old rule of Spartan discipline was gradually relaxed.

Conspiracy against the States.

It was then, shortly after the accession of Agesilaus to the throne, on the death of Agis, that a dangerous conspiracy broke out in Sparta itself, headed by Cinadon, a man of strength and courage, who saw that men of his class were excluded from the honors and distinctions of the State by the oligarchy—the ephors and the senate. But the rebellion, though put down by the energy of Agesilaus, still produced a dangerous discontent which weakened the power of the State.

Lacedæmonian fleet threatened. Naval victory over the Lacedæmonians.

The Lacedæmonian naval power, at this crisis, was seriously threatened by the union of the Persian and Athenian fleet under Conon. That remarkable man had escaped from the disaster of Ægospotami with eight triremes, and sought the shelter of Cyprus, governed by his friend Evagoras, where he remained until the war between Sparta and the Persians gave a new direction to his enterprising genius. He joined Pharnabazus, enraged with the Spartans on account of the invasion of his satrapy by Lysander and Agesilaus, and by him was intrusted with the command of the Persian fleet. He succeeded in detaching Rhodes from the Spartan alliance, and gained, some time after, a decisive victory over Pisander—the Spartan admiral, off Cnidus, which weakened the power of Sparta on the sea, B.C. 394. More than half of the Spartan ships were captured and destroyed.

Revolt of Thebes.

This great success emboldened Thebes and other States to throw off the Spartan yoke. Lysander was detached from his command at the Hellespont to act against Bœotia, while Pausanias conducted an army from the Peloponnesus. The Thebans, threatened by the whole power of Sparta, applied to Athens, and Athens responded, no longer under the control of the Thirty Tyrants. Lysander was killed before Haliartus, an irreparable blow to Sparta, since he was her ablest general. Pausanias was compelled to evacuate Bœotia, and the enemies of Sparta took courage. An alliance between Athens, Corinth, Thebes, and Argos was now made to carry on war against Sparta.

Renewed power of the city.

Thebes at this time steps from the rank of a secondary power, and gradually rises to the rank of an ascendant city. Her leading citizen was Ismenias, one of the great organizers of the anti-Spartan movement— the precursor of Pelopidas and Epaminondas. He conducted successful operations in the northern part of Bœotia, and captured Heracleia.

Battle of Coronæa.

Such successes induced the Lacedæmonians to recall Agesilaus from Asia, and to concentrate all their forces against this new alliance, of which Thebes and Corinth were then the most powerful cities. The allied forces were also considerable—some twenty-four thousand hoplites, besides light troops and cavalry, and these were mustered at Corinth, where they took up a defensive position. The Lacedæmonians advanced to attack them, and gained an indecisive victory, B.C. 394, which secured their ascendency within the Peloponnesus, but no further. Agesilaus advanced from Asia through Thrace to co-operate, but learned, on the confines of Bœotia, the news of the great battle of Cnidus. At Coronæa another battle was fought between the Spartan and anti-Spartan forces, which was also indecisive, but in which the Thebans displayed great heroism. This battle compelled Agesilaus, with the Spartan forces, which he commanded, to retire from Bœotia.

Decline of Sparta.

This battle was a moral defeat to Sparta. Nearly all her maritime allies deserted her—all but Abydos, which was held by the celebrated Dercyllidas. Pharnabazus and Conon now sailed with their fleet to Corinth, but the Persian satrap soon left and Conon remained sole admiral, assisted with Persian money. With this aid he rebuilt the long walls of Athens, with the hearty co-operation of those allies which had once been opposed to Athens.

Corinth becomes the seat of war.

Conon had large plans for the restoration of the Athenian power. He organized a large mercenary force at Corinth, which had now become the seat of war. But as many evils resulted from the presence of so many soldiers in the city, a conspiracy headed by the oligarchal party took place, with a view of restoring the Lacedæmonian power. Pasimelus, the head of the conspirators, admitted the enemy within the long walls of the city, which, as in Athens, secured a communication between the city and the port. And between these walls a battle took place, in which the Lacedæmonians were victorious with a severe loss. They pulled down a portion of the walls between Corinth and the port of Lechæum, sallied forth, and captured two Corinthian dependencies, but the city of Corinth remained in the hands of their gallant defenders, under the Athenian Iphicrates. The long walls were soon restored, by aid of the Athenians, but were again retaken by Agesilaus and the Spartans, together with Lechæum. This success alarmed Thebes, which unsuccessfully sued for peace. The war continued, with the loss, to the Corinthians, of Piræum, an important island port, which induced the Thebans again to open negotiations for peace, which were contemptuously rejected.

Great disaster to Sparta.

In the midst of these successes, tidings came to Agesilaus of a disaster which was attended with important consequences, and which spoiled his triumph. This was the destruction of a detachment of six hundred Lacedæmonian hoplites by the light troops of Iphicrates—an unprecedented victory—for the hoplites, in their heavy defensive armor, held in contempt the peltarts with their darts and arrows, even as the knights of mediæval Europe despised an encounter with the peasantry. This event revived the courage of the anti-Spartan allies, and intensely humiliated the Lacedæmonians. It was not only the loss of the aristocratic hoplites, but the disgrace of being beaten by peltarts. Iphicrates recovered the places which Agesilaus had taken, and Corinth remained undisturbed.

Sparta invokes the aid of Persia.

Sparta, in view of these great disasters, now sought to detach Persia from Athens. She sent Antalcidas to Ionia, offering to surrender the Asiatic Greeks, and promising a universal autonomy throughout the Grecian world. These overtures were disliked by the allies, who sent Conon to counteract them. But Antalcidas gained the favor of the Persian satrap Tiribasus, who had succeeded Tissaphernes, and he privately espoused the cause of Sparta, and seized Conon and caused his death. Tiribasus, however, was not sustained by the Persian court, which remained hostile to Sparta. Struthas, a Persian general, was sent into Ionia, to act more vigorously against the Lacedæmonians. He gained a victory, B.C. 390, over the Spartan forces, commanded by Thimbron, who was slain.

Death of Thrasybulus.

The Lacedæmonians succeeded, after the death of Conon, in concentrating a considerable fleet near Rhodes. Against this, Thrasybulus was sent from Athens with a still larger one, and was gaining advantages, when he was slain near Aspendus, in Pamphylia, in a mutiny, and Athens lost the restorer of her renovated democracy, and an able general and honest citizen, without the vindictive animosities which characterized the great men of his day.

Investment of Rhodes. Evil consequences of the rivalries of the Grecian States.

Rhodes still held out against the Lacedæmonians, who were now commanded by Anaxibius, in the place of Dercyllidas. He was surprised by Iphicrates, and was slain, and the Athenians, under this gallant leader, again became masters of the Hellespont. But this success was balanced by the defection of Ægina, which island was constrained by the Lacedæmonians into war with Athens. I need not detail the various enterprises on both sides, until Antalcidas returned from Susa with the treaty confirmed between the Spartans and the court of Persia, which closed the war between the various contending parties, B.C. 387. This treaty was of great importance, but it indicates the loss of all Hellenic dignity when Sparta, too, descends so far as to comply with the demands of a Persian satrap. Athens and Sparta, both, at different times, invoked the aid of Persia against each other—the most mournful fact in the whole history of Greece, showing how much more powerful were the rivalries of States than the sentiment of patriotism, which should have united them against their common enemy. The sacrifice of Ionia was the price which was paid by Sparta, in order to retain her supremacy over the rest of Greece, and Persia ruled over all the Greeks on the Asiatic coast. Sparta became mistress of Corinth and of the Corinthian Isthmus. She organized anti-Theban oligarchies in the Bœotian cities, with a Spartan harmost. She decomposed the Grecian world into small fragments. She crushed Olythus, and formed a confederacy between the Persian king and the Dionysius of Syracuse. In short, she ruled with despotic sway over all the different States.

We have now to show how Sparta lost the ascendency she had gained, and became involved in a war with Thebes, and how Thebes became, under Pelopidas and Epaminondas, for a time the dominant State of Greece.

CHAPTER XXII
THE REPUBLIC OF THEBES

Thebes.

After Sparta and Athens, no State of Greece arrived at pre-eminence, until the Macedonian empire arose, except Thebes, the capital of Bœotia; and the empire of this city was short, though memorable, from the extraordinary military genius of Epaminondas.

In the year B.C. 370, Sparta was the ascendant power of Greece, and was feared, even as Athens was in the time of Pericles. She had formed an alliance with the Persian king and with Dionysius of Syracuse. All Greece, within and without the Peloponnesus, except Argos and Attica and some Thessalian cities, was enrolled in a confederacy under the lead of Sparta, and Spartan governors and garrisons occupied the principal cities.

Under the domination of Sparta.

Thebes especially was completely under Spartan influence and control, and was apparently powerless. Her citadel, the Cadmea, was filled with Spartan soldiers, and the independence of Greece was at an end. Confederated with Macedonians, Persians, and Syracusans, nobody dared to call in question the headship of Sparta, or to provoke her displeasure.

Invectives of the orators against Sparta.

This destruction of Grecian liberties, with the aid of the old enemies of Greece, kindled great indignation. The orator Lysias, at Athens, gave vent to the general feeling, in which he veils his displeasure under the form of surprise, that Sparta, as the chief of Greece, should permit the Persians, under Artaxerxes, and the Syracusans, under Dionysius, to enslave Greece. The orator Isocrates spoke still more plainly, and denounced the Lacedæmonians as "traitors to the general security and freedom of Greece, and seconding foreign kings to aggrandize themselves at the cost of autonomous Grecian cities—all in the interest of their own selfish ambition." Even Xenophon, with all his partiality for Sparta, was still more emphatic, and accused the Lacedæmonians with the violation of their oaths.

Discontent in Thebes.

In Thebes the discontent was most apparent, for their leading citizens were exiled, and the oligarchal party, headed by Leontiades and the Spartan garrison, was oppressive and tyrannical. The Theban exiles found at Athens sympathy and shelter. Among these was Pelopidas, who resolved to free his country from the Spartan yoke. Holding intimate correspondence with his friends in Thebes, he looked forward patiently for the means of effecting deliverance, which could only be effected by the destruction of Leontiades and his colleagues, who ruled the city. Philidas, secretary of the polemarchs, entered into the conspiracy, and, being sent in an embassy to Athens, concocted the way for Pelopidas and his friends to return to Thebes and effect a revolution. Charon, an eminent patriot, agreed to shelter the conspirators in his house until they struck the blow. Epaminondas, then living at Thebes, dissuaded the enterprise as too hazardous, although all his sympathies were with the conspirators.

Rebellion under Philidas. Its success.

When all was ready, Philidas gave a banquet at his house to the polemarchs, agreeing to introduce into the company some women of the first families of Thebes, distinguished for their beauty. In concert with the Theban exiles at Athens, Pelopidas, with six companions, crossed Cithæron and arrived at Thebes, in December, B.C. 379, disguised as hunters, with no other arms than concealed daggers. By a fortunate accident they entered the gates and sought shelter in the house of Charon until the night of the banquet. They were introduced into the banqueting chamber when the polemarchs were full of wine, disguised in female attire, and, with the aid of their Theban conspirators, dispatched three of the polemarchs with their daggers. Leontiades was not present, but the conspirators were conducted secretly to his house, and effected their purpose. Leontiades was slain, in the presence of his wife. The conspirators then proceeded to the prison, slew the jailer, and liberated the prisoners, and then proclaimed, by heralds, in the streets, at midnight, that the despots were slain and Thebes was free. But the Spartans still held possession of the citadel, and, apprised of the *coup d'etat*, sent home for re-enforcements. But before they could arrive Pelopidas and the enfranchised citizens stormed the Cadmea, dispersed the garrison, put to death the oligarchal Thebans, and took full possession of the city.

The Theban revolution produces a great sensation. Thebes forms an alliance with Athens.

This unlooked-for revolution was felt throughout Greece like an electric shook, and had a powerful moral effect. But the Spartans, although it was the depth of winter, sent forth an expedition, under King Cleombrotus—Agesilaus being disabled—to reconquer Thebes. He conducted his army along the Isthmus of Corinth, through Megara, but did nothing, and returned, leaving his lieutenant, Sphodrias, to prosecute hostilities. Sphodrias, learning that the Piræus was undefended, undertook to seize it, but failed, which outrage so incensed the Athenians, that they dismissed the Lacedæmonian envoys, and declared war against Sparta. Athens now exerted herself to form a second maritime confederacy, like that of Delos, and Thebes enrolled herself a member. As the Athenian envoys, sent to the islands of the Ægean, promised the most liberal principles, a new confederacy was formed. The confederates assembled at Athens and threatened war on an extensive scale. A resolution was passed to equip twenty thousand hoplites, five hundred horsemen, and two hundred triremes. A new property-tax was imposed at Athens to carry on the war.

Theban government.

At Thebes there was great enthusiasm, and Pelopidas, with Charon and Melon, were named the first bœotrarchs. The Theban government became democratic in form and spirit, and the military force was put upon a severe training. A new brigade of three hundred hoplites, called the Sacred Band, was organized for the special defense of the citadel, composed of young men from the best families, distinguished for strength and courage. The Thebans had always been good soldiers, but the popular enthusiasm raised up the best army for its size in Greece.

Epaminondas. His accomplishments.

Epaminondas now stands forth as a leader of rare excellence, destined to achieve the greatest military reputation of any Greek, before or since his time, with the exception of Alexander the Great—a kind of Gustavus Adolphus, introducing new tactics into Grecian warfare. He was in the prime of life, belonging to a poor but honorable family, younger than Pelopidas, who was rich. He had acquired great reputation for his gymnastic exercises; and was the most cultivated man in Thebes, a good musician, and a still greater orator. He learned to play on both the lyre and flute from the teachings of the best masters, sought the conversation of the learned, but was especially eloquent in speech, and effective, even against the best Athenian opponents. He was modest, unambitious, patriotic, intellectual, contented with poverty, generous, and disinterested. When the Cadmea was taken, he was undistinguished, and his rare merits were only known to Pelopidas and his friends. He was among the first to join the revolutionists, and was placed by Pelopidas among the organizers of the military force.

Sparta attacks Thebes.

The Spartans now made renewed exertions, and King Agesilaus, the greatest military man of whom Sparta can boast, marched with a large army, in the spring of B.C. 378, to attack Thebes. He established his head-quarters in Thespiæ, from which he issued to devastate the Theban territory.

The Thebans and Athenians, unequal in force, still kept the field against him, acting on the defensive, declining battle, and occupying strong positions. After a month of desultory warfare, Agesilaus retired, leaving Phœbidas in command at Thespiæ, who was slain in an incautious pursuit of the enemy.

Second unsuccessful expedition of Agesilaus.

In the ensuing summer Agesilaus undertook a second expedition into Bœotia, but gained no decided advantage, while the Thebans acquired experience, courage, and strength. Agesilaus having strained his lame leg, was incapacitated for active operation, and returned to Sparta, leaving Cleombrotus to command the Spartan forces. He was unable to enter Bœotia, since the passes over Mount Cithæron were held by the Thebans, and he made an inglorious retreat, without even reaching Bœotia.

Naval victory of the Athenians. Victory of Pelopidas.

The Spartans now resolved to fit out a large naval force to operate against Athens, by whose assistance the Thebans had maintained their ground for two years. The Athenians, on their part, also fitted out a fleet, assisted by their allies, under the command of Chabrias, which defeated the Lacedæmonian fleet near Naxos, B.C. 376. This was the first great victory which Athens had gained since the Peloponnesian war, and filled her citizens with joy and confidence, and led to a material enlargement of their maritime confederacy. Phocion, who had charge of a squadron detached from the fleet of Chabrias, also sailed victorious round the Ægean, took twenty triremes, three thousand prisoners, with one hundred and ten talents in money, and annexed seventeen cities to the confederacy. Timotheus, the son of Conon, was sent with the fleet of Chabrias, to circumnavigate the Peloponnesus, and alarm the coast of Laconia. The important island of Corcyra entered into the confederation, and another Spartan fleet, under Nicolochus, was defeated, so that the Athenians became once again the masters of the sea. But having regained their ascendency, Athens became jealous of the growing power of Thebes, now mistress of Bœotia, and this jealousy, inexcusable after such reverses, was increased when Pelopidas gained a great victory over the Lacedæmonians near Tegyra, which led to the expulsion of their enemies from all parts of Bœotia, except Orchomenus, on the borders of Phocis. That territory was now attacked by the victorious Thebans, upon which Athens made peace with the Lacedæmonians.

The jealousy of the Grecian republics.

It would thus seem that the ancient Grecian States were perpetually jealous of any ascendant power, and their policy was not dissimilar from that which was inaugurated in modern Europe since the treaty of Westphalia— called the balance of power. Greece, thus far, was not ambitious to extend her rule over foreign nations, but sought an autonomous independence of the several States of which she was composed. Had Greece united under the leadership of Sparta or Athens, her foreign conquests might have been considerable, and her power, centralized and formidable, might have been a match even for the Romans. But in the anxiety of each State to secure its independence, there were perpetual and unworthy jealousies of each rising State, when it had reached a certain point of prosperity and glory. Hence the various States united under Sparta, in the Peloponnesian war, to subvert the ascendency of Athens. And when Sparta became the dominant power of Greece, Athens unites with Thebes to break her domination. And now Athens becomes jealous of Thebes, and makes peace with Sparta, in the same way that England in the eighteenth century united with Holland and other States, to prevent the aggrandizement of France, as different powers of Europe had previously united to prevent the ascendency of Austria.

Humiliation of Sparta.

The Spartan power was now obviously humbled, and one of the greatest evidences of this was the decline of Sparta to give aid to the cities of Thessaly, in danger of being conquered by Jason, the despot of Pheræ, whose formidable strength was now alarming Northern Greece.

Hostilities between Athens and Sparta. Peace between Athens and Sparta.

The peace which Sparta had concluded with Athens was of very short duration. The Lacedæmonians resolved to attack Corcyra, which had joined the Athenian confederation. An armament collected from the allies, under Mnasippus, in the spring of B.C. 373, proceeded against Corcyra. The inhabitants, driven within the walls of the city, were in danger of famine, and invoked Athenian aid. Before it arrived, however, the Corcyræans made a successful sally upon the Spartan troops, over-confident of victory, in which Mnasippus was slain, and the city became supplied with provisions. After the victory, Iphicrates, in command of the Athenian fleet, which had been delayed, arrived and captured the ships which Dionysius of Syracuse had sent to the aid of the Lacedæmonians. These reverses induced the Spartans to send Antalcidas again to Persia to sue for fresh intervention, but the satraps, having nothing more to gain from Sparta, refused aid. But Athens was not averse to peace, since she no longer was jealous of Sparta, and was jealous of Thebes. In the mean time Thebes seized Platæa, a town of Bœotia, unfriendly to her ascendency, and expelled the inhabitants who sought shelter in Athens, and increased the feeling of disaffection toward the rising power. This event led to renewed negotiations for peace between Athens and Sparta, which was effected at a congress held in the latter city. The Athenian orator Callistratus, one of the envoys, proposed that Sparta and Athens should divide the headship of Greece between them, the former having the supremacy on land, the latter on the sea. Peace was concluded on the basis of the autonomy of each city.

Epaminondas at the congress of Sparta.

Epaminondas was the Theban deputy to this congress. He insisted on taking the oath in behalf of the Bœotian confederation, even as Sparta had done for herself and allies. But Agesilaus required he should take the oath for Thebes alone, as Athens had done for herself alone. He refused, and made himself memorable for his eloquent speeches, in which he protested against the pretensions of Sparta. "Why," he maintained, "should not Thebes respond for Bœotia, as well as Sparta for Laconia, since Thebes had the same ascendency in Bœotia that Sparta had in Laconia?" Agesilaus, at last, indignantly started from his seat, and said to Epaminondas: "Speak plainly. Will you, or will you not, leave to each of the Bœotian cities its separate autonomy?" To which the other replied: "Will you leave each of the Laconian towns autonomous?" Without saying a word, Agesilaus struck the name of the Thebans out of the roll, and they were excluded from the treaty.

Renewal of hostilities between Sparta and Thebes.

The war now is to be prosecuted between Sparta and Thebes, since peace was sworn between all the other States. The deputies of Thebes returned home discouraged, knowing that their city must now encounter, single-handed, the whole power of the dominant State of Greece. "The Athenians — friendly with both, yet allies with neither — suffered the dispute to be fought out without interfering." The point of it was, whether Thebes was in the same relation to the Bœotian towns that Sparta was to the Laconian cities. Agesilaus contended that the relations between Thebes and other Bœotian cities was the same as what subsisted between Sparta and her allies. This was opposed by Epaminondas.

Great preparations of Sparta.

After the congress of B.C. 371, both Sparta and Athens fulfilled the conditions to which their deputies had sworn. The latter gave orders to Iphicrates to return home with his fleet, which had threatened the Lacedæmonian coast; the former recalled her harmosts and garrisons from all the cities which she occupied, while she made preparations, with all her energies, to subdue Thebes. It was anticipated that so powerful a State as Sparta would soon accomplish her object, and few out of Bœotia doubted her success.

Defeat of a Theban force.

King Cleombrotus was accordingly ordered to march out of Phocis, where he was with a powerful force, into Bœotia. Epaminondas, with a body of Thebans, occupied a narrow pass near Coronea, between a spur of Mount Helicon and the Lake Copais. But instead of forcing this pass, the Spartan king turned southward by a mountain road, over Helicon, deemed scarcely practicable, and defeated a Theban division which guarded it, and marched to Creusis, on the Gulf of Alcyonis, and captured twelve Theban triremes in the harbor. He then left a garrison to occupy the post, and proceeded over a mountainous road in the territory of Thespiæ, on the eastern declivity of Helicon, to Leuctra, where he encamped. He was now near Thebes, having a communication with Sparta through the port of Creusis. The Thebans were dismayed, and it required all the tact and eloquence of Epaminondas and Pelopidas to rally them. They marched out at length from Thebes, under their seven bœotrarchs, and posted themselves opposite the Spartan camp. Epaminondas was one of these generals, and urged immediate battle, although the Theban forces were inferior.

Military tactics of Epaminondas. Great victory obtained by Thebes.

It was through him that a change took place in the ordinary Grecian tactics. It was customary to fight simultaneously along the whole line, in which the opposing armies were drawn up. Departing from this custom, he disposed his troops obliquely, or in échelon, placing on his left chosen Theban hoplites to the depth of fifty, so as to bear with impetuous force on the Spartan right, while his centre and right were kept back for awhile from action. Such a combination, so unexpected, was completely successful. The Spartans could not resist the concentrated and impetuous assault made on their right, led by the Sacred Band, with fifty shields propelling behind. Cleombrotus, the Spartan king, was killed, with the most distinguished of his staff, and the Spartans were driven back to their camp. The allies, who fought without spirit or heart, could not be rallied. The victory was decisive, and made an immense impression throughout Greece; for it was only twenty days since Epaminondas had departed from Sparta, excluded from the general peace. The Spartans bore the defeat with their characteristic fortitude, but their prestige was destroyed. A new general had arisen in Bœotia, who carried every thing before him. The Athenians heard of the victory with ill-concealed jealousy of the rising power.

The Spartans evacuate Bœotia.

Jason, the tyrant of Pheræ, now joined the Theban camp and the Spartan army was obliged to evacuate Bœotia. The great victory of Leuctra gave immense extension to the Theban power, and broke the Spartan rule north of the Peloponnesus. All the cities of Bœotia acknowledged the Theban supremacy, while the harmosts which Sparta had placed in the Grecian cities were forced to return home. Sparta was now discouraged and helpless, and even many Peloponnesian cities put themselves under the presidency of Athens. None were more affected by the Spartan overthrow than the Arcadians, whose principal cities had been governed by an oligarchy in the interest of Sparta, such as Tegea and Orchomenus, while Mantinea was broken up into villages. The Arcadians, free from Spartan governors, and ceasing to look henceforth for victory and plunder in the service of Sparta, became hostile, and sought their political independence. A Pan-Arcadian union was formed.

Agesilaus marches into Arcadia. Epaminondas invades Sparta.

Sparta undertook to recover her supremacy over Arcadia, and Agesilaus was sent to Mantinea with a considerable force, for the city had rebuilt its walls, and resumed its former consolidation, which was a great offense in the eyes of Sparta. The Arcadians, invaded by Spartans, first invoked the aid of Athens, which being refused, they turned to Thebes, and Epaminondas came to their relief with a great army of auxiliaries—Argeians, Elians, Phocians, Locrians, as well as Thebans, for his fame now drew adventurers from every quarter to his standard. These forces urged him to invade Laconia itself, and his great army, in four divisions, penetrated the country through different passes. He crossed the Eurotas and advanced to Sparta, which was in the greatest consternation, not merely from the near presence of Epaminondas with a powerful army of seventy thousand men, but from the discontent of the Helots. But Agesilaus put the city in the best possible defense, while every means were used to secure auxiliaries from other cities. Epaminondas dared not to attempt to take the city by storm, and after ravaging Laconia, returned into Arcadia. This insult to Sparta was of great moral force, and was an intense humiliation, greater even than that felt after the battle of Leuctra.

Restores the independence of Messenia. The Spartan kingdom dismembered.

This expedition, though powerless against Sparta herself, prepared Epaminondas to execute the real object which led to the assistance of the Arcadians. This was the re-establishment of Messenia, which had been conquered by Sparta two hundred years before. The new city of Messenia was built on the site of Mount Ithome, where the Messenians had defended themselves in their long war against the Laconians, and the best masons and architects were invited from all Greece to lay out the streets, and erect the public edifices, while Epaminondas superintended the fortifications. All the territory westward and south of Ithome—the southwestern corner of the Peloponnesus, richest on the peninsula, was now subtracted from Sparta, while the country to the east was protected by the new city in Arcadia, Megalopolis, which the Arcadians built. This wide area, the best half of the Spartan territory, was thus severed from Sparta, and was settled by Helots, who became free men, with inextinguishable hatred of their old masters. But these Helots were probably the descendants of the old Messenians whom Sparta had conquered. This renovation of Messenia, and the building of the two cities, Messenia and Megalopolis, was the work of Epaminondas, and were the most important events of the day. The latter city was designed as the centre of a new confederacy, comprising all Arcadia.

Sparta forms an alliance with Athens.

Sparta being thus crippled, dismembered, and humbled, Epaminondas evacuated the Peloponnesus, filled, however, with undiminished hostility. Sparta condescends to solicit aid from Athens, so completely was its power broken by the Theban State, and Athens consents to assist her, in the growing fear and jealousy of Thebes, thereby showing that the animosities of the Grecian States grew out of political jealousy rather than from revenge or injury. To rescue Sparta was a wise policy, if it were necessary to maintain a counterpoise against the ascendency of Thebes. An army was raised, and Iphicrates was appointed general. He first marched to Corinth, and from thence into Arcadia, but made war with no important results.

Greece emancipated from the Spartan yoke.

Such were the great political changes which occurred within two years under the influence of such a hero as Epaminondas. Laconia had been invaded and devastated, the Spartans were confined within their walls, Messenia had been liberated from Spartan rule, two important cities had been built, to serve as great fortresses to depress Sparta, Helots were converted into freemen, and Greece generally had been emancipated from the Spartan yoke. Such were the consequences of the battle of Leuctra.

And this battle, which thus destroyed the prestige of Sparta, also led to renewed hopes on the part of the Athenians to regain the power they had lost. Athens already had regained the ascendency on the sea, and looked for increased maritime aggrandizement. On the land she could only remain a second class power, and serve as a bulwark against Theban ascendency.

Athens seeks to recover Amphipolis. A part of Thessaly under the protection of Thebes.

Athens sought also to recover Amphipolis—a maritime city, colonized by Athenians, at the head of the Strymonican Gulf, in Macedonia, which was taken from her in the Peloponnesian war, by Brasidas. Amyntas, the king of Macedonia, seeking aid against Jason of Pheræ, whose Thessalian dominion and personal talents and ambition combined to make him a powerful potentate, consented to the right of Athens to this city. But Amyntas died not long after the assassination of Jason, and both Thessaly and Macedonia were ruled by new kings, and new complications took place. Many Thessalian cities, hostile to Alexander, the son of Jason, invoked the aid of Thebes, and Pelopidas was sent into Thessaly with an army, who took Larissa and various other cities under his protection. A large part of Thessaly thus came under the protection of Thebes. On the other hand, Alexander, who succeeded Amyntas in Macedonia, found it difficult to maintain his own dominion without holding Thessalian towns in garrison. He was also harassed by interior commotions, headed by Pausanias, and was slain. Ptolemy, of Alorus, now became regent, and administered the kingdom in the name of the minor children of Amyntas—Perdiccas and Philip. The mother of these children, Eurydice, presented herself, with her children, to Iphicrates, and invoked protection. He declared in her favor, and expelled Pausanias, and secured the sceptre of Amyntas, who had been friendly to the Athenians, to his children, under Ptolemy as regent. The younger of these children lived to overthrow the liberties of Greece.

The Theban supremacy in Thessaly and Macedonia.

But Iphicrates did not recover Amphipolis, which was a free city, and had become attached to the Spartans after Brasidas had taken it. Iphicrates was afterward sent to assist Sparta in the desperate contest with Thebes. The Spartan allied army occupied Corinth, and guarded the passes which prevented the Thebans from penetrating into the Peloponnesus. Epaminondas broke through the defenses of the Spartans, and opened a communication with his Peloponnesian allies, and with these increased forces was more than a match for the Spartans and Athenians. He ravaged the country, induced Sicyon to abandon Sparta, and visited Arcadia to superintend the building of Megalopolis. Meanwhile Pelopidas, B.C. 368, conducted an expedition into Thessaly, to protect Larissa against Alexander of Pheræ, and to counterwork the projects of that despot, who was in league with Athens. He was successful, and then proceeded to Macedonia, and made peace with Ptolemy, who was not strong enough to resist him, taking, among other hostages to Thebes, Philip, the son of Amyntas. The Thebans and Macedonians now united to protect the freedom of Amphipolis against

Athens. Pelopidas returned to Thebes, having extended her ascendency over both Thessaly and Macedonia.

Thebes now aspires to the leadership of Greece.

Thebes, now ambitious for the headship of Greece, sent Pelopidas on a mission to the Persian king at Susa, who obtained a favorable rescript. The States which were summoned to Thebes to hear the rescript read refused to accept it; and even the Arcadian deputies protested against the headship of Thebes. So powerful were the sentiments of all the Grecian States, from first to last, against the complete ascendency of any one power, either Athens, or Sparta, or Thebes. The rescript was also rejected at Corinth. Pelopidas was now sent to Thessaly to secure the recognition of the headship of Thebes; but in the execution of his mission he was seized and detained by Alexander of Pheræ.

The Thebans then sent an army into Thessaly to rescue Pelopidas. Unfortunately, Epaminondas did not command it. Having given offense to his countrymen, he was not elected that year as bœotrarch, and served in the ranks as a private hoplite. Alexander, assisted by the Athenians, triumphed in his act of treachery, and treated his illustrious captive with harshness and cruelty, and the Theban army, unsuccessful, returned home.

Thebes rescues Pelopidas. Complicated political relations of the Grecian States.

The Thebans then sent another army, under Epaminondas, into Thessaly for the rescue of Pelopidas, and such was the terror of his name, that Alexander surrendered his prisoner, and sought to make peace. But the rescue of Pelopidas disabled Thebes from prosecuting the war in the Peloponnesus. As soon, however, as this was effected, Epaminondas was sent as an envoy into Arcadia to dissuade her from a proposed alliance with Athens, and there had to contend with the Athenian orator Callistratus. The complicated relations of the different Grecian States now became so complicated, that it is useless, in a book like this, to attempt to unravel them. Negotiations between Athens and Persia, the efforts of Corinth and other cities to secure peace, the ambition of Athens to maintain ascendency on the sea, the creation of a Theban navy—these and other events must be passed by.

But we can not omit to notice the death of Pelopidas.

Death of Pelopidas. Grief of the Thebans.

He had been sent with an army into Thessaly against Alexander of Pheræ, who was at the height of his power, holding in dependence a considerable part of Thessaly, and having Athens for an ally. In a battle which took place between Pelopidas and Alexander, near Pharsalus, the Thessalians were routed. Pelopidas, seeing his enemy apparently within his reach, and remembering only his injuries, sallied forth, unsupported, like Cyrus, on the field of Cunaxa, at the sight of his brother, to attack him when surrounded by his guards, and fell while fighting bravely. Nothing could exceed the grief of the victorious Thebans in view of this disaster, which was the result of inexcusable rashness. He was endeared by uninterrupted services from the day he slew the Spartan governors and recovered the independence of his city. He had taken a prominent part in all the struggles which had raised Thebes to unexpected glory, and was second in abilities to Epaminondas alone, whom he ever cherished with more than fraternal friendship, without envy and without reproach. All that Thebes could do was to revenge his death. Alexander was stripped of all his Thessalian dependencies, and confined to his own city, with its territory, near the Gulf of Pegasæ.

Orchomenus revolts from Thebes. Unfortunate fate of the city.

It was while Pelopidas was engaged in his Thessalian campaign, that a conspiracy against the power of Thebes took place in the second city of Bœotia—Orchomenus, on Lake Copais. This city was always disaffected, and in the absence of Pelopidas in Thessaly, and Epaminondas with a fleet on the Hellespont, some three hundred of the richest citizens undertook to overthrow the existing government. The plot was discovered before it was ripe for execution, the conspirators were executed, the town itself was destroyed, the male adults were killed, and the women and children were sold into slavery. This barbarous act was but the result of long pent up Theban hatred, but it kindled a great excitement against Thebes throughout Greece. The city, indeed, sympathized with the Spartan cause, and would have been destroyed before but for the intercession of Epaminondas, whose policy was ever lenient and magnanimous. It was a matter of profound grief to this general, now re-elected as one of the bœotarchs, that Thebes had stained her name by this cruel vengeance, since he knew it would intensify the increasing animosity against the power which had arrived so suddenly to greatness.

Renewed hostilities. Epaminondas attempts to surprise Sparta. His great victory over the Lacedæmonians at Mantinea. His death.

Hostilities, as he feared, soon broke out with increased bitterness between Sparta and Thebes. And these were precipitated by difficulties in Arcadia, then at war with Elis, and the appropriation of the treasures of Olympia by the Arcadians. Sparta, Elis, and Achaia formed an alliance, and Arcadia invoked the aid of Thebes. The result was that Epaminondas marched with a large army into the Peloponnesus, and mustered his forces at Tegea, which was under the protection of Thebes. His army comprised, besides Thebans and Bœotians, Eubœans, Thessalians, Locrians, and other allies from Northern Greece. The Spartans, allied with Elians, Achæans, and Athenians, united at Mantinea, under the command of Agesilaus, now an old man of eighty, but still vigorous and strong. Tegea lay in the direct road from Sparta to Mantinea, and while Agesilaus was moving by a more circuitous route to the westward, Epaminondas resolved to attempt a surprise on Sparta. This movement was unexpected, and nothing saved Sparta except the accidental information which Agesilaus received of the movement from a runner, in time to turn back to Sparta and put it in a condition of defense before Epaminondas arrived, for Tegea was only about thirty miles from Sparta. The Theban general was in no condition to assault the city, and his enterprise failed, from no fault of his. Seeing that Sparta was defended, he marched back immediately to Tegea, and dispatched his cavalry to surprise Mantinea, about fifteen miles distant. The surprise was baffled by the unexpected arrival of Athenian cavalry. An encounter took place between these two bodies of cavalry, in which the Athenians gained an advantage. Epaminondas saw then no chance left for striking a blow but by a pitched battle, with all his forces. He therefore marched from Tegea toward the enemy, who did not expect to be attacked, and was unprepared. He adopted the same tactics that gave him success at Leuctra, and posted himself, with his Theban phalanx on the left, against the opposing right, and bore down with irresistible force, both of infantry and cavalry, while he kept back the centre and right, composed of his trustworthy troops, until the battle should be decided. His column, not far from fifty shields in depth, pressed upon the opposing column of only eight shields in depth, like the prow of a trireme impelled against the midships of an antagonist in a sea-fight. This mode of attack was completely successful. Epaminondas broke through the Lacedæmonian line, which turned and fled, but he himself, pressing on to the attack, at the head of his column, was mortally wounded. He was pierced with a spear—the handle broke, leaving the head sticking in his breast. He at once fell, and his own troops gathered around his bleeding body, giving full expression to their grief and lamentations.

His great military genius. His character.

Thebes gained, by the battle of Mantinea, the preservation of her Arcadian allies and of her anti-Spartan frontier; while Sparta lost, beyond hope, her ancient prestige and power. But the victory was dearly purchased by the death of Epaminondas, who has received, and probably deserves, more unmingled admiration than any hero whom Greece ever produced. He was a great military genius, and introduced new tactics into the art of war. He was a true patriot, thinking more of the glory of his country than his own exaltation. He was a man of great political insight, and merits the praise of being a great statesman. He was, above all, unsullied by vices, generous, devoted, merciful in war, magnanimous in victory, and laborious in peace. He was also learned, eloquent, and wise, ruling by moral wisdom as well as by genius. His death was an irreparable loss—one of those great men whom his country could not spare, and whose services no other man could render. Of modern heroes he most resembles Gustavus Adolphus. And as the Thirty Years in Germany loses all its interest after the battle of Leutzen, when the Swedish hero laid down his life in defense of his Protestant brethren, so the Theban contest with Sparta has no great significance after the battle of Mantinea. The only great blunder which Epaminondas made was to encourage his countrymen to compete with Athens for the sovereignty of the seas. That sovereignty was the natural empire of Athens, even as the empire of the land was the glory of Sparta. If these two powers had been contented with their own peculiar sphere, and joined in a true alliance with each other, the empire of Greece might have resisted the encroachments of Philip and Alexander, and defied the growing ascendency of Rome.

Death of Agesilaus. Death of Artaxerxes.

Shortly after the death of Epaminondas, B.C. 362, the greatest man of Spartan annals disappeared from the stage of history. Agesilaus died in Egypt, having gone there to assist the king in his revolt from Persia. He also possessed all the great qualities of a prince, a soldier, a statesman and a man. He, too, was ambitious, but only to perpetuate the power of Sparta. It was his misfortune to contend with a greater man, but he did all that was in the power of a king of Sparta to retrieve her fortunes, and died deeply lamented and honored. Artaxerxes died B.C. 358, after having subdued the revolt of his satraps and of Egypt, having reigned forty-five years, and Ochus succeeded to his throne, taking his father's name.

Philip of Macedon.

Athens recovered, during the wars between Sparta and Thebes, much of her former maritime power, and succeeded in retaking the Chersonese. But another great character now arises to our view—Philip of Macedon, who succeeded in overturning the liberties of Greece. But before we present his career, that of Dionysius of Syracuse, demands a brief notice, and the great power of Sicily, as a Grecian State, during his life.

CHAPTER XXIII
DIONYSIUS AND SICILY

We have already seen how the Athenian fleet was destroyed at the siege of Syracuse, where Nicias and Demosthenes were so lamentably defeated, which defeat resulted in the humiliation of Athens and the loss of her power as the leading State of Greece.

The destruction of this great Athenian armament in September, B.C. 413, created an intoxication of triumph in the Sicilian cities. Nearly all of them had joined Syracuse, except Naxos and Catana, which sided with Athens. Agrigentum was neutral.

Syracuse after the failure of Nicias.

The Syracusans were too much exhausted by the contest to push their victory to the loss of the independence of these cities, but they assisted their allies, the Lacedæmonians, with twenty triremes against Athens, under Hermocrates, while Rhodes furnished a still further re-enforcement, under Dorieus. But the Peloponnesian war was not finished as soon as the Syracusans anticipated. Even the combined Peloponnesian and Syracusan fleets sustained two defeats in the Hellespont. The battle of Cyzicus was even still more calamitous, since the Spartan admiral Mindarus was slain, and the whole of his fleet was captured and destroyed. The Syracusans suffered much by this latter defeat, and all their triremes were burned to prevent them falling into the hands of their enemies, and the seamen were left destitute on the Propontis, in the satrapy of Pharnabazus. These adverse events led to the disgrace of Hermocrates, who stimulated the movement and promised what he could not perform. But his conduct had been good, and his treatment was unjust and harsh. War recognizes only success, whatever may be the virtues and talents of the commanders; and this is one of the worst phases of war, when accident and circumstances contribute more to military rewards than genius itself.

Internal condition of the city.

The banishment of Hermocrates was followed by the triumph of the democratical party, and Diocles, an influential citizen, was named, with a commission of ten, to revise the constitution and the laws. The laws of

Diocles did not remain in force long, and were exceeding severe in their penalties. But they were afterward revived, and copied by other Sicilian cities, and remained in force to the Grecian conquest of the island.

The wars of the Syracusans with Carthage.

The Syracusans then prosecuted war with vigor against Naxos, which sided with Athens, until it was brought to a sudden close by an invasion of the Carthaginians, the ancient foes of Greece. As far back as the year 480 B.C.—that year which witnessed the invasion of Greece by Xerxes—the Carthaginians had invaded Sicily, with a mercenary army under Hamilcar, for the purpose of reinstating the tyrant of Himera, expelled by Theron of Agrigentum. The Carthaginian army was routed, and Hamilcar was slain by Gelon, the tyrant of Syracuse. This defeat was so signal, that it was seventy years before the Carthaginians again invaded Sicily, shortly after the destruction of Athenian power at Syracuse. No sooner was the protecting naval power of Athens withdrawn from Greece, than the Persians and the Carthaginians pressed upon the Hellenic world.

Carthage. Its maritime power.

It is singular that so little is known of the early history of Carthage, which became the great rival of Rome. It was founded by the Phœnicians, and became a considerable commercial city before Athens had reached the naval supremacy of Greece. Her possessions were extensive on the coast of Africa, both east and west, comprehending Sardinia and the Balearic isles. At the maximum of her power, before the first Punic war, the population was nearly a million of people. It was built on a fortified peninsula of about twenty miles in circumference, with the isthmus. Upon this isthmus was the citadel Byrsa, surrounded with a triple wall, and crowned at its summit by a magnificent temple of Æsculapius. It possessed three hundred tributary cities in Libya, which was but a small part of the great empire which belonged to it in the fourth century before Christ. All the towns on the coast, even those founded by the Phœnicians, like Hippo and Utica, were tributary, with the exception of Utica. Although the Carthaginians were averse to land service, yet no less than forty thousand hoplites, with one thousand cavalry and two thousand war chariots, marched out from the gates to resist an enemy. But the Carthaginian armies were mostly composed of mercenaries—Gauls, Iberians, and Libyans, and forming a discordant host in language and custom.

Its political constitution.

The political constitution of Carthage was oligarchal. Two kings were elected annually, and presided over the Senate, of three hundred persons, made up from the principal families. The great families divided between them, as in Rome, the offices and influence of the State, and maintained an insolent distinction from the people. It was an aristocracy, based on wealth, and created by commerce, as in Venice, in the Middle Ages. There was a demos, or people, at Carthage, who were consulted on particular occasions; but, whether numerous or not, they were kept in dependence to the rich families by banquets and lucrative employments. The government was stable and well conducted, both for internal tranquillity and commercial aggrandizement.

Its eminent men.

The first eminent historical personage was Mago, B.C. 500, who greatly extended the dominions of Carthage. Of his two sons, Hamilcar was defeated and slain by Gelon of Syracuse. The other son, Hasdrubal, perished in Sardinia. His sons remained the most powerful citizens of the State, carrying on war against the Moors and other African tribes. Hannibal, grandson of Hamilcar, distinguished himself in an invasion of Sicily, B.C. 410, and with a large army, of one hundred thousand men, stormed and took Selinus, and killed one hundred and sixty thousand of the inhabitants, and carried away captive five thousand more. He then laid siege to Himera, which he also took, and slaughtered three thousand of the inhabitants, in expiation of the memory of his grandfather. These were Grecian cities, and the alarm throughout Greece was profound for this new enemy. These events look place about the time that Hermocrates was banished for an unsuccessful maritime war. Hermocrates afterward attempted to enter Syracuse, but was defeated and slain.

Dionysius at Syracuse.

At this period Dionysius appears upon the stage—for the next generation the most formidable name in the Grecian world. He had none of the advantages of family or wealth—but was well educated, and espoused the cause of Hermocrates, and rose to distinction during the intestine commotions which resulted from the death of Hermocrates and the banishment of Diocles, the lawgiver.

Carthaginians invade Sicily.

In 406 B.C., Sicily was again invaded by a large force from Carthage, estimated by some writers as high as three hundred thousand men, who were chiefly mercenaries. Hannibal was the leader of these forces. All the Greek cities now prepared for vigorous war. The Syracusans sent to Sparta and the Italian Greek cities for aid. Agrigentum was most in danger, and most alarmed of the Greek Sicilian cities. It was second only to Syracuse in numbers and wealth, having a population of eight hundred thousand people, though this is probably an exaggeration. It was rich in temples and villas and palaces; its citizens were wealthy, luxurious, and hospitable.

Rise of Dionysius.

The army of Hannibal advanced against this city, which was strongly fortified, and re-enforced by a strong body of troops from Syracuse, under Daphneus. He defeated the Iberian mercenaries, but did not preserve his victory, so that the Carthaginians were enabled to take and plunder Agrigentum. There was, of course, bitter complaint against the Syracusan generals, who might have prevented this calamity. In the discontent which succeeded, Dionysius was elevated to the command. He procured a vote to restore the Hermocratean exiles, and procured, also, a body of paid guards, and established himself as despot of Syracuse; and he arrived at this power by demagogic arts, allying himself with the ultra democratic party.

Defeated by the Carthaginians.

Soon after his elevation, the Carthaginians advanced, under Imoleo, to attack Gela, which was relieved by Dionysius with a force of fifty thousand men. Intrenching himself between Gela and the sea, opposite the Carthaginians, he resolved to attack the invaders, but was defeated and obliged to retreat, so that Gela fell into the hands of the Carthaginians, who perpetrated their usual cruelties. This defeat occasioned a mutiny at Syracuse, and his house was plundered of the silver and gold and valuables which he had already collected. But he rapidly returned to Syracuse, and punished the mutineers, and became master of the city, driving away the rich citizens who had vainly obstructed his elevation. He abolished every remnant of freedom, and ruled despotically with the aid of his mercenaries, and the common people who rallied to his standard.

Carthaginians make peace.

It was fortunate for him that the Carthaginians, although victors at Gela, made proposals of peace, which were accepted. Dionysius accepted a peace, the terms of which were favorable to Carthage, in order to secure his own power. He betrayed the interests of Sicily to an enemy from selfish and unworthy motives. The whole south of Sicily was consigned to the Carthaginians, and Syracuse to Dionysius.

Dionysius centralizes his power.

Dionysius now concentrated all his efforts to centralize and maintain his power. He greatly strengthened the fortifications of Syracuse. He constructed a new wall, with lofty towers and elaborate defenses, outside the mole which connected the islet Ortygia with Sicily. He also erected a citadel. He then had an impregnable stronghold, powerful for attack and defense. The fortress he erected in the islet of Ortygia he filled with his devoted adherents, consisting mostly of foreigners, to whom he assigned a permanent support and residence. He distributed anew the Syracusan territory, reserving the best lands for his friends, who thus became citizens. By this wholesale confiscation he was enabled to support ten thousand mercenary troops, devoted to him and his tyranny. The contributions he extorted were enormous, so that in five years twenty per cent of the whole property of Syracuse was paid into his hands.

Marches against the Sikels. His critical condition. Strengthens the fortifications of Syracuse. His vast military preparations.

Having thus strengthened his power in Syracuse, he marched against the Sikels, in the interior of the island. But his absence was taken advantage of by the discontented citizens, who attempted to regain their freedom. He returned at once to Syracuse, and intrenched himself in his fortress, where he was besieged by the insurgents. The tyrant was now driven to desperation, and nothing saved him but the impregnable fortifications which he had erected. But his situation was so desperate that his adherents melted away, and he began to abandon all hope of retaining his position. As a last resource, he purchased the aid of a body of Campanian cavalry, in the Carthaginian service, which was stationed at Gela, while he amused the Syracusans, to gain time, by a pretended submission. They agreed to allow him to depart with five triremes, and relaxed the siege, supposing him already subdued. Meanwhile the Carthaginian mercenaries arrived and defeated the Syracusans, already dispersed and divided. Dionysius, finding himself rescued and re-established in his dominions, strengthened the fortifications of Ortygia, and employed his forces, now that Syracuse was subdued, in conquering the Grecian cities of Naxos, Catana, and Leontini. Strengthened at home and in the interior, Dionysius then prepared to attack the Carthaginians, but previously took measures to insure the defensibility of Syracuse. Six thousand persons were employed on a wall three and a half miles in length, from the fort of Trogilus to Euryalus, the summit of the slope of Epipolæ, a high cliff, which commanded the roads to the city. Six thousand teams of oxen were employed in drawing the stones from the quarries. This wall was not like Ortygia, a guard-house against the people of Syracuse, but a defense against external enemies. As it was a great public work of defense, the citizens worked with cheerfulness and vigor, and so enthusiastically did they labor, that the work was completed in twenty days. The city being now impregnable, he commenced preparations for offensive war, and changed his course toward the citizens, pursuing a mild, and conciliatory policy. He made peace with Messene and Rhegium, and married a lady from Locri. He collected all the best engineers, mechanics, and artisans from Sicily and

Italy, constructed immense machines, provided arms from every nation around the Mediterranean, so that he collected or fabricated one hundred and forty thousand shields and fourteen thousand breastplates, destined for his body-guard and officers, together with a vast number of helmets, spears, and daggers. All these were accumulated in his impregnable fortress of Ortygia. His naval preparations were equally stupendous. The docks of Syracuse were filled with workmen, and two hundred triremes were added to the one hundred and ten which already were housed in the docks. The trireme was the largest ship of war which for three hundred years had sailed in the Grecian or Mediterranean waters. But Dionysius constructed triremes with five banks of oars, and had a navy vastly superior to what Athens ever possessed. He now hired soldiers from every quarter, enlisting Syracusans and the inhabitants of the cities depending upon her. He sent envoys to Italy and the Peloponnesus for recruits, offering the most liberal pay.

His marriage. Marches against the Carthaginians.

When all his preparations were completed, he married, on the same day, two wives—the Locrian (Doris), and the Syracusan (Aristomache), and both of these women lived with him at the same table in equal dignity. He had three children by Doris, the oldest of whom was Dionysius the Younger, and four by Aristomache. When his nuptials had been celebrated with extraordinary magnificence, and banquets, and fetes, in which the whole population shared, he convoked a public assembly, and exhorted the citizens to war against Carthage, as the common enemy of Greece, B.C. 397. He then granted permission to plunder the Carthaginian ships in the harbor, and shortly after marched out from Syracuse with an army against the Carthaginians in Sicily, consisting of eighty thousand men, while a fleet of two hundred triremes and five hundred transports accompanied his march along the coast—the largest military force hitherto assembled under Grecian command.

His success.

The first place he attacked was Motya, north of Cape Lilybæum, in the western extremity of the island, all the Grecian cities under Carthaginian leadership having revolted. This city was both populous and wealthy, built on an islet, which was separated from Sicily by a narrow strait two-thirds of a mile in width, bridged over by a narrow mole. The Motyans, seeing the approach of so formidable an army, broke up their mole, and insulated themselves from Sicily. The Carthaginians sent a large fleet to assist Motya, under Imilco, but being inferior to that of Dionysius, it could not venture on a pitched battle. Motya made a desperate defense, but a road across the strait being built by the besiegers, the new engines of war carried over it were irresistible, the town was at length carried and plundered, and the inhabitants slaughtered or sold as slaves.

He returns to Syracuse. His naval defeat at Catana.

The siege occupied the summer, and Dionysius, triumphant, returned to Syracuse. But Imilco being elevated to the chief magistracy of Carthage, brought over to Sicily an overwhelming force, collected from all Africa and Iberia, amounting to one hundred thousand men, afterward re-enforced by thirty thousand more, at the lowest estimate, with four hundred ships and six hundred transports. This army disembarked at Panormus, on the northwestern side of the island (Palermo) retook Motya, regained Eryx, then marched east and captured Messene, at the extreme eastern part of the island near Italy, which prevented Dionysius from getting aid from Italy. The Sikels also rebelled, and Dionysius, greatly disquieted by the loss of all his conquests, and by approaching dangers, strengthened the fortifications of Syracuse, to which he had retired, and made preparations to resist the enemy. He had still a force of thirty thousand foot and three thousand horse, and one hundred and eighty ships of war. He sent also to Sparta for aid. He then advanced to Catana. A naval battle took place off this city, gained by the Carthaginians, from superior numbers. One hundred of the Syracusan ships were destroyed, with twenty thousand men, B.C. 395.

Imilco lays siege to Syracuse.

After this defeat, Dionysius retreated to Syracuse with his land forces, amid great discontent, and invoked the aid of Sparta and Corinth. Imilco advanced also to Syracuse, while his victorious fleet occupied the great harbor—a much more imposing armament than that the Athenians had at the close of the Persian war. The total number of vessels was two thousand. Imilco established his head-quarters at the temple of Zeus Olympius, one mile and a half from the city, and allowed his troops thirty days for plunder over the Syracusan territory; then he established fortified posts, and encircled his camp with a wall, and set down in earnest to reduce the city to famine. But as he was not master of Epipolæ, as Nicias was, Syracuse was able to communicate with the country around, both west and north, and also found means to secure supplies by sea.

Disasters of the Carthaginians. They retire from Syracuse.

Meanwhile the Syracusans defeated a portion of the Carthaginian fleet, and a terrific pestilence overtook the army before the city. The military strength of the Carthaginians was prostrated by the terrible malady, which swept away one hundred and fifty thousand persons in the camp. When thus weakened and demoralized, the Carthaginians were attacked by the Syracusans, and were completely routed. The fleet was also defeated and set on fire, and the conflagration reached the camp, which was thus attacked by pestilence, fire, and sword. The disaster was fatal to the Carthaginians, and retreat was necessary. Imilco dispatched a secret envoy to Dionysius, offering three hundred talents if the fleet was allowed to sail away unmolested to Africa. This could not be permitted, but Imilco and the native Carthaginians were allowed to retire. The remaining part of the army, deprived of their head, was destroyed, with the exception of the Sikels, who knew the roads, and made good their escape.

Death of Imilco.

This immense disaster, greater than that the Athenians had suffered under Nicias, produced universal mourning and distress at Carthage, while the miserable Imilco vainly endeavoring to disarm the wrath of his countrymen, shut himself up in his house, and starved himself to death. This misfortune led also to a revolt of the African allies, which was subdued with difficulty, while the power of Carthage in Sicily was reduced to the lowest ebb. Dionysius was now left to push his conquests in other directions, and Syracuse was rescued from impending ruin.

Financial embarrassments of Dionysius.

Dionysius had now reigned eleven years, with absolute power. The pestilence, and the treachery of Imilco, had freed him of the Carthaginians. But a difficulty arose as to the payment of his mercenaries, which he compromised by giving them the rich territory of Leontini, so that ten thousand quitted Syracuse, and took up their residence in the town. The cost of maintaining a large standing army was exceeding burdensome, and we only wonder how the tyrant found means to pay it, and prosecute at the same time such great improvements.

Makes himself master of Messene.

He now directed his attention to the Sikels, in the interior of the island, and took several of their towns, but from one of them he met with desperate resistance, find came near losing his life from a wound by a spear which penetrated his cuirass. This repulse caused the Carthaginians to rally in the west of the island, under Magon, with an army of eighty thousand. But he was repulsed by Dionysius, and concluded a truce with him, which gave the latter leisure to make himself master of Messene and Taurominium—the two most important maritime posts on the Italian side of Sicily, and thus prepare for the invasion of the Greek cities in the south of Italy, B.C. 391.

Invades Italy.

Dionysius departed from Syracuse, B.C. 389, with a powerful force, to subdue the Italiot Greeks, and laid siege to Caulonia. He defeated their army, and slew their general. The victor treated the defeated Greeks with lenity, and then laid siege to Rhegium, to which he granted peace on severe terms. Caulonia and Hipponeum, two cities whose territory occupied the breadth of the Calabrian peninsula, fell into his hands. Rhegium surrendered after a desperate defense, and Phyton, who commanded the town, was treated with brutal inhumanity. The town was dismantled, and all the territory of Southern Calabria was united to Locri. It was at this time that the peace of Antalcidas took place, which put an end to the Spartan wars in Asia Minor. The ascendant powers of Greece were now Sparta and Syracuse, each fortified by alliance with the other.

Conquers Croton.

Croton, the largest city in Magna Grecia, was now conquered by Dionysius, who plundered the temple of Ilere, near Cape Lacinium, and among its treasure was a splendid robe, decorated in the most costly manner, which the conqueror sold to the Carthaginians, which long remained one of the ornaments of their city. The value and beauty of the robe may be estimated at the price paid for it—one hundred and twenty talents, more than one hundred thousand dollars.

Becomes master of Southern Italy. Hissed at the Grecian games.

He now undertook a maritime expedition along the coast of Latium and Etruria, and pillaged the rich temple at Agylla, stripping it of gold and ornaments to the value of one thousand talents. So great was the celebrity he acquired, that the Gauls of Northern Italy, who had recently sacked Rome, proffered their alliance and aid. Master of Sicily and Southern Italy, he inspired, by his unscrupulous plundering of temples, the greatest terror and dislike throughout Central Greece. He then entered as competitor at the festivals of Greece for the prize of tragic poetry. But so contemptible were his poems, they were disgracefully hissed and ridiculed. Especially those poems which were recited at Olympeia—where he sent legations decked in the richest garments, furnished with gold and silver, and provided with splendid tents—were received with a storm of hisses, which plunged him in an agony of shame and grief, and drove him nearly mad, and made him conscious of the deep hatred which everywhere existed toward him. All his rich displays, which surpassed every thing that had ever before been seen in that holy plain, were worse than a failure—because they came from him. Not all his grandeur in Syracuse could save him from the disgrace and insults which he had received in Olympeia.

Dion.

It was at this time, B.C. 387, that Plato visited Sicily on a voyage of inquiry and curiosity, chiefly to see Mount Ætna, and was introduced to

Dion, then a young man in Syracuse, and brother-in-law to Dionysius. Dion was so impressed with the conversation of Plato, that he invited the tyrant to talk with him also. Plato discoursed on virtue and justice, showing that happiness belonged only to the virtuous, and that despots could not lay claim even to the merit of true courage—most unpalatable doctrine to the tyrant, who became bitterly hostile to the philosopher. He even caused Plato to be exposed in the market as a slave, and sold for twenty minæ, which his friends paid and released him. On his voyage home, through the influence of the tyrant, he was again sold at Egina, and again repurchased, and set at liberty. So bitter are tyrants of the virtues which contrast with their misdeeds; and so vindictive especially was the despot who reigned at Syracuse.

Power and wealth of Dionysius.

Dionysius was now occupied, by the new defenses and fortifications of his capital, so that the whole slope of Epipolæ was bordered and protected by massive walls and towers, and five divisions of the city had each its separate fortifications, so that it was the largest fortified city in all Greece—larger than Athens herself.

Defeated in a war with Carthage.

The plunder the tyrant had accumulated enabled him to make new preparations for a war with Carthage. But he was defeated in a great battle at Cronium, with terrible loss, by the youthful son of Magon, which compelled him to make peace, and cede to Carthage all the territory of Sicily west of the river Halycus, and pay a tribute of one thousand talents.

Again defeated. Gains a prize for poetry, dies from a fit of debauchery. His character.

Very little is recorded of Dionysius after this peace, B.C. 382, for thirteen years, during which the Spartans had made themselves master of Thebes, and placed a garrison in Cadmea. In the year 368 he made war again with Carthage, but was defeated near Lilybæum, and forced to return to Syracuse. In the year 367 it would seem that he was at last successful with his poems, for he gained the prize of tragedy at the Lenæan festival at Athens, which so intoxicated him with joy, that he invited his friends to a splendid banquet, and died from the effects of excess and wine, after a reign of thirty-eight years. He was a man of restless energy and unscrupulous ambition. His personal bravery was great, and he was vigilant and long sighted—a man of great abilities, sullied by cruelty and jealousy. In his spare time he composed tragedies to compete for prizes. No other Greek had ever arrived at so great power from a humble position, or achieved so striking exploits abroad, or preserved his grandeur so unimpaired at his death. But he was greatly favored by fortune, especially when the pestilence destroyed the hosts of Imilco. He maintained his power by intimidation of his subjects, careful organization, and liberal pay to his mercenaries. He cared nothing for money excepting as a means to secure dominion. His exactions were exorbitant, and his rapacity boundless. He trusted no one, and his suspicion was extended even to his wives. He allowed no one to shave him, and searched his most intimate friends for concealed weapons before they were allowed in his presence. He made Syracuse a great fortress, to the injury of Sicily and Italy, and fancied that he left his dominions fastened by chains of adamant. He could point to Ortygia with its impregnable fortifications, to a large army of mercenaries—to four hundred ships of war, and to vast magazines of arms and military stores.

Dion.

He left no successor competent to rivet the chains he had forged. His son Dionysius succeeded to his throne at the age of twenty-five. His brother-in-law Dion was the next prominent member of his family, and possessed a fortune of one hundred talents—a man of great capacity, ambitious, luxurious, but fond of literature and philosophy. He was, however, so much influenced by Plato, whose Socratic talk and democratic principles enchained and fascinated him, that his character became essentially modified, and he learned to hate the despotism under which he grew up, and formed large schemes for political reform. He aspired to cleanse Syracuse of slavery, and clothe her in the dignity of freedom, by establishing an improved constitutional polity, with laws which secured individual rights. He exchanged his luxurious habits for the simple fare of a philosopher. Never before had Plato met with a pupil who so profoundly and earnestly profited from his instructions. The harsh treatment which Plato received from the tyrant was a salutary warning to Dion. He saw that patience was imperatively necessary, and he so conducted as to maintain the favor of Dionysius.

Dionysius II. His feeble character. Plato visits Syracuse. His injudicious teachings.

Dionysius II. was twenty-five years old when his father died, and though he possessed generous impulses, was both weak and vain, given to caprice, and insatiate of praise. He had been kept from business from the excessive jealousy of his father, and his life had been passed in idleness and luxury at the palace of Ortygia. His father's taste for poetry had introduced guests to his table whose conversation opened his mind to generous sentiments, but the indecision of his character prevented his profiting from any serious studies. Dion supported this feeble novice on the throne of his father, and tried to gain influence over him, and frankly suggested the measures to be adopted, and Dionysius listened at first to his wise counsels. Dion wished to make Syracuse a free city, with good laws, to expel the Carthaginians from Sicily, and replant the semi-barbarian Hellenic cities. He also endeavored to reform the life of Dionysius as well as Syracuse, and actually wrought a signal change in his royal pupil, so that he desired to see and converse with the great sage who had so completely changed the life of Dion, and inspired him with patriotic enthusiasm. Accordingly, Plato was sent for, who reluctantly consented to visit Syracuse. He had no great faith in the despot who sought his wisdom, and he did not wish, at sixty-one, to leave his favorite grove, with admiring disciples from every part of Greece, where he reigned as monarch of the mind. He went to Syracuse, not with the hope so much of converting a weak tyrant, as from unwillingness to desert his friend, and be taunted with the impotence of his philosophy. He was received with great distinction at court, and a royal carriage conveyed him to his lodgings. The banquets of the Acropolis became distinguished for simplicity, and the royal pupil commenced at once in taking lessons in geometry. The old courtiers were alarmed, and disgusted. "A single Athenian sophist," they said, "with no force but his tongue and reputation, has achieved the conquest of Syracuse." Dionysius seemed to have abdicated in favor of Plato, and the noble objects for which Dion labored seemed to be on the way of fulfillment. But Plato acted injudiciously, and spoiled his influence by unreasonable vigor. It was absurd to expect that the despot would go to school like a boy, and insist upon a mental regeneration before he gave him lessons of practical wisdom in politics. All the necessary reforms were postponed on the ground that the royal pupil was not yet ripe for them, and every influence was exerted to show him his own unworthiness—that his whole past life had been vicious—delicate ground for any teacher to assume, since he irritated rather than reformed. He was even averse to any political changes until Dionysius had gone through his schooling. Plato also maintained a proud, philosophical dignity, showing no respect to persons, and refusing to the defects of his pupil any more indulgence than he granted to those who listened to his teachings at home.

Banishment of Dion. Second visit of Plato.

Such a mistake was attended soon with difficulties. The old courtiers recovered their influence. Dion was calumniated and slandered, as seeking to usurp the sovereign powers, and that Plato was brought to Syracuse as an agent in the conspiracy. Plato tried to counterwork this mischief, but in vain. Dionysius lost all inclination to reform, and Dion was hated, for he was superior to his nephew in dignity and ability, and was haughty and austere in his manners. He was accordingly banished from Syracuse, and Plato was retained *in the Acropolis*, but was otherwise well treated, and entreated to remain. The tyrant, however, refused to recall Dion, but consented to the departure of Plato. Another visit to Syracuse, which he made with the hope of securing the recall of Dion, was a splendid captivity, and although he was treated with extraordinary deference, he was not at rest until he obtained permission to depart. He had failed in his mission of benevolence and friendship. All the vast possessions of Dion were confiscated, and Plato had the mortification to hear of this injury in the very palace to which he went as a reformer.

Dion in exile. Meditates the overthrow of Dionysius.

Incensed at the seizure of his property, and hopeless of permission to return, and of all those reforms which he had projected, Dion now meditated the overthrow of the power of Dionysius, and his own restoration at the point of the sword. During his exile he had chiefly resided in Athens, enjoying the teaching of his friend Plato, and dispensing his vast wealth in generous charities. Nor did Plato fully approve of his plans for the overthrow of Dionysius, anticipating little good from such violence, although he fully admitted his wrongs. But other friends, less judicious and more interested, warmly seconded his projects. With aid from various sources, he at last could muster eight hundred veterans, with which he ventured to attack the most powerful despot in Greece, and in his own stronghold. And so enthusiastic was Dion, all disparity of forces was a matter of indifference. Moreover, he accounted it glory and honor to perish in so just and noble a cause as the liberation of Sicily from a weak and cruel despot, every way inferior to his father in character, though as strong in resources.

He lands in Sicily.

But the friends of Dion did not dream of throwing away their lives. They calculated on a rising of the Syracusans to throw off an insupportable yoke, and they had utter contempt for the tyrant himself, knowing his drunken habits, and effeminate character, and personal incompetency. So, after ten years' exile, Dion, with his followers, landed in Sicily, at Heracleia, also in the absence of Dionysius, who had quitted Syracuse for Italy, with eighty triremes, so that the city was easy of access.

Enters Syracuse in triumph.

This unaccountable mistake of the tyrant in leaving his capital at such a crisis, was regarded with great joy by the small army of Dion, which marched out at once from Heracleia, and was joined in the Agrigentian territory with two hundred horsemen. As he approached Syracuse, other bands joined him, so that he had five thousand men as he approached the capital. Timocrates, the husband of Dion's late wife, for his wife was taken away from him, was left in command at Syracuse with a large force of mercenaries. But as Dion advanced to the city, there was a general rising of the citizens, and Timocrates was obliged to return, leaving the fortresses garrisoned. Dion entered the city by the principal street, which was decorated as on a day of jubilee, and proclaimed liberty to all. He was also chosen general, with his brother Megacles, and approached Ortygia, and challenged the garrison to come out and fight. He then succeeded in capturing Epipolæ and Eurylæ, those fortified quarters, and erected a cross wall from sea to sea to block up Ortygia.

Demands the abdication of Dionysius.

At the end of seven days, when all these results had been accomplished, Dionysius returned to Syracuse, but Ortygia was the only place which remained to him, and that, too, shut up on the land side by a blockading wall. The rest of the city was in possession of his enemies, though those enemies were subjects. His abdication was imperatively demanded by Dion, who refused all conciliation and promises of reform. Rallying, then, his soldiers, he made a sally to surprise the blockading wall, and was nearly successful, but Dion, at length, repulsed his forces, and recovered the wall. Ortygia was again blockaded, but as Dionysius was still master of the sea, he ravaged the coasts for provisions, and maintained his position, until the arrival of Heraclides, with a Peloponnesian fleet, gave the Syracusans a tolerable naval force. Philistus commanded the fleet of Dionysius, but in a battle with Heraclides, he lost his life.

Dionysius resorts to intrigues. Unpopularity of Dion. But Ortygia surrenders to him.

Dionysius now lost all hope of recovering his power by force, and resorted to intrigues, stimulating the rivalry of Heraclides, and exposing the defeats of Dion, whose arrogance and severity were far from making him popular. Calumnies now began to assail Dion, and he was mistrusted by the Syracusans, who feared only an exchange of tyrants. There was also an unhappy dissension between Dion and Heraclides, which resulted in the deposition of Dion, and he was forced to retreat from Syracuse, and seek shelter with the people of Leontini, who stood by him. Dionysius again had left Ortygia for Italy, leaving his son in command, and succeeded in sending re-enforcements from Locri, under Nypsius, so that the garrison of Ortygia was increased to ten thousand men, with ample stores. Nypsius sallied from the fortress, mastered the blockading wall, and entered Neapolis and Achradina, fortified quarters of the city. The Syracusans, in distress, then sent to Leontini to invoke the aid of Dion, who returned as victor, drove Nypsius into his fortress, and saved Syracuse. He also magnanimously pardoned Heraclides, and prosecuted the blockade of Ortygia, and was again named general. Still Heraclides, who was allowed to command the fleet, continued his intrigues, and frustrated the operations against Dionysius. At last, Ortygia surrendered to Dion, who entered the fortress, where he found his wife and sister, from whom he had been separated twelve years. At first, Arete, his wife, who had consented to marry Timocrates, was afraid to approach him, but he received her with the tenderest emotion and affection. His son, however, soon after died, having fallen into the drunken habits of Dionysius.

Dion master of Syracuse. His mistakes. His death. His character.

Dion was now master of Syracuse, and on the pinnacle of power. His enterprise had succeeded against all probabilities. But prosperity, which the Greeks were never able to bear, poisoned all his good qualities and exaggerated his bad ones. He did not fall into the luxury of his predecessors. He still wore the habit of a philosopher, and lived with simplicity, but he made public mistakes. His manners, always haughty, became repulsive. He despised popularity. He conferred no real liberty. He retained his dictatorial power. He preserved the fortifications of Ortygia. He did not meditate a permanent despotism, but meant to make himself king, with a modified constitution, like that of Sparta. He had no popular sympathies, and sought to make Syracuse, like Corinth, completely oligarchial. He took no step to realize any measure of popular freedom, and, above all, refused to demolish the fortress, behind whose fortifications the tyrants of Syracuse had intrenched themselves in danger. He also caused Heraclides to be privately assassinated, so that the Syracusans began to hate him as cordially as they had hated Dionysius. This unpopularity made him irritable, and suspicious and disquieted. A conspiracy, headed by Callippus, put an end to his reign. He was slain by the daggers of assassins. Thus perished one of the noblest of the Greeks, but without sufficient virtue to bear success. His great defect was inexperience in government, and it may be doubted whether Plato himself could have preserved liberty in so corrupt a city as Syracuse. The character of Dion also changed greatly by his banishment, since vindictive sentiments were paramount in his soul. He had a splendid opportunity of becoming a benefactor to his country, but this was thrown away, and instead of giving liberty he only ruled by force, and moved from bad to worse, until he made a martyr of the man whom once he magnanimously forgave. Had he lived longer, he probably would have proved a remorseless tyrant like Tiberius. So rare is it for men to be temperate in the use of power, and so much easier is it to give expression to grand sentiments than practice the self-restraint which has immortalized the few Washingtons of the world.

Dionysius recovers Ortygia. Syracuse invokes the aid of Corinth. Timoleon sent as general.

The Athenian Callippus, who overturned Dion, remained master of Syracuse for more than a year, but its condition was miserable and deplorable, convulsed by passions and hostile interests. In the midst of the anarchy which prevailed, Dionysius contrived to recover Ortygia, and establish himself as despot. The Syracusans endured more evil than before, for the returned tyrant had animosities to gratify. There was also fresh danger from Carthage, so that the Syracusans appealed to their mother city, Corinth, for aid. Timoleon was chosen as the general of the forces to be sent—an illustrious citizen of Corinth, then fifty years of age, devoted to the cause of liberty, with hatred of tyrants and wrongs, who had even slain his brother when he trampled on the liberties of Corinth—and a brother whom he loved. But he was forced to choose between him and his country, and he chose his country, securing the gratitude of Corinth, but the curses of his mother and the agonies of self-reproach, so that he left for years the haunts of men, and buried himself in the severest solitude. Twenty years elapsed from the fratricide to his command of a force to relieve the Syracusans from their tyrant Dionysius.

His wonderful successes.

Timoleon commenced his preparations of ships and soldiers with alacrity, but his means were scanty, not equal even to those of Dion when he embarked on his expedition. He was prevented with his small force from reaching Sicily by a Carthaginian fleet of superior force, but he effected his purpose by stratagem, and landed at Taurominium under great discouragements. He defeated Hicetas, who had invoked the aid of Carthage, at Adranum, and marched unimpeded to the walls of Syracuse. Dionysius, blocked up at Ortygia, despaired of his position, and resolved to surrender the fortress, stipulating for a safe conveyance and shelter at Corinth. This tyrant, broken by his drunken habits, did not care to fight, as his father did, for a sceptre so difficult to be maintained, and only sought his ease and self-indulgence. So he passed into the camp of Timoleon with what money he could raise, and the fortress was surrendered. A re-enforcement from Corinth enabled Timoleon to maintain his ground.

Dionysius an exile in Corinth.

The appearance of the fallen tyrant in Corinth produced a great sensation. Some from curiosity, others from sympathy, and still more from derision, went to see a man who had enjoyed so long despotic power, now suing only for a humble domicile. But his conduct, considering his drunken habits, was marked by more dignity than was to be expected from so weak a man. He is said to have even opened a school to teach boys to read, and to have instructed the public singers in reciting poetry. His career, at least, was an impressive commentary on the mutability of fortune, to which the Greeks were fully alive.

Timoleon demolishes the stronghold of tyranny. His noble administration.

Timoleon, in possession of Ortygia, with its numerous stores, found himself able to organize a considerable force to oppose the Carthaginians who sought to get possession of the fortress. Hicetas, now assisted by a Carthaginian force under Magon, attacked Ortygia, but was defeated by the Corinthian Neon, who acquired Achradina, and joined it by a wall to Ortygia. But Magon now distrusted Hicetas, and suddenly withdrew his army. Timoleon thus became master of Syracuse, and Hicetas was obliged to retire to Leontini. Timoleon ascribed his good fortune to the gods, but purchased a greater hold on men's minds than fortune gave him by his moderation in the hour of success—a striking contrast to Dion and the elder Dionysius. He invited the Syracusans to demolish the stronghold of tyranny, where the despots had so long intrenched themselves. He erected courts of justice on its site. He recalled the exiles, and invited new colonists to the impoverished city, so that sixty thousand immigrants arrived. He relieved the poverty and distress of the people by selling the public lands, and employed his forces to expel remaining despots from the island.

His great victory over the Carthaginians.

But Hicetas again invited the Carthaginians to Sicily. They came, with a vast army of seventy thousand men and twelve hundred ships, under Hasdrubal and Hamilcar, B.C. 340. Timoleon could only assemble twelve thousand to meet this overwhelming force, but with these he marched against the Carthaginians, and gained a great victory, by the aid of a terrible storm which pelted the Carthaginians in the face. No victory was ever more complete than this at Crimisus. Ten thousand of the invaders were slain, and fifteen thousand made prisoners, together with an enormous spoil.

He lays down his power.

Timoleon had now to deal with two Grecian enemies—Hicetas and Mamercus—tyrants of Leontini and Catana. Over these he gained a complete victory, and put them to death. He then, after having delivered Syracuse, and defeated his enemies, laid down his power, and became a private citizen. But his influence remained, as it ought to have been, as great as ever, for he was a patriot of most exalted virtue, a counselor whom all could trust—a friend who sacrificed his own interests. And he exerted his influence for the restoration of Syracuse, for the introduction of colonists, and the enforcement of wise laws. The city was born anew, and the gratitude and admiration of the citizens were unbounded. In his latter years he became blind, but his presence could not then even be spared when any serious difficulty arose—ruling by the moral power of wisdom and sanctity—one of the best and loftiest characters of all antiquity. And nothing was more remarkable than his patience under contradiction, and his eagerness to insure freedom of speech, even against himself.

His death and character.

Thus, by the virtues and wisdom of this remarkable man, were freedom and comfort diffused throughout Sicily for twenty-four years, until the despotism of Agathocles. Timoleon died B.C. 337—a father and benefactor—and the Syracusans solemnized his funeral with lavish honors, which was attended by a countless procession, and passed a vote to honor him for all future time with festive matches, in music and chariot-races, and such gymnastics as were practiced at the Grecian games. A magnificent monument was erected to his memory. "The mournful letters written by Plato after the death of Dion contrasts strikingly with the enviable end of Timoleon, and with the grateful inscription of the Syracusans on his tomb."

CHAPTER XXIV
PHILIP OF MACEDON

Unexpected Rise of Macedonia.

No one would have supposed, B.C. 400, that the destruction of Grecian liberties would come from Macedonia—a semi-barbarous kingdom which, during the ascendency of Sparta, had so little political importance. And if any new power threatened to rise over the ruins of the Spartan State, and become paramount in Greece, it was Thebes. The successes of Pelopidas and Epaminondas had effectually weakened the power of Sparta. She no longer enjoyed the headship of Greece. She no longer was the leader of dependent allies, submitting to her dictation in all external politics, serving under the officers she appointed, administering their internal affairs by oligarchies devoted to her purposes, and even submitting to be ruled by governors whom she put over them. She had lost her foreign auxiliary force and dignity, and even half of her territory in Laconia. The Peloponnesians, who once rallied around her were disunited, and Megalopolis and Messene were hostile. Corinth, Sicyon, Epidaurus, and other cities, formerly allies, stood aloof, and the grand forces of Hellas now resided outside of the Peloponnesus. Athens and Thebes were the new seats of power. Athens had regained her maritime supremacy, and Thebes was formidable on the land, having absorbed one-third of the Bœotian territory, and destroyed three or four autonomous cities, and secured powerful allies in Thessaly.

Philip of Macedon.

When the battle of Mantinea was fought, at which Epaminondas lost his life, Perdiccas, son of Amyntas, was the king of Macedonia. He was slain, in the flower of his life, in a battle with the Illyrians, B.C. 359. On the advice of Plato, who had been his teacher, he was induced to bestow upon his brother Philip a portion of territory in Macedonia, who for three years preceding had been living in Thebes as a hostage, carried there by Pelopidas at fifteen years of age, when he had reduced Macedonia to partial submission.

Philip at Thebes.

At Thebes the young prince was treated with courtesy, and resided with one of the principal citizens, and received a good education. He was also favored with the society of Pelopidas and Epaminondas, and witnessed with great interest the training of the Theban forces by these two remarkable men—one the greatest organizer, and the other the greatest tactician of the age. When transferred from Thebes to a subordinate government of a district in his brother's kingdom, he organized a military force on the principles he had learned in Thebes. The unexpected death of Perdiccas, leaving an infant son, opened to him the prospect of succeeding to the throne. He first assumed the government as guardian of his young nephew Amyntas, but the difficulties with which he was surrounded, having many competitors from other princes of the family of Amyntas, his father, that he assumed the crown, putting to death one of his half brothers, while the other two fled into exile.

Surrender of Amphipolis.

His first proceeding as king was to buy the Thracians, his enemies, by presents and promises, so that only the Athenians and the Illyrians remained formidable. But he made peace with Athens by yielding up Amphipolis, for the possession of which the Athenians had made war in Macedonia.

Revolt from Athens of Lesbos, Chios, Samos, &c. Death of Timotheus.

The Athenians, however, neglected to take possession of Amphipolis, being engaged in a struggle to regain the island of Eubœa, then under the dominion of Thebes. It also happened that a revolt of a large number of the islands of the Ægean, which belonged to the confederacy of which Athens was chief, took place—Lesbos, Chios, Samos, Cos, and Rhodes, including Byzantium. This revolt is called the social war, caused by the selfishness of Athens in acting more for her own interest than that of her allies, and neglecting to pay the mercenaries in her service. The revolt was also stimulated by the intrigues of the Carian prince, Mausolus. But it was a serious blow to the foreign ascendency of Athens, and in a battle to recover these islands, the Athenians, under Chabrias, were defeated at Chios. They were also unsuccessful on the Hellespont from quarrels among their generals—Timotheus, Iphicrates, and Chares. The popular voice at Athens laid the blame of defeat on the two former unjustly, in consequence of which Timotheus was fined one hundred talents, the largest fine ever imposed at Athens, and shortly after died in exile—a distinguished man, who had signally maintained the honor and glory of his country. Iphicrates also was never employed again. The loss of these two generals could scarcely be repaired. Soon after, peace was made with the revolted cities, by which their independence and autonomy were guaranteed. This was an inglorious result of the war to Athens, and fatally impaired her power and dignity, so that she was unable to make a stand against the aggressions of Philip.

Philip lays siege to Amphipolis. Fall of the city.

One of the first things he did after defeating the Illyrians was to lay siege to Amphipolis, although he had ceded the city to Athens. For this treachery there was no other reason than ambition and the weakened power of Athens. Amphipolis had long remained free, and was not disposed to give up its liberties, and sent to Athens for aid. Philip, an arch politician, contrived by his intrigues to prevent Athens from giving assistance. The neglect of Athens was a great mistake, for Amphipolis commanded the passage over the Strymon, and shut up Macedonia from the east, and was, moreover, easily defensible by sea. Deprived of aid from Athens, the city fell into the hands of Philip, and was an acquisition of great importance. It was the most convenient maritime station in Thrace, and threw open to him all the country east of the Strymon, and especially the gold region near Mount Pangreus. This place henceforward became one of the bulwarks of Macedonia, until the Roman conquest.

Duplicity of Philip.

Having obtained this place, he commenced, without a declaration of war against Athens, a series of hostile measures, while he professed to be her friend. He deprived her of her hold upon the Thermaic Gulf, conquered Pydna and Potidæa, and conciliated Olynthus. His power was thus so far increased that he founded a new city, called Philippi, in the regions where his gold mines yielded one thousand talents yearly. He then married Olympias, daughter of a prince of the Molossi, who gave birth, in the year B.C. 356, to a son destined to conquer the world.

War with Athens.

The capture of Amphipolis by Philip was, of course, followed by war with Athens, which lasted twelve years. And this war commenced at a time Athens was in great embarrassments, owing to the social war.

The sacred war.

But he was aided by another event of still greater importance—the sacred war, which for a time convulsed the Hellenic world, and which grew out of the accusation of Thebes, before the Amphictyonic Council, that Sparta had seized her citadel in time of profound peace. The sentence of the council, that Sparta should pay a fine of five hundred talents, was a departure of Grecian custom, and Sparta refused to pay it, which refusal led to her exclusion from the council, the Delphic temple, and the Pythian games, and this exclusion again arrayed the different States of Greece against each other, as to the guardianship of the Oracle itself.

Philip of Macedon seized this opportunity, when so many States were engaged in war, to prosecute his schemes. He attacked Methone, the last remaining possession of Athens on the Macedonian coast, and captured the city, and then advanced into Thessaly against the despots of Pheræ, who invoked the aid of Onomarchus, now very powerful.

Demosthenes. His accomplishments. His great eloquence.

It was at this time, B.C. 353, that Demosthenes, the orator, appeared before the Athenian people. He was about twenty-seven years of age, and the wealth of his father secured him great advantages in education. His father died while he was young, and his property was confided to the care of guardians, named in his father's will. But they administered the property with such negligence, that only a small sum came to Demosthenes when he attained his civil majority, at the age of sixteen. After repeated complaints, he brought a judicial action against one of the guardians, and obtained verdict against him to the extent of ten talents. But the guardian delayed the payment, and Demosthenes lost nearly all his patrimony. He had, however, received a good education, and in spite of a feeble constitution, he mastered all the learning of the age. His family influence enabled him to get an early introduction to public affairs, and he proceeded to train himself as a speaker, and a writer of speeches for others. He put himself under the teaching of a famous rhetorician, Iænus, and profited by the discourses of Plato and Isocrates then in the height of their fame. He also was a great student of Thucydides, and copied his whole history, with his own hand, eight times. He still had to contend against a poor voice, and an ungraceful gesticulation; but by unwearied labor he overcame his natural difficulties so as to satisfy the most critical Athenian audience. But this conquest in self-education was only made by repeated trials and humiliations, and it is said he even spoke with pebbles in his mouth, and prepared himself to overcome the noise of the Assembly by declaiming in stormy weather on the sea-shore. He sometimes passed two or three mouths in a subterranean chamber, practicing by day and by night, both in composition and declamation, such pains did those old Greeks take to perfect themselves in art; for public speaking is an art, as well as literary composition. He learned Sophocles by heart, and took lessons from actors even to get the true accent. It was several years before he was rewarded with success, and then his delivery was full of vehemence and energy, but elaborate and artificial. But it was not more labor which made Demosthenes the greatest orator of antiquity, and perhaps, of all ages and nations, but also natural genius. His self-training merely developed the great qualities of which he was conscious, as was Disraeli when he made his early failures in Parliament. Without natural gifts of eloquence, he might have worked till doomsday without producing the extraordinary effect which is ascribed to him, for his speeches show great insight, genius, and natural force, as well as learning, culture, and practice; so that they could be read like the speeches of Burke and Webster, with great effect. He had great political sagacity, moral wisdom, elevation of sentiment, and patriotic ardor, as well as art. He would have been great, if he had stammered all his life. He composed speeches for other great orators before he had confidence in his own eloquence.

Phocion.

In contrast with Demosthenes, who was rich, was Phocion, who remained poor, and would receive neither money nor gifts. He went barefoot, like Socrates, and had only one female slave in his household, was personally incorruptible, and also brave in battle, so that he was elected to the office of strategus, or general, forty-five times, without ever having solicited place or been present at the election. He had great contempt of fine speeches, yet was most effective as an orator for his brevity, good sense, and patriotism, and despised the "warlike eloquence, un-warlike despotism, paid speech-writing, and delicate habits of Demosthenes."

Different policy of these two leaders.

This Athenian, with Spartan character and habits, was opposed to the war with Philip, and was therefore the leading opponent of Demosthenes, whose foresight and sagacity led him to penetrate the schemes of the Macedonian king. But the Athenians were generally induced to a peace policy in degenerate times, and did not sympathize with the lofty principles which Demosthenes declared, and hence the influence of Phocion, though of commanding patriotism and morality, was mischievous, while that of Demosthenes was good. The citizens of Athens, enriched by commerce and enervated by leisure, were at this time averse to the burdens of military service, and formed a striking contrast to their ancestors one hundred years earlier, in the time of Pericles. In the time of Demosthenes, they sought home pleasures, the refinements of art, and the enjoyments of cultivated life, not warlike enterprises. And this decline in military spirit was equally noticeable in the cities of the Peloponnesus. And hence the cities of Greece resorted to mercenaries, like Carthage, and intrusted to them the defense of their liberties. The warlike spirit of ancient Sparta and Athens now was pre-eminent in Macedonia, where the people were poor, hardy, adventurous and bold.

It was against these warlike Macedonians, rude and hardy, that the refined Athenians were now to contend, led by a prince of uncommon military talents and insatiable ambition, and who joined craft to bravery and genius. Demosthenes in vain invoked the ancient spirit which had inspired the heroes of Marathon.

Conquests of Philip to Thessaly. Threatens Central Greece.

In the year 383 B.C., Philip attacked Lyeophron, of Pheræ, in Thessaly. Onomarchus, then victorious over the Thebans, advanced against Philip, and defeated him in two battles, so that the Macedonian army withdrew from Thessaly. But Philip repaired his losses, marched again into Thessaly, defeated the Phocians, and slew Onomarchus. His conquest of Pheræ was now easy, and he rapidly made himself master of all Thessaly, and expelled Lycophron. He then marched to Thermopylæ, to the great alarm of Athens, which sent a force to resist him, which force succeeded in defending the pass, and keeping Philip, for a time, from entering Southern Greece. The Phocians also rallied, again availed themselves of the treasure of Delphi, and melted down the golden ornaments and vessels which Crœsus, the Lydian king, had given one hundred years before, among which were three hundred and sixty golden goblets, from the proceeds of which a new army of mercenaries was raised.

No generals fit to cope with him.

The power of Philip was now exceedingly formidable, and his successes inspired great alarm throughout Greece, as would appear from the first Philippic of Demosthenes, delivered in B.C. 352. But the Grecian States had no general able to cope with him on the land, while he created a navy to annoy the Athenians at sea.

Philip conquers the Olynthians. Revolt of Eubœa. Ravages of Philip.

For a time, however, the efforts of Philip were diverted from Southern and Central Greece, in order to conquer the Olynthians. They were his neighbors, and had been his allies; but the expulsion of the Athenians from the coast of Thrace and Macedonia now alarmed the Olynthians, together with the increasing power of Philip, so that they concluded a treaty of peace with Athens. Hostilities broke out in the year 350 B.C., and Demosthenes put forward all his eloquence to excite his countrymen to vigorous war. Athens, partially aroused, sent a body of mercenaries to the assistance of Olynthus, one of the most flourishing of the cities of Chalcidia, southeast of Macedonia. But before effective aid could he rendered, the island of Eubœa, through the intrigues of Philip, revolted from Athens. It was in an expedition to recover that island that Demosthenes served as a hoplite in the army, under Phocion as general. It was not till the summer of B.C. 348 that this territory was recovered by Athens. In the year following, Athens made great exertions in behalf of Olynthus, and amid great financial embarrassments. Three expeditions were sent into Chalcidia, under the command of Chares, numbering altogether four thousand Athenians and ten thousand mercenaries. But they were powerless against the conquering arms of Philip, who completely overran and devastated the peninsula, taking thirty-two cities, and selling the people for slaves. At last Olynthus fell, B.C. 347, and the spoils of this old Hellenic city were divided among the soldiers of the conqueror, who celebrated his victories by a splendid festival.

No such calamity had befallen Greece for a century as the conquest of Chalcidia, and it filled Athens with unspeakable alarms. Æschines, the rival of Demosthenes as an orator, now joined with him in denouncing Philip as the common enemy of Greece. Aristodemus was sent to him with propositions of peace, and Philip professed to entertain them favorably, with his characteristic duplicity.

The temple of Delphi robbed. Encroachments of Philip. His duplicities and intrigues. Philip obtains possession of the pass of Thermopylæ.

Meanwhile the sacred war had impoverished the Phocians, and there were dissensions among themselves. Their temple of Delphi had already been stripped of the enormous sum of ten thousand talents, eleven million five hundred thousand dollars, probably equal in our times to two hundred and thirty million dollars; so that it must have been richer, when the relative value of gold and silver is considered, than any church in Christendom. The treasures of the temple, enriched for three hundred years by offerings from all parts of the world, still enabled the Phocians to maintain war with Thebes. At last the Thebans invoked the aid of Philip, and a Macedonian army, under Parmenio, advanced as far as Thessaly. But the Phocians, in alarm, entreated both Sparta and Athens for assistance. The crisis was great, for if Philip should once secure the Pass of Thermopylæ, all Southern Greece was in imminent danger. The whole defense of Greece now turned upon this Pass, of as much importance to Philip as to Athens and Sparta, for it was the only road into Greece. Envoys were again sent from Athens to Philip, to learn on what conditions peace could be secured, among whom were Demosthenes and Æschines. But he would grant no better terms than that each party should retain what they already possessed, and the Athenians consented. Philip reaped all the advantages of a peace, which gave him the possession of the cities and territory he had taken. The Phocians were left out in the negotiations, a fatal step, since it required the united forces of Greece from preventing the further encroachments of the Macedonian king. He had now leisure for the completion of the conquest of Thrace. When this was completed, he marched toward Thermopylæ, which was held by the Phocians, carefully veiling his real intentions, and even pretending that his advance to the south was for the purpose of reconstituting the Bœotian cities and putting down Thebes. His real object was to surprise the Pass, for he was a man who had very little respect to treaties, promises, or oaths. All this while he contrived to deceive Athens and the Phocians, with the connivance of Æschines, whom he had bribed or cheated. But he did not deceive Demosthenes, who entreated his countrymen to make a stand against him, even at the eleventh hour, for he was then within three days' march of the Pass. But the eloquence and warnings of Demosthenes were in vain. The people went with Æschines, who persuaded them that Philip was friendly to Athens and only hostile to Thebes. It was the design of Philip to detach Athens from the Phocians, and thus make his conquest easier; and he succeeded by his falsehoods and intrigues. Under these circumstances, the Phocians surrendered to Philip the pass, which they ought to have defended at all hazard, and the king retired to Phocis, but still professed the greatest friendship for Athens, with whom he made peace.

And is master of the keys of Greece.

Master now of Phocis, with a triumphant army, he openly joined the Thebans and restored the Temple of Delphi to its inhabitants, and convoked the Amphictyonic Council, which dispossessed the Phocians of their place in the assembly, and conferred it upon Philip. The unhappy Phocians were now reduced to a state of utter ruin. Their towns were dismantled, and their villages were not allowed to contain over fifty houses each. They were stripped, and slain, and their fields laid waste. Philip was now master of the keys of Greece, and the recognized leader of the Amphictyonic Council. Athens had secured an inglorious peace with her enemy, through the corruption of her own envoys, B.C. 346, and was soon to reap the penalty of her credulity and indolence. She allowed herself to be deceived, and Philip, in co-operation with Thebes, the enemy of Athens, presently threw off the mask and disgracefully renewed the war with Athens, He had gained his object by bribery and falsehood. It is mournful that the Athenians should not have listened to the warnings of the most sagacious patriot who adorned those degenerate times, but the influence of Æschines was then paramount, and he was sold to Philip. He cried peace, when there was no peace. The great error of Athens was in not rendering timely assistance to the Phocians, who possessed the Pass of Thermopylæ, although they had brought upon themselves the indignation of Greece by the seizure of the Delphic treasures.

Lamentations of Demosthenes.

The victories and encroachments of Philip, within the line of common Grecian defense, were profoundly lamented by Demosthenes, and he now felt that it was expedient to keep on terms of peace with so powerful and unscrupulous and cunning a man. Isocrates wished Philip to reconcile the four great cities of Greece, Sparta, Athens, Thebes, and Argos, put himself at the head of their united forces, and Greece generally, invade Persia, and liberate the Asiatic Greeks. But this was putting the Hellenic world under one man, and renouncing the independence of States and the autonomy of cities—the great principles of Grecian policy from the earliest historic times, and therefore a complete subversion of Grecian liberties, and the establishment of a centralized power under Philip, whose patrimonial kingdom was among the least civilized in Greece.

Philip's continued encroachments. His insatiate ambition.

The peace between Philip and Athens lasted, without any formal renunciation, for six years, during which the Macedonian king pursued his aggressive policy and his intrigues in all the States of Greece. His policy was precisely that of Rome when it meditated the conquest of the world, only his schemes were confined chiefly to Greece. Every year his power increased, while the States of Greece remained inactive and uncombined—a proof of the degeneracy of the times—certainly in regard to self-sacrifices to secure their independence. Demosthenes plainly saw the approaching absorption of Greece in the Macedonian dominion, unless the States should unite for common defense; and he took every occasion to denounce Philip, not only in Athens, but to the envoys of the different States. The counsels of the orator were a bitter annoyance to the despot, who sent to Athens letters of remonstrance.

Athens at last aroused by Demosthenes. Siege of Perinthus. Philip withdraws from Byzantium.

At last an occasion was presented for hostilities by the refusal of the Athenians to allow Philip to take possession of the island of Halicarnassus, claiming the island as their own. Reprisals took place, and Philip demanded the possession of the Hellespont and Bosphorus, and the Greek cities on their coast, of the greatest value to Athens, since she relied upon the possession of the straits for the unobstructed importation of corn. The Athenians now began to realize the encroaching ambition of Philip, and to listen to Demosthenes, who, about this time, B.C. 341, delivered his third Philippic. From this time to the battle of Chæronea, the influence of Demosthenes was greater than that of any other man in Athens, which too late listened to his warning voice. Through his influence, Eubœa was detached from Philip, and also Byzantium, and they were brought into alliance with Athens. Philip was so much chagrined that he laid siege to Perinthus, and marched through the Chersonese, which was part of the Athenian territory, upon which Athens declared war. Philip, on his side, issued a manifesto declaring his wrongs, as is usual with conquerors, and announced his intention of revenge. The Athenians fitted out a fleet and sent it under Chares to the Hellespont. Philip prosecuted, on his part, the siege of Perinthus, on the Propontis, with an army of thirty thousand men, with a great number of military engines. One of his movable towers was one hundred and twenty feet high, so that he was able to drive away the defenders of the walls by missiles. He succeeded in driving the citizens of this strong town into the city, and it would have shared the fate of Olynthus, had it not been relieved by the Byzantine and Grecian mercenaries. Philip was baffled, after a siege of three months, and turned his forces against Byzantium, but this town was also relieved by the Athenians, and the inhabitants from the islands of the Ægean. These operations lasted six mouths, and were the greatest adverses which Philip had as yet met with. A vote of thanks was decreed by the Athenians to Demosthenes, who had stimulated these enterprises. Philip was obliged to withdraw from Byzantium, and retreated to attack the Scythians. An important reform in the administration of the marine was effected by Demosthenes, although opposed by the rich citizens and by Æschines.

Another sacred war. Ruinous to Grecian liberties.

While these events transpired, a new sacred war was declared by the Amphictyonic Council against the Locrians of Amphissa, kindled by Æschines, which more than compensated Philip for his repulse at Byzantium, bringing advantage to him and ruin to Grecian liberty. But the Athenians stood aloof from this suicidal war, when all the energies of Greece were demanded to put down the encroachments of Philip. As was usual in these intestine troubles, the weaker party invoked the aid of a foreign power, and the Amphictyonic Assembly, intent on punishing Amphissa, sought assistance from Philip. He, of course, accepted the invitation, and marched south through Thermopylæ, proclaiming his intention to avenge the Delphian god. In his march he took Nicæa from the Thebans, and entered Phocis, and converted Elatea into a permanent garrison. Hitherto he had only proclaimed himself as a general acting under the Amphictyonic vote to avenge the Delphian god,—now he constructed a military post in the heart of Greece.

Alliance of Thebes and Athens. Renewed military preparations of Philip.

Thebes, ever since the battle of Leuctra, had been opposed to Athens, and even now unfriendly relations existed between the two cities, and Philip hoped that Thebes would act in concert with him against Athens. But this last outrage of Philip exceedingly alarmed Athens, and Demosthenes stood up in the Assembly to propose an embassy to Thebes with offers of alliance. His advice was adopted, and he was dispatched with other envoys to Thebes. The Athenian orator, in spite of the influence of the Macedonian envoys, carried his point with the Theban Assembly, and an alliance was formed between Thebes and Athens. The Athenian army marched at once to Thebes, and vigorous measures were made at Athens for the defensive war which so seriously threatened the loss of Grecian liberty. The alliance was a great disappointment to Philip, who remained at Phocis, and sent envoys to Sparta, inviting the Peloponnesians to join him against Amphissa. But the Thebans and Athenians maintained their ground against him, and even gained some advantages. Among other things, they reconstituted the Phocian towns. The Athenians and their allies had a force of fifteen thousand infantry and two thousand cavalry, and Demosthenes was the war minister by whom these forces were collected. These efforts on the part of Thebes and Athens led to renewed preparations on the part of Philip. He defeated a large body of mercenaries, and took Amphissa. Unfortunately, the Athenians had no general able to cope with him, and it was the work of Demosthenes merely to keep up the courage of his countrymen and incite them to effort.

Battle of Chæronea. Its decisive character. Macedonian phalanx.

At last, in the month of August, Philip, with thirty thousand foot and two thousand horse, met the allied Greeks at Chæronea, the last Bœotian town on the frontiers of Phocis. The command of the armies of the allies was shared between the Thebans and Athenians, but their movements were determined by a council of civilians and generals, of which Demosthenes was the leading spirit. Philip, in this battle, which decided the fortunes of Greece, commanded the right wing, opposed to the Athenians, and his son Alexander, the left wing, opposed to the Thebans. The Macedonian phalanx, organized by Philip, was sixteen deep, with veteran soldiers in the front. The Theban "Sacred Band" was overpowered and broken by its tremendous force, much increased by the long pikes which projected in front of the foremost soldiers. But the battle was not gained by the phalanx alone. The organization of the Macedonian army was perfect, with many other sorts of troops, bodyguards, light hoplites, light cavalry, bowmen, and slingers. One thousand Athenians were slain, and two thousand more were made captives. The Theban loss was still greater.

Desperate measures of Athens.

Unspeakable was the grief and consternation of Athens, when the intelligence reached her of this decisive victory. A resolution was at once taken for a vigorous defense of the city. All citizens sent in their contributions, and every hand was employed on the fortifications. The temples were stripped of arms, and envoys were sent to various places for aid.

Fall of Thebes.

Thebes was unable to rally, and fell into the hands of the victors, and a Macedonian garrison was placed in the Cadmea, or citadel. From Athens, envoys were sent to Philip for peace, which was granted on the condition that he should be recognized as the chief of the Hellenic world. It was a great humiliation to Athens to concede this, after having defeated the Persian hosts, and keeping out so long all foreign domination. But times had changed, and the military spirit had fled.

Athens was not prostrated by the battle of Chæronea. She still retained her navy, and her civic rights. Thebes was utterly prostrated, and never rallied again.

Philip invades the Peloponnesus. Collects a large force against the Persians.

Philip, having now subjugated Thebes, and constrained Athens into submission, next proceeded to carry his arms into the Peloponnesus. He found but little resistance, except in Laconia. The Corinthians, Argeians, Messenians, Elians, and Arcadians submitted to his power. Even Sparta could make but feeble resistance. He laid waste Laconia, and then convened a congress of Grecian cities at Corinth, and announced his purpose to undertake an expedition against the king of Persia, avenge the invasion of Greece by Xerxes, and liberate the Asiatic Greeks. A large force of two hundred thousand foot and fifteen thousand horse was promised him, and all the States of Greece concurred, except Sparta, which held aloof from the congress. Athens was required to furnish a well equipped fleet. All the States, and all the islands, and all the cities of Greece, were now subservient to Philip, and no one State could exercise control over its former territories.

Death of Philip.

It was in the year B.C. 337, that this great scheme for the invasion of Persia was concerted, which created no general enthusiasm, since Persia was no longer a power to be feared. The only power to be feared now was Macedonia. While preparations were going on for this foolish and unnecessary expedition, the prime mover of it was assassinated, and his career, so disastrous to Grecian liberty, came to an end. It seems that he had repudiated his wife, Olympias, disgusted with the savage impulses of her character, and married, for his last wife, for he had several, Cleopatra, which provoked bitter dissensions among the partisans of the two queens, and also led to a separation between himself and his son Alexander, although a reconciliation afterward took place. It was while celebrating the marriage of his daughter by Olympias, with Alexander, king of Epirus, and also the birth of a son by Cleopatra, that Pausanias, one of the royal body-guard, who nourished an implacable hatred of Philip, chose his opportunity, and stabbed him with a short sword he had concealed under his garment.

Alexander. Character of Philip.

Alexander, the son of Philip by Olympias, was at once declared king, whose prosecution of the schemes of his father are to be recounted in the next chapter. Philip perished at the age of forty-seven, after a most successful reign of twenty-three years. On his accession he found his kingdom a narrow territory around Pella, excluded from the sea-coast. At his death the Macedonian kingdom was the most powerful in Greece, and all the States and cities, except Sparta, recognized its ascendency. He had gained this great power, more from the weakness and dissensions of the Grecian States, than from his own strength, great as were his talents. He became the arbiter of Greece by unscrupulous perjury and perpetual intrigues. But he was a great organizer, and created a most efficient army. Without many accomplishments, he affected to be a patron of both letters and religion. His private life was stained by character or drunkenness, gambling, perfidy, and wantonness. His wives and mistresses were as numerous as those of an Oriental despot. He was a successful man, but it must be borne in mind that he had no opponents like Epaminondas, or Agesilaus, or Iphicrates. Demosthenes was his great opponent, but only in counsels and speech. The generals of Athens, and Sparta, and Thebes had passed away, and with the decline of military spirit, it is not remarkable that Philip should have ascended to a height from which he saw the Grecian world suppliant at his feet.

CHAPTER XXV
ALEXANDER THE GREAT

Alexander the Great. Sent by Providence to do a great work.

We come now to consider briefly the career of Alexander, the son of Philip—the most successful, fortunate, and brilliant hero of antiquity. I do not admire either his character or his work. He does not compare the with Cæsar or Napoleon in comprehensiveness of genius, or magnanimity, or variety of attainments, or posthumous influences. He was a meteor—a star of surprising magnitude, which blazed over the whole Oriental world with unprecedented brilliancy. His military genius was doubtless great—even transcendent, and his fame is greater than his genius. His prestige is wonderful. He conquered the world more by his name than by his power. Only two men, among military heroes, dispute his pre-eminence in the history of nations. After more than two thousand years, his glory shines with undiminished brightness. His conquests extended over a period of only twelve years, yet they were greater and more dazzling than any man ever made before in a long reign. Had he lived to be fifty, he might have subdued the whole world, and created a universal empire equal to that of the Cæsars—which was the result of five hundred years' uninterrupted conquests by the greatest generals of a military nation. Though we neither love nor reverence Alexander, we can not withhold our admiration, for his almost superhuman energy, courage, and force of will. He looms up as one of the prodigies of earth—yet sent by Providence as an avenger—an instrument of punishment on those effeminated nations, or rather dynasties, which had triumphed over human misery. I look upon his career, as the Christians of the fifth century looked upon that of Alaric or Attila, whom they called the scourge of God.

Which was prepared by his father. Extent of the Persian empire. The accumulation of riches in the royal cities.

His conquests and dominions were, however, prepared by one perhaps greater than himself in creative genius, and as unscrupulous and cruel as he. Philip found his kingdom a little brook; he left it a river—broad, deep, and grand. Under Alexander, this river became an irresistible torrent, sweeping every thing away which impeded its course. Philip created an army, and a military system, and generals, all so striking, that Greece succumbed before him, and yielded up her liberties. Alexander had only to follow out his policy, which was to subdue the Persians. The Persian empire extended over all the East—Asia Minor, Syria, Egypt, Parthia, Babylonia, Mesopotamia, Armenia, Bactria, and other countries—the one hundred and twenty provinces of Nebuchadnezzar and Cyrus, from the Mediterranean to India, from the Euxine and Caspian Seas to Arabia and the Persian Gulf—a monstrous empire, whose possession was calculated to inflame the monarchs who reigned at Susa and Babylon with more than mortal pride and self-sufficiency. It had been gradually won by successive conquerors, from Nimrod to Darius. It was the gradual absorption of all the kingdoms of the East in the successive Assyrian, Babylonian, and Persian empires—for these three empires were really one under different dynasties, and were ruled by the same precedents and principles. The various kingdoms which composed this empire, once independent, yielded to the conquerors who reigned at Babylon, or Nineveh, or Persepolis, and formed satrapies paying tribute to the great king. The satraps of Cyrus were like the satraps of Nebuchadnezzar, members or friends of the imperial house, who ruled the various provinces in the name of the king of Babylon, or Persia, without much interference with the manners, or language, or customs, or laws, or religion of the conquered, contented to receive tribute merely, and troops in case of war. And so great was the accumulation of treasure in the various royal cities where the king resided part of the year, that Darius left behind him on his flight, in Ecbatana alone, one hundred and eighty thousand talents, or two hundred million dollars. It was by this treasure that the kings of Persia lived in such royal magnificence, and with it they were able to subsidize armies to maintain their power throughout their vast dominions, and even gain allies like the Greeks, when they had need of their services. Their treasures were inexhaustible—and were accumulated with the purpose of maintaining empire, and hence were not spent, but remained as a sacred deposit.

Philip had aspired to overturn the empire. Knowing its internal weakness.

It was to overthrow this empire that Philip aspired, after he had conquered Greece, in part to revenge the injuries inflicted by the Persian invasions, but more from personal ambition. And had he lived, he would have succeeded, and his name would have been handed down as the great conqueror, rather than that of his more fortunate son. Philip knew what a rope of sand the Persian military power was. Xenophon had enlightened the Greeks as to the inefficiency of the Persian armies, if they needed any additional instruction after the defeat of Xerxes and his generals. The vast armies of the Persians made a grand show, and looked formidable when reviewed by the king in his gilded chariot, surrounded by his nobles, the princes of his family, and the women of his harem. And these armies were sufficient to keep the empire together. The mighty prestige attending victories for one thousand years, and all the pomp of millions in battle array, was adequate to keep the province together, for the system of warfare and the character of the forces were similar in all the provinces. It was external enemies, with a different system of warfare, that the Persian kings had to dread—not the revolt of enervated States, and unwarlike cities. The Orientals were never warlike in the sense that Greece and Rome were. The armies of Greece and Rome were small, but efficient. It was seldom that any Grecian or Roman army exceeded fifty thousand men, but they were veterans, and they had military science and skill and discipline. The hosts of Xerxes or Darius were undisciplined, and they were mercenaries, unlike the original troops of Cyrus.

But this work is reserved for Alexander. Who was the conqueror of the Oriental world? What constituted his military genius.

Now it was the mission of Alexander to overturn the dynasties which reigned so ingloriously on the banks of the Euphrates—to overrun the Persian empire from north to south and east to west—to cut it up, and form new kingdoms of the dismembered provinces, and distribute the hoarded treasures of Susa, Persepolis, and Ecbatana—to introduce Greek satraps instead of Persian—to favor the spread of the Greek language and institutions—to found new cities where Greeks might reign, from which they might diffuse their spirit and culture. Alexander spent only one year of his reign in Greece, all the rest of his life was spent in the various provinces of Persia. He was the conqueror of the Oriental world. He had no hard battles to fight, like Cæsar or Napoleon. All he had to do was to appear with his troops, and the enemy fled. Cities were surrendered as he approached. The two great battles which decided the fate of Persia—Issus and Arbela—were gained at the first shock of his cavalry. Darius fled from the field, in both instances, at the very beginning of the battle, and made no real resistance. The greater the number of Persian soldiers, the more disorderly was the rout. The Macedonian soldiers fought retreating armies in headlong flight. The slaughter of the Persians was mere butchery. It was something like collecting a vast number of birds in a small space, and shooting them when collected in a corner, and dignifying the slaughter with a grand name—not like chasing the deer over rocks and hills.

It was his passion to conquer, not reconstruct.

The military genius of Alexander was seen in the siege of the few towns which *did* resist, like Tyre and Gaza; in his rapid marches; in the combination of his forces; in the system, foresight, and sagacity he displayed, conquering at the light time, marching upon the right place, husbanding his energies, wasting no time in expeditions which did not bear on the main issue, and concentrating his men on points which were vital and important. Philip, if he had lived, might have conquered the Persian empire; but he would not have conquered so rapidly as Alexander, who knew no rest, and advanced from conquering to conquer, in some cases without ulterior objects, as in the Indian campaigns—simply from the love and excitement of conquest. He only needed time. He met no enemies who could oppose him—more, I apprehend, from the want of discipline among his enemies, than from any irresistible strength of his soldiers, for he embodied the conquered soldiers in his own army, and they fought like his own troops, when once disciplined. Nor did he dream of reconstruction, or building up a great central power. He would, if he had lived, have overrun Arabia, and then Italy, and Gaul. But he did not live to measure his strength with the Romans. His mission was ended when he had subdued the Persian world. And he left no successor. His empire was divided among his generals, and new kingdoms arose on the ruins of the Persian empire.

His early history. His conquest of the Grecian States.

"Alexander was born B.C. 356, and like his father, Philip, was not Greek, but a Macedonian and Epirot, only partially imbued with Grecian sentiment and intelligence." He inherited the ambition of Philip, and the violent and headstrong temperament of his furious mother, Olympias. His education was good, and he was instructed by his Greek tutors in the learning common to Grecian princes. His taste inclined him to poetry and literature, rather than to science and philosophy. At thirteen he was intrusted to the care of the great Aristotle, and remained under his teaching three years. At sixteen he was left regent of the Macedonian kingdom, whose capital was Pella, while his father was absent in the siege of Byzantium. At eighteen he commanded one of the wings of the army at the battle of Chæronea. His prospects were uncertain up to the very day when Philip was assassinated, on account of family dissensions, and the wrath of his father, whom he had displeased. But he was proclaimed king on the death of Philip, B.C., 336 and celebrated his funeral with great magnificence, and slew many of his murderers. The death of Philip had excited aspirations of freedom in the Grecian States, but there was no combination to throw off the Macedonian yoke. Alexander well understood the discontent of Greece, and his first object was to bring it to abject submission. With the army of his father he marched from State to State, compelling submission, and punishing with unscrupulous cruelty all who resisted. After displaying his forces in various portions of the Peloponnesus, he repaired to Corinth and convened the deputies from the Grecian cities, and was chosen to the headship of Greece, as his father, Philip, had been. He was appointed the keeper of the peace of Greece. Each Hellenic city was declared free, and in each the existing institutions were recognized, but no new despot was to be established, and each city was forbidden to send armed vessels to the harbor of any other, or build vessels, or engage seamen there. Such was the melancholy degradation of the Grecian world. Its freedom was extinguished, and there was no hope of escaping the despotism of Macedonia, but by invoking aid from the Persian king. Had he been wise, he would have subsidized the Greeks with a part of his vast treasures, and raised a force in Greece able to cope with Alexander. But he was doomed, and the Macedonian king was left free to complete the conquest of all the States. He first marched across Mount Hæmus, and subdued the Illyrians, Pæonians, and Thracians. He even crossed the Danube, and defeated the Gætæ.

He annihilates the Theban power. Moral effect of his merciless severity. He is master of Greece.

Just as he had completed the conquest of the barbarians north of Macedonia, he heard that the Thebans had declared their independence, being encouraged by his long absence in Thrace, and by reports of his death. But he suddenly appeared with his victorious army, and as the Thebans had no generals equal to Pelopidas and Epaminondas, they were easily subdued. Thebes was taken by assault, and the population was massacred — even women and children, whether in their houses or in temples. Thirty thousand captives were reserved for sale. The city was razed to the ground, and the Cadmea alone was preserved for a Macedonian garrison. The Theban territory was partitioned among the reconstructed cities of Orchomenus and Platæa. This severity was unparalleled in the history of Greece, but the remorseless conqueror wished to strike with terror all other cities, and prevent rebellion. He produced the effect he desired. All the cities of Greece hastened to make peace with so terrible an enemy. He threatened a like doom on Athens because she refused to surrender the anti-Macedonian leaders, including Demosthenes, but was finally appeased through the influence of Phocion, since he did not wish to drive Athens to desperate courses, which might have impeded his contemplated conquest of Persia, for the city was still strong in naval defenses, and might unite with the Persian king. So Athens was spared, but the empire of Thebes was utterly destroyed. He then repaired to Corinth to make arrangements for his Persian campaign, and while in that city he visited the cynical philosopher, Diogenes, who lived in a tub. It is said that when the philosopher was asked by Alexander if he wished any thing, he replied: "Nothing, except that you would stand a little out of my sunshine"—a reply which extorted from the conqueror the remark: "If I were not Alexander, I would be Diogenes."

Prepares to invade Persia.

It took Alexander a year and a few months to crush out what little remained of Grecian freedom, subdue the Thracians, and collect forces for his expedition into Persia. In the spring of 334 B.C., his army was mustered between Pella and Amphipolis, while his fleet was at hand to render assistance. In April he crossed the strait from Sestos to Abydos, and never returned to his own capital—Pella—or to Europe. The remainder of his life, eleven years and two months, was spent in Asia, in continued and increasing conquests; and these were on such a gigantic scale that Greece dwindled into insignificance.

He marshals his forces in Asia. His phalanx and the armor of his troops.

When marshalled on the Asiatic shore, the army of Alexander presented a total of thirty thousand infantry, and four thousand five hundred cavalry—a small force, apparently, to overthrow the most venerable and extensive empire in the world. But these troops were veterans, trained by Philip, and commanded by able generals. Of these troops twelve thousand were Macedonians, armed with the sarissa, a long pike, which made the phalanx, sixteen deep, so formidable. The sarissa was twenty-one feet in length, and so held by both hands as to project fifteen feet before the body of the pikeman. The soldier of the phalanx was also provided with a short sword, a circular shield, a breastplate, leggings, and broad-brimmed hat. But, besides the phalanx of heavy armed men, there were hoplites lightly armed, hypaspists for the assault of walled places, and troops with javelins and with bows. The cavalry was admirable, distributed into squadrons, among whom were the body-guards—all promoted out of royal pages and the picked men of the army, sons of the chief people in Macedonia, and these were heavily armed.

His generals.

The generals who served under Alexander were all Macedonians, and had been trained by Philip. Among these were Hephæstion, the intimate personal friend of Alexander, Ptolemy, Perdiccas, Antipater, Clitus, Parmenio, Philotas, Nicanor, Seleucus, Amyntas, Phillipes, Lysimachus, Antigonas, most of whom reached great power. Parmenio and Antipater were the highest in rank, the latter of whom was left as viceroy of Macedonia, Eumenes was the private secretary of Alexander, the most long-headed man in his army.

Alexander is unobstructed in crossing the Hellespont. Error of the Persians. Battle of the Granicus. Alexander dispenses with his fleet. Fall of Miletus.

Alexander had landed, unopposed, against the advice of Memnon and Mentor—two Rhodians, in the service of Darius, the king—descendants of one of the brothers of Artaxerxes Mnemon—the children of King Ochus, after his assassination, having all been murdered by the eunuch Bagoas. As the Persians were superior by sea to the Macedonians, it was an imprudence to allow Alexander to cross the Hellespont without opposition; but Memnon was overruled by the Persian satraps, who supposed that they were more than a match for Alexander on the land, and hoped to defeat him. Arsites, the Phrygian satrap, commanded the Persian forces, assisted by other satraps, and Persians of high rank, among whom were Spithridates, satrap of Lydia and Ionia. The cavalry of the Persians greatly outnumbered that of the Macedonians, but the infantry was inferior. Memnon advised the satraps to avoid fighting on the land, and to employ the fleet for aggressive movements in Macedonia and Greece, but Arsites rejected his advice. The Persians took post on the river Granicus, near the town of Parium, on one of the declivities of Mount Ida. Alexander at once resolved to force the passage of the river, taking the command of the right wing, and giving the left to Parmenio. The battle was fought by the cavalry, in which Alexander showed great personal courage. At one time he was in imminent danger of his life, from the cimeter of Spithridates, but Clitus saved him by severing the uplifted arm of the satrap from his body with his sword. The victory was complete, and great numbers of the satraps were slain. There remained no force in Asia Minor to resist the conqueror, and the Asiatics submitted in terror and alarm. Alexander then sent Parmenio to subdue Dascyleum, the stronghold of the satrap of Phrygia, while he advanced to Sardis, the capital of Lydia, and the main station of the Persians in Asia Minor. The citadel was considered impregnable, yet such was the terror of the Persians, that both city and citadel surrendered without a blow. Phrygia and Lydia then fell into his hands, with immense treasure, of which he stood in need. He then marched to Ephesus, and entered the city without resistance, and thus was placed in communication with his fleet, under the command of Nicanor. He found no opposition until he reached Miletus, which was encouraged to resist him from the approach of the Persian fleet, four hundred sail, chiefly of Phœnician and Cyprian ships, which, a few weeks earlier, might have prevented his crossing into Asia. But the Persian fleet did not arrive until the city was invested, and the Macedonian fleet, of one hundred and sixty sail, had occupied the harbor. Alexander declined to fight on the sea, but pressed the siege on the land, so that the Persian fleet, unable to render assistance, withdrew to Halicarnassus. The city fell, and Alexander took the resolution of disbanding his own fleet altogether, and concentrating all his operations on the land—doubtless a wise, but desperate measure. He supposed, and rightly, that after he had taken the cities on the coast, the Persian fleet would be useless, and the country would be insured to his army.

The siege of Halicarnassus. Conquest of Asia Minor.

Alexander found some difficulty at the siege of Halicarnassus, from the bravery of the garrison, commanded by Memnon, and the strength of the defenses, aided by the Persian fleet. But his soldiers, "protected from missiles by movable pent-houses, called tortoises, gradually filled up the deep and wide ditch round the town, so as to open a level road for his engines (rolling towers of wood) to come up close to the walls." Then the battering-rams overthrew the towers of the city wall, and made a breach in them, so that the city was taken by assault. Memnon, forced to abandon his defenses, withdrew the garrison by sea, and Alexander entered the city. The ensuing winter months were employed in the conquest of Lydia, Pamphylia, and Pisidia, which was effected easily, since the terror of his arms led to submission wherever he appeared. At Gordium, in Phrygia, he performed the exploit familiarly known as the cutting of the Gordian knot, which was a cord so twisted and entangled, that no one could untie it. The oracle had pronounced that to the person who should untie it, the empire of Persia was destined. Alexander, after many futile attempts to disentangle the knot, in a fit of impatience, cut it with his sword, and this was accepted as the solution of the problem.

The Persians resolve on offensive operations.

Meanwhile Memnon, to whom Darius had intrusted the guardianship of the whole coast of Asia Minor, with a large Phœnician fleet and a considerable body of Grecian mercenaries, acquired the important island of Chios, and a large part of Lesbos. But in the midst of his successes, he died of sickness, and no one was left able to take his place. Had his advice been taken, Alexander could not have landed in Asia. His death was an irreparable loss to Persian cause, and with his death vanished all hope of employing the Persian force with wisdom and effect. Darius now changed his policy, and resolved to carry on offensive measures on the land. He therefore summoned a vast army, from all parts of his empire, of five hundred thousand infantry, and one hundred thousand cavalry. An eminent Athenian, Charidemus, advised the Persian king to employ his great treasure in subsidizing the Greeks, and not to dream, with his undisciplined Asiatics, to oppose the Macedonians in battle. But the advice was so unpalatable to the proud and self-reliant king, in the midst of his vast forces, that he looked upon Charidemus as a traitor, and sent him to execution.

Neglect to guard the mountain passes. Which Alexander passes through unobstructed. Infatuation and errors of the Persians. The Persians advance to Issus.

It would not have been difficult for Darius to defend his kingdom, had he properly guarded the mountain passes through which Alexander must needs march to invade Persia. Here again Darius was infatuated, and he, in his self-confidence, left the passes over Mount Taurus and Mount Amanus undefended. Alexander, with re-enforcements from Macedonia, now marched from Gordium through Paphlagonia and Cappadocia, whose inhabitants made instant submission, and advanced to the Cilician Gates—an impregnable pass in the Taurus range, which opened the way to Cilicia. It had been traversed seventy years before by Cyrus the Younger, with the ten thousand Greeks, and was the main road from Asia Minor into Cilicia and Syria. The narrowest part of this defile allowed only four soldiers abreast, and here Darius should have taken his stand, even as the Greeks took possession of Thermopylæ in the invasion of Xerxes. But the pass was utterly undefended, and Alexander marched through unobstructed without the loss of a man. He then found himself at Tarsus, where he made a long halt, from a dangerous illness which he got by bathing in the river Cydnus. When he recovered, he sent Parmenio to secure the pass over Mount Amanus, six days' march from Tarsus, called the Cilician Gates. These were defended, but the guard fled at the approach of the Macedonians, and this important defile was secured. Alexander then marched through Issus to Myriandrus, to the south of the Cilician Gates, which he had passed. The Persians now advanced from Sochi and appeared in his rear at Issus—a vast host, in the midst of which was Darius with his mother, his wife, his harem, and children, who accompanied him to witness his anticipated triumph, for it seemed to him an easy matter to overwhelm and crush the invaders, who numbered only about forty thousand men. So impatient was Darius to attack Alexander that he imprudently advanced into Cilicia by the northern pass, now called Beylan, with all his army, so that in the narrow defiles of that country his cavalry was nearly useless. He encamped near Issus, on the river Pinarus. Alexander, learning that Darius was in his rear, retraced his steps, passed north through the Gates of Cilicia, through which he had marched two days before, and advanced to the river Pinarus, on the north bank of which Darius was encamped. And here Darius resolved to fight. He threw across the river thirty thousand cavalry and twenty thousand infantry, to insure the undisturbed formation of his main force. His main line was composed of ninety thousand hoplites, of which thirty thousand were Greek in the centre. On the mountain to his left, he posted twenty thousand, to act against the right wing of the Macedonian army. He then recalled the thirty thousand cavalry and twenty thousand infantry, which he had sent across the river, and awaited the onset of Alexander, Darius was in his chariot, in the centre, behind the Grecian hoplites. But the ground was so uneven, that only a part of his army could fight. A large proportion of it were mere spectators.

The great and decisive battle of Issus.

Alexander advanced to the attack. The left-wing was commanded by Parmenio, and the right by himself, on which were placed the Macedonian cavalry. The divisions of the phalanx were in the centre, and the Peloponnesian cavalry and Thracian light infantry on the left. The whole front extended only one and a half mile. Crossing the river rapidly, Alexander, at the head of his cavalry, light infantry, and some divisions of the phalanx, fell suddenly upon the Asiatic hoplites which were stationed on the Persian left. So impetuous and unexpected was the charge, that the troops instantly fled, vigorously pressed by the Macedonian right. Darius, from his chariot, saw the flight of his left wing, and, seized with sudden panic, caused his chariot to be turned, and fled also among the foremost fugitives. In his terror he cast away his bow, shield, and regal mantle. He did not give a single order, nor did he remain a moment after the defeat of his left, as he ought, for he was behind thirty thousand Grecian hoplites, in the centre, but abandoned himself to inglorious flight, and this was the signal for a general flight also of all his troops, who turned and trampled each other down in their efforts to get beyond the reach of the enemy.

The mistakes of the Persians, and the cowardice of Darius.

Thus the battle was lost by the giving way of the Asiatic hoplites on the left, and the flight of Darius in a few minutes after. The Persian right showed some bravery, till Alexander, having completed the rout of the left, turned to attack the Grecian mercenaries in the flank and rear, when all fled in terror. The slaughter of the fugitives was prodigious. The camp of Darius was taken, with his mother, wife, sister, and children. One hundred thousand Persians were slain, not in *fight*, but in *flight*, and among them were several eminent satraps and grandees. The Persian hosts were completely dispersed, and Darius did not stop till he had crossed the Euphrates. The booty acquired was immense, in gold, silver, and captives.

Important consequences of the battle.

Such was the decisive battle of Issus, where the cowardice and incompetency of Darius were more marked than the generalship of Alexander himself. No victory was ever followed by more important consequences. It dispersed the Persian hosts, and opened Persia to a victorious enemy, and gave an irresistible prestige to the conqueror. The fall of the empire was rendered probable, and insured successive triumphs to Alexander.

The flight and inaction of Darius.

But before he proceeded to the complete conquest of the Persian empire, Alexander, like a prudent and far-reaching general, impetuous as he was, concluded to subdue first all the provinces which lay on the coast, and thus make the Persian fleet useless, and ultimately capture it, and leave his rear without an enemy. Accordingly he sent Parmenio to capture Damascus, where were collected immense treasures. It was surrendered without resistance though it was capable of sustaining a siege. There were captured vast treasures, with prodigious numbers of Persians of high rank, and many illustrious Greek exiles. Master of Damascus, Alexander, in the winter of B.C. 331, advanced upon Phœnicia, the cities of which mostly sent letters of submission. While at Maranthus, Darius wrote to Alexander, asking for the restitution of his wife, mother, sister, and daughter, and tendering friendship, to which Alexander replied in a haughty letter, demanding to be addressed, not as an equal, but as lord of Asia.

The siege of Tyre. Its fall.

The last hope of Darius was in the Phœnicians, who furnished him ships; and one city remained firm in its allegiance — Tyre — the strongest and most important place in Phœnicia. But even this city would have yielded on fair and honorable conditions. This did not accord with Alexander's views, who made exorbitant demands, which could not be accepted by the Tyrians without hazarding their all. Accordingly they prepared for a siege, trusting to the impregnable defenses of the city. It was situated on an islet, half a mile from the main land, surrounded by lofty walls and towers of immense strength and thickness. But nothing discouraged Alexander, who loved to surmount difficulties. He constructed a mole from the main land to the islet, two hundred feet wide, of stone and timber, which was destroyed by a storm and by the efforts of the Tyrians. Nothing daunted, he built another, still wider and stronger, and repaired to Sidon, where he collected a great fleet, with which he invested the city by sea, as well as land. The doom of the city was now sealed, and the Tyrians could offer no more serious obstructions. The engines were then rolled along the mole to the walls, and a breach was at last made, and the city was taken by assault. The citizens then barricaded the streets, and fought desperately until they were slain. The surviving soldiers were hanged, and the women and children sold as slaves. Still the city resisted for seven months, and its capture was really the greatest effort of genius that Alexander had shown, and furnished an example to Richelieu in the siege of La Rochelle.

Offer of Darius. Rejected by Alexander.

On the fall of this ancient and wealthy capital, whose pride and wealth are spoken of in the Scriptures, Alexander received a second letter from Darius, offering ten thousand talents, his daughter in marriage, with the cession of all the provinces of his empire west of the Euphrates, for the surrender of his family. To which the haughty and insolent conqueror replied: "I want neither your money nor your cession. All your money and territory are mine already, and you are tendering me a part instead of the whole. If I choose to marry your daughter I *shall* marry her, whether you give her to me or not. Come hither to me, if you wish for friendship."

Who conquers Egypt.

Darius now saw that he must risk another desperate battle, and summoned all his hosts. Yet Alexander did not immediately march against him, but undertook first the conquest of Egypt. Syria, Phœnicia, and Palestine were now his, as well as Asia Minor. He had also defeated the Persian fleet, and was master of all the islands of the Ægean. He stopped on his way to Egypt to take Gaza, which held out against him, built on a lofty artificial mound two hundred and fifty feet high, and encircled with a lofty wall. The Macedonian engineers pronounced the place impregnable, but the greater the difficulty the greater the eagerness of Alexander to surmount it. He accordingly built a mound all around the city, as high as that on which Gaza was built, and then rolled his engines to the wall, effected a breach, and stormed the city, slew all the garrison, and sold all the women and children for slaves. As for Batis, the defender of the city, he was dragged by a chariot around the town, as Achilles, whom Alexander imitated, had done to the dead body of Hector. The siege of these two cities, Tyre and Gaza, occupied nine months, and was the hardest fighting that Alexander ever encountered.

Founding of Alexandria.

He entered and occupied Egypt without resistance, and resolved to found a new city, near the mouth of the Nile, not as a future capital of the commercial world, but as a depot for his ships. While he was preparing for this great work, he visited the temple of Jupiter Ammon in the desert, and was addressed by the priests as the Son of God, not as a mortal, which flattery was agreeable to him, so that ever afterward he claimed divinity, in the arrogance of his character, and the splendor of his successes, and even slew the man who saved his life at the Granicus, because he denied his divine claims—the most signal instance of self-exaggeration and pride recorded in history, transcending both Nebuchadnezzar and Napoleon.

Alexander marches to the Euphrates.

After arranging his affairs in Egypt, and obtaining re-enforcements of Greeks and Thracians, he set out for the Euphrates, which he crossed at Thapsacus, unobstructed—another error of the Persians. But Darius was paralyzed by the greatness of his misfortunes, and by the capture of his family, and could not act with energy or wisdom. He collected his vast hosts on a plain near Arbela, east of the Tigris, and waited for the approach of the enemy. He had one million of infantry, forty thousand cavalry, and two hundred scythed chariots, besides a number of elephants. He placed himself in the centre, with his choice troops, including the horse and foot-guards, and mercenary Greeks. In the rear stood deep masses of Babylonians, and on the left, and right, Bactrians, Cadusians, Medes, Albanians, and troops from the remote provinces. In the front of Darius, were the scythed chariots with advanced bodies of cavalry.

Marshalling of the armies at Arbela.

Alexander, as he approached, ranged his forces with great care and skill, forty thousand foot and seven thousand horse. His main line was composed, on the right, of choice cavalry; then, toward the left, of hypaspists; then the phalanx, in six divisions, which formed the centre; then Greek cavalry on the extreme left. Behind the main line was a body of reserves, intended to guard against attack on the flanks and rear. In front of the main line were advanced squadrons of cavalry and light troops. The Thracian infantry guarded the baggage and camp. He himself commanded the right, and Parmenio the left.

Utter discomfiture of Darius. His inglorious flight. The battle of Arbela a death-blow to Persia. Military genius of the conqueror.

Darius, at the commencement of the attack, ordered his chariots to charge, and the main line to follow, calculating on disorder. But the horses of the chariots were terrified and wounded by the Grecian archers and darters in front, and most turned round, or were stopped. Those that pressed on were let through the Macedonian lines without mischief. As at Issus, Alexander did not attack the centre, where Darius was surrounded with the choicest troops of the army, but advanced impetuously upon the left wing, turned it, and advanced by a flank movement toward the centre, where Darius was posted. The Persian king, seeing the failure of the chariots, and the advancing troops of Alexander, lost his self-possession, turned his chariot, and fled, as at Issus. Such folly and cowardice led, of course, to instant defeat and rout; and nothing was left for the victor, but to pursue and destroy the disorderly fugitives, so that the slaughter was immense. But while the left and centre of the Persians were put to flight, the right fought vigorously, and might have changed the fortune of the day, had not Alexander seasonably returned from the pursuit, and attacked the left in the rear and flank. Then all was lost, and headlong flight marked the Persian hosts. The battle was lost by the cowardice of Darius, who insisted, with strange presumption, on commanding in person. Half the troops, under an able general, would have overwhelmed the Macedonian army, even with Alexander at the head. But the Persians had no leader of courage and skill, and were a mere rabble. According to some accounts, three hundred thousand Persians were slain, and not more than one hundred Macedonians. There was no attempt on the part of Darius to rally or collect a new army. His cause and throne were irretrievably lost, and he was obliged to fly to his farthest provinces, pursued by the conqueror. The battle of Arbela was the death-blow to the Persian empire. We can not help feeling sentiments of indignation in view of such wretched management on the part of the Persians, thus throwing away an empire. But, on the other hand, we are also compelled to admit the extraordinary generalship of Alexander, who brought into action every part of his army, while at least three-quarters of the Persians were mere spectators, so that his available force was really great. His sagacious combinations, his perception of the weak points of his adversary, and the instant advantage which he seized—his insight, rapidity of movement, and splendid organization, made him irresistible against any Persian array of numbers, without skill. Indeed, the Persian army was too large, since it could not be commanded by one man with any effect, and all became confusion and ruin on the first misfortune. The great generals of antiquity, Greek and Roman, rarely commanded over fifty thousand men on the field of battle; and fifty thousand, under Alexander's circumstances, were more effective, perhaps, than two hundred thousand. In modern times, when battles are not decided by personal bravery, but by the number and disposition of cannon, and the excellence of firearms, an army of one hundred thousand can generally overwhelm an army of fifty thousand, with the same destructive weapons. But in ancient times, the impetuous charge of twenty thousand men on a single point, followed by success, would produce a panic, and then a rout, when even flight is obstructed by numbers. Thus Alexander succeeded both at Issus and Arbela. He concentrated forces upon a weak point, which, when carried, produced a panic, and especially sent dismay into the mind of Darius, who had no nerve or self-control. Had he remained firm, and only fought on the defensive, the Macedonians might not have prevailed. But he fled; and confusion seized, of course, his hosts.

Surrender of Babylon and Susa.

Both Babylon and Susa, the two great capitals of the empire, immediately surrendered after the decisive battle of Arbela, and Alexander became the great king and Darius a fugitive. The treasure found at Susa was even greater than that which Babylon furnished—about fifty thousand talents, or fifty million dollars, one-fifth of which, three years before, would have been sufficient to subsidize Greece, and present a barrier to the conquests of both Philip and Alexander.

The enormous treasures of the Persian Kings.

The victor spent a month in Babylon, sacrificing to the Babylonian deities, feasting his troops, and organizing his new empire. He then marched into Persia proper, subdued the inhabitants, and entered Persepolis. Though it was the strongest place in the empire, it made no resistance. Here were hoarded the chief treasures of the Persian kings, no less than one hundred and twenty thousand talents, or about one hundred and twenty million dollars of our money—an immense sum in gold and silver in that age, a tenth of which, judiciously spent, would have secured the throne to Darius against any exterior enemy. He was now a fugitive in Media, and thither Alexander went at once in pursuit, giving himself no rest. He established himself at Ecbatana, the capital, without resistance, and made preparations for the invasion of the eastern part of the Persian empire, beyond the Parthian desert, even to the Oxus and the Indus, inhabited by warlike barbarians, from which were chiefly recruited the Persian armies.

Successive conquests of Alexander.

It would be tedious to describe the successive conquests of Sogdiana, Margiana, Bactriana, and even some territory beyond the Indus. Alexander never met from these nations the resistance which Cæsar found in Gaul, nor were his battles in these eastern countries remarkable. He only had to appear, and he was master. At last his troops were wearied of these continual marchings and easy victories, when their real enemies were heat, hunger, thirst, fatigue, and toil. They refused to follow their general and king any further to the east, and he was obliged to return. Yet some seven years were consumed in marches and conquests in these remote countries, for he penetrated to Scythia at the north, and the mouth of the Indus to the south.

He kills his friend Clitus. Agony and remorse of Alexander.

It was in the expeditions among these barbarians that some of the most disgraceful events of his life took place. He seldom rested, but when he had leisure he indulged in great excesses at the festive board. His revelries with his officers were prolonged often during the night, and when intoxicated, he did things which gave him afterward the deepest remorse and shame. Thus he killed, with his own hand, Clitus, at a feast, because Clitus ventured to utter some truths which were in opposition to his notions of omnipotence. But the agony of remorse was so great, that he remained in bed three whole days and nights immediately after, refusing all food and drink. He also killed Philotas, one of his most trusted generals, and commander of his body-guard, on suspicion of treachery, and then, without other cause than fear of the anger of his father, Parmenio, he caused that old general to be assassinated at Ecbatana, in command of the post—the most important in his dominions—where his treasures were deposited. He savagely mutilated Bessus, the satrap, who stood out against him in Bactria. Callisthenes, one of the greatest philosophers of the age, was tortured and assassinated for alleged complexity in a conspiracy, but he really incurred the hatred of the monarch for denying his claim to divinity.

He penetrates to the Indus. Porus.

In the spring of B.C. 326, Alexander crossed the Indus, but met with no resistance until he reached the river Hydaspes (Jhylum) on the other side of which, Porus, an Indian prince, disputed his passage, with a formidable force and many trained elephants—animals which the Macedonians had never before encountered. By a series of masterly combinations Alexander succeeded in crossing the river, and the combat commenced. But the Indians could not long withstand the long pikes and close combats of the Greeks, and were defeated with great loss. Porus himself, a prince of gigantic stature, mounted on an elephant, was taken, after having fought with great courage. Carried into the presence of the conqueror, Alexander asked him what, he wished to be done for him, for his gallantry and physical strength excited admiration. Porus replied that he wished to be treated as a king, which answer still more excited the admiration of the Greeks. He was accordingly treated with the utmost courtesy and generosity, and retained as an ally. Alexander was capable of great magnanimity, when he was not opposed. He was kind to the family of Darius, both before and after his assassination by the satrap Bessus. And his munificence to his soldiers was great, and he never lost their affections. But he was cruel and sanguinary in his treatment of captives who had made him trouble, putting thousands to the sword in cold blood.

The soldiers of Alexander refuse to advance further to the East.

As before mentioned, the soldiers were wearied with victories and hardships, without enjoyments, and longed to return to Europe. Hence Sangala, in India, was the easternmost point to which he penetrated. On returning to the river Hydaspes, he constructed a fleet of two thousand boats, in which a part of his army descended the river with himself, while another part marched along its banks. He sailed slowly down the river to its junction with the Indus, and then to the Indian ocean. This voyage occupied nine months, but most of the time was employed in subduing the various people who opposed his march. On reaching the ocean, he was astonished and interested by the ebbing and flowing of the tide—a new phenomenon to him. The fleet was conducted from the mouth of the Indus, round by the Persian Gulf to the mouth of the Tigris—a great nautical achievement in those days; but he himself, with the army, marched westward through deserts, undergoing great fatigues and sufferings, and with a great loss of men, horses, and baggage. At Carmania he halted, and the army for seven days was abandoned to drunken festivities.

He returns to Persepolis. His abandonment to pleasure.

On returning to Persepolis, in Persia, he visited and repaired the tomb of Cyrus, the greatest conqueror the world had seen before himself. In February, B.C. 324, he marched to Susa, where he spent several months in festivities and in organizing his great government, since he no longer had armies to oppose. He now surrounded himself with the pomp of the Persian kings, wore their dress, and affected their habits, much to the disgust of his Macedonian generals. He had married a beautiful captive—Roxana, in Bactria, and he now took two additional wives, Statira, daughter of Darius, and Parysatis, daughter of King Ochus. He also caused his principal officers to marry the daughters of the old Persian grandees, and seemed to forget the country from which he came, and which he was destined never again to see. Here also he gave a donation to his soldiers of twenty thousand talents—about five hundred dollars to each man. But even this did not satisfy them, and when new re-enforcements arrived, the old soldiers mutinied. He disbanded the whole of them in anger, and gave them leave to return to their homes, but they were filled with shame and regret, and a reconciliation took place.

Death of Hephæstion and grief of Alexander.

It was while he made a visit to Ecbatana, in the summer of B.C. 324, that his favorite, Hephæstion, died. His sorrow and grief were unbounded. He cast himself upon the ground, cut his hair close, and refused food and drink for two days. This was the most violent grief he ever manifested, and it was sincere. He refused to be comforted, yet sought for a distraction from his grief in festivals and ostentation of life.

His entrance into Babylon. Splendor of the funeral of Hephæstion. Death of Alexander.

In the spring of B.C. 323, he marched to Babylon, where were assembled envoys from all the nations of the known world to congratulate him for his prodigious and unprecedented successes, and invoke his friendship, which fact indicates his wide-spread fame. At Babylon he laid plans and made preparations for the circumnavigation and conquest of Arabia, and to found a great maritime city in the interior of the Persian Gulf. But before setting out, he resolved to celebrate the funeral obsequies of Hephæstion with unprecedented splendor. The funeral pile was two hundred feet high, loaded with costly decorations, in which all the invention of artists was exhausted. It cost twelve thousand talents, or twelve million dollars of our money. The funeral ceremonies were succeeded by a general banquet, in which he shared, passing a whole night in drinking with his friend Medius. This last feast was fatal. His heated blood furnished fuel for the raging fever which seized him, and which carried him off in a few days, at the age of thirty-two, and after a reign of twelve years and eight months, June, B.C. 323.

His boundless ambition. His death a fortunate event. Effects of his conquests.

He indicated no successor. Nor could one man have governed so vast an empire with so little machinery of government. His achievements threw into the shade those of all previous conquerors, and he was, most emphatically, the Great King—the type of all worldly power. "He had mastered, in defiance of fatigue, hardship, and combat, not merely all the eastern half of the Persian empire, but unknown Indian regions beyond. Besides Macedon, Greece, and Thrace, he possessed all the treasures and forces which rendered the Persian king so formidable," and he was exalted to all this power and grandeur by conquest at an age when a citizen of Athens was intrusted with important commands, and ten years less than the age for a Roman consul. But he was unsatisfied, and is said to have wept that there were no more worlds to conquer. He would, had he lived, doubtless have encountered the Romans, and all their foes, and added Italy and Spain and Carthage to his empire. But there is a limit to human successes, and when his work of chastisement of the nations was done, he died. But he left a fame never since surpassed, and "he overawes the imagination more than any personage of antiquity." He had transcendent merits as a general, but he was much indebted to fortunate circumstances. He thought of new conquests, rather than of consolidating what he had made, so that his empire must naturally be divided and subdivided at his death. Though divided and subdivided, the effect of those conquests remained to future generations, and had no small effect on civilization, and yet, instead of Hellenizing Asia, he rather Asiatized Hellas. That process, so far as it was carried out, is due to his generals—the Diadochi—Antigonas, Ptolemy, Seleucus, Lysimachus, &c., who divided between them the empire. But Hellenism in reality never to a great extent passed into Asia. The old Oriental habits and sentiments and intellectual qualities remained, and have survived all succeeding conquests. Oriental habits and opinions rather invaded the western world with the progress of wealth and luxury. Asia, by the insidious influences of effeminated habits, undermined Greece, and even Rome, rather than received from Europe new impulses or sentiments, or institutions. A new and barbarous country may prevail, by the aid of hardy warriors, adventurous and needy, over the civilized nations which have been famous for a thousand years, but the conquered country almost invariably has transmitted its habits and institutions among the conquerors, so much more majestic are ideas than any display of victorious brute forces. Dynasties are succeeded by dynasties, but civilization survives, when any material exists on which it can work.

Athens was never a greater power in the world than at the time her political ruin was consummated. Hence the political changes of nations, which form the bulk of all histories, are insignificant in comparison with those ideas and institutions which gradually transform the habits and opinions of ordinary life. Yet it is these silent and gradual changes which escape the notice of historians, and are the most difficult to be understood and explained, for lack of sufficient and definite knowledge. Moreover, it is the feats of extraordinary individuals in stirring enterprise and heroism which have thus far proved the great attraction of past ages to ordinary minds. No history, truly philosophical, would be extensively read by any people, in any age, and least of all by the young, in the process of education.

The remaining history of Greece has little interest until the Roman conquests, which will be presented in the next book.